A HISTORY OF JORD

Though a small state, Jordan has frequently found itself at the centre of conflict and crisis in the modern Middle East. It has been a central protagonist in the wars of the region, notably the 1948 and 1967 Arab–Israeli wars, and has also been at the forefront of peace-making, signing a separate peace with Israel in 1994. Philip Robins' survey of Jordan's political history begins in the early 1920s, continues through the years of the British mandate, and traces events over the next half century to the present day. Throughout the latter period the country's fortunes were closely identified with its head of state, King Hussein, until his death in 1999. In the early days, as the author testifies, his prospects were often regarded as grim. However, both King and country survived a variety of existential challenges, from assassination attempts and internal subversion to a civil war with the Palestine Liberation Organisation. In the 1970s and 1980s the country emerged as an apparently stable and prosperous state. However, King Hussein's death, the succession of his son, Abdullah II, and the recent upheavals in the region have plunged the country back into uncertainty. This is an incisive account, compellingly told, about one of the most important countries in the Middle East.

Philip Robins is University Lecturer in Politics with special reference to the Middle East in the Department of Politics and International Relations at the University of Oxford and a Fellow of St Antony's College. His most recent book is *Suits and Uniforms: Turkish Foreign Policy since the Cold War* (2003).

A HISTORY OF JORDAN

PHILIP ROBINS

University of Oxford

CAMBRIDGE
UNIVERSITY PRESS

PUBLISHED BY THE PRESS SYNDICATE OF THE UNIVERSITY OF CAMBRIDGE
The Pitt Building, Trumpington Street, Cambridge, United Kingdom

CAMBRIDGE UNIVERSITY PRESS
The Edinburgh Building, Cambridge, CB2 2RU, UK
40 West 20th Street, New York, NY 10011–4211, USA
477 Williamstown Road, Port Melbourne, VIC 3207, Australia
Ruiz de Alarcón 13, 28014 Madrid, Spain
Dock House, The Waterfront, Cape Town 8001, South Africa

http://www.cambridge.org

First published 2004

Printed in the United States of America

Typeface Adobe Garamond 11/12.5 pt.   *System* LATEX 2$_\varepsilon$ [TB]

A catalogue record for this book is available from the British Library

National Library of Australia Cataloguing in Publication data
Robins, Philip.
A history of Jordan.
Bibliography.
Includes index.
ISBN 0 521 59117 1 (hbk.).
ISBN 0 521 59895 8 (pbk.).
1. Hussein, King of Jordan, 1935– .
2. Jordan – Politics and government.
I. Title.

956.95043

ISBN 0 521 59117 1 hardback
ISBN 0 521 59895 8 paperback

For my daughter Isabel

Contents

Illustrations

Tables and maps

Acknowledgements

It is well over two decades since I first went to Jordan, initially to live and work as a journalist and then to return to undertake doctoral research under the supervision of the redoubtable Tim Niblock. Since 1986, when I ceased to reside in the country, I have been a frequent visitor, most recently to conduct my current research into the field of illegal drugs. During this long association with the country I have talked with several hundreds of people, Jordanians, Palestinians and expatriates, many of them numerous times over. With hardly an exception, they have been kind and generous with their time, hospitality and insights. My thanks are due to each one of them. While to mention any by name is hard on the others, there are certain people whose assistance compels special mention. Nigel Denby, Paul and Jane Dracott, Keith and Janet Fraser-Smith, Tony and Alison Harpur, Declan and Liz Mannion, Alastair MacNeil, Dina Matar, Hana Muasher, Peter and Fenella Raftery, Mike and Maureen Ryan, and Alison Woods were all pivotal figures in my life at different times during my various stints in Jordan, and many remain close and valued friends. Debts of gratitude are particularly owed to Nasser Abu Nab, Lamis Andoni, Jalal Azzeh, Ian Chandler, Hiyyam Fakhoury, Yusuf al-Khadra, Rami and Ellen Khouri, David Oston and Sheila Oston, Rana Sabbagh, Jamal and Mary Sha'ir, Muraiwid and Ruth Tell, Ara Voskian, P. V. Vivekenand and Nidal Zayaddin for providing me with humour, sanctuary and good company. During the early days I learnt a lot about Jordan from associates who became more than just good contacts, and whose conversation was especially valuable and rich in insight, particularly Asad Abdul Rahman, Bill Burns, Alan Charlton, Fahd al-Fanek, Abdullah Hasanat, George Hawatmeh, Saji Salamah Khalil, Ahmad Mango, Marwan Muasher, Isam al-Tal and Tariq al-Tell. More recently Bassam Asfour, Ibrahim Izzedin, Musa Keilani, Sir John Moberly, Salameh Ne'matt, Amal Sabbagh, Asher Susser and Suhail al-Twal have continued to remind me how much understanding there is still to be done.

Of course, romance and Jordan is not a new thing. I am pleased to say, though, that, unlike for some others, romance in Jordan for me found a personal rather than political fulfilment, as it was while working there that I met my wife, Helen. For that reason alone, this book would have been a labour of love.

Though in many ways a product of more than 20 years of working on Jordan, the book was written after I joined the Middle East Centre (MEC) at St Antony's College in the mid-1990s. I would like to thank Eugene Rogan, Avi Shlaim and the other fellows and members of the Centre for their stimulation and support, not least in the field of Jordan studies. Graduate students, both past and present, have helped turn the MEC into a centre of excellence as far as the study of Jordan is concerned. I should like in particular to thank Yoav Alon, Paul Kingston, Paul Lalor, Robert Satloff, Lawrence Tal, Tariq al-Tell and Basma Talal for convening and taking part in the numerous discussions of Jordan, past and present, in which I have been involved at the Centre. Lastly, I would also like to thank the staff of the MEC, not least the librarian, Mostan Ebtihaj, for her cheerful help in providing the necessary research sources to support my work, and the archivist, Debbie Usher, who was especially helpful in securing the bulk of the photos contained within this work.

As for the book itself, I would like to thank Marigold Acland for commissioning it, for her patience in its preparation, and for her well-judged promptings during its writing. I would also like to thank Amanda Pinches and Karen Hildebrandt for their help in bringing the book to publication, and to Roger Bourke for his editing. With respect to the manuscript, Mary Wilson was kind enough to read it in its entirety. I am especially grateful to her, both for her detailed specific comments and her general observations. Helen also read the manuscript and made many judicious comments and suggestions based on her knowledge of the country. I am also especially grateful to Ahmad Khalidi and Tony Reeve who read and commented on specific chapters. As is usual on these occasions, I am happy to own up to responsibility for the final version.

Chronology

1867	Ottoman control is reimposed upon the lands of Transjordan
1906	The Hijaz Railway reaches Amman
1920	April: The San Remo conference establishes the mandate system, of which Transjordan is to be part
	August: British High Commissioner Sir Herbert Samuel announces the creation of autonomous administrations in Transjordan
	November: the future ruler, Amir Abdullah bin Hussein, arrives in Maan in the south
1921	Cairo conference under Churchill gives Abdullah jurisdiction over Transjordan
1923	September: The Adwan 'revolt'
1924	August: Abdullah accepts the Ultimatum on British administrative supervision
	October: Hijaz falls to the Saudis
1925	November (2nd): Hadda Agreement signed with the Saudis
1925–7	Druze Rebellion in southern Syria
1928	February: Agreement signed between Britain and Abdullah recognises the Amir as head of Transjordan
	April: Organic Law, effectively a constitution, passed, establishing a Legislative Council
	July: First meeting of the oppositionist Transjordan National Congress
1930	November: Major John Glubb establishes the Desert Patrol
1933	March: Legislative Council passes a consolidated land tax
1936–39	Revolt by the Arab population in Palestine
1939	Glubb replaces Peake as commander of the Arab Legion
	Alec Kirkbride replaces Cox as British Resident
1941	Middle East Supply Centre established

	April: Rashid Ali al-Kailani coup in Iraq; Arab Legion participates in its suppression
1945	Arab League established, with Transjordan as a founding member
1946	May (25th): Hashemite Kingdom of Jordan proclaimed
	August: Secret meetings begin between Abdullah and the Jewish Agency
1947	November (29th): UN General Assembly passes partition plan
1948	March (15th): Anglo-Jordanian treaty signed
	May: Britain terminates Palestine mandate
	May–June: First phase of the war: Jordan holds Arab Jerusalem
	July: Second phase of the war: Jordan forfeits Lydda and Ramle
	October–January (1949): Third phase of the war: Israel attacks Egypt rather than Jordan
	October: First National Palestine Congress convened in Amman prepares the way for annexation
	December: Jericho Congress opts for unity of the West Bank with Jordan
1949	April (3rd): Israeli–Jordanian armistice concluded
1950	April (25th): Jordanian parliament passes unification resolution
1951	July (20th): King Abdullah assassinated in Jerusalem
	September (6th): Prince Talal proclaimed king
1952	January (1st): New, liberal constitution ratified
	July (23rd): Nasser leads Free Officers' coup in Egypt
	August (11th): King Talal abdicates on the grounds of ill-health
1953	May (2nd): King Hussein formally accedes
1954	October (16th): General election subject to gross interference
1955	New municipal law adopted
	December: After sustained rioting, Jordan decides not to join Baghdad Pact
1956	March (1st): Glubb Pasha dismissed as head of the Arab Legion
	October: General election results in largely radical parliament; leader of National Socialists, Suleiman Nabulsi, invited to form government
	July–November: The Suez crisis

1957   January (19th): Arab Solidarity Agreement struck, whereby
Arab states would replace Britain as Jordan's paymaster
January: Eisenhower Doctrine against Communism unveiled
March (14th): Anglo-Jordanian treaty abrogated
April: Following reports of army unrest, the king sacks the
Nabulsi government and faces down the disturbances at the
Zarqa army camp
Martial law follows the convening of the 'Patriotic
Congress', an attempt to rally the opposition

1958   February (1st): Egypt and Syria unite to form the United
Arab Republic
February (14th): Iraq and Jordan respond by establishing the
Arab Federation
July (14th): Revolution in Baghdad brings down the
Hashemite monarchy in Iraq
Hussein invites in British troops to stabilise Jordan

1960   August (29th): Prime minister Hazza al-Majali assassinated
by Syrian agents

1962   January: First premiership of technocratic, reformist Wasfi
al-Tall
September: Start of Yemeni civil war

1963   February and March: Nationalist revolutions in Baghdad
and Damascus respectively

1964   January: First Arab summit creates the Palestine liberation
movement
September: Arab summit establishes unified Arab military
command

1966   November (13th): Israel undertakes devastating raid on
Samu

1967   May (30th): King Hussein flies to Cairo; signs Joint Defence
Agreement with Egypt
June (5th–10th): Six day war results in devastation of
Jordanian military; loss of the West Bank
August–September: Khartoum Arab summit adopts peaceful
strategy for rectifying Arab–Israeli problems
November (22nd): UN Security Council adopts Resolution
242, based on principle of land for peace

1968   March (21st): Jordanian and Palestinian fighters face down
the Israeli army at the Battle of Karamah

1970   September: PFLP's Dawson's Field hijackings precipitate
Jordanian–Palestinian clashes

	'Black September' defeat for Palestinian guerrillas in a civil war
1971	July: Remainder of Palestinian guerrillas driven out of Jordan
	The Allon Plan symbolises Israel's preference for the 'Jordanian option' with regard to the future of the West Bank
1972	March (15th): Hussein unveils his United Arab Kingdom vision for East Bank–West Bank relations
1973	September: Jordan warns Israel of imminent Arab attack
	October: Jordan participates belatedly in October (6th–26th) War on the Syrian front
1974	Army unrest over food prices results in establishment of the ministry of supply
	October: Rabat Arab summit recognises the PLO as representative of the Palestinians, at Jordan's expense
	November: Parliament suspended in light of Rabat resolution
1976	Arafat and Hussein meet at Cairo Arab summit, marking the start of a post-civil war, post-Rabat thaw
1977	PLO body reverses policy on regime change in Amman
1978	April: National Consultative Council established while parliament in abeyance
	September (17th): Camp David Accords signed, envisaging role for Jordan
	November: Baghdad Arab summit pledges $1.25 billion a year to Jordan in return for steadfastness
1979	December: Sharif Abdul Hamid Sharaf appointed prime minister
1982	June: Israeli invasion of Lebanon
	September (1st): Reagan peace plan is unveiled
1983	Jordanian Central Bank provides revolving credit line to maintain trade with Iraq
	March: Parliament restored; Islamist successes in by-elections
1984	November: PLO's national council meets in Amman
1985	February (11th): Peace process coordinating agreement forged with PLO
1986	February: Peace process agreement collapses in recrimination
	August: Jordan unveils still-born development plan for the West Bank
1987	April: King Hussein and Shimon Peres conclude London Agreement on peace process
	December: First uprising begins in Palestinian territories

1988   July (31st): King Hussein cuts administrative and legal ties with the West Bank

1989   February: Jordan is a founder member of four-state Arab Cooperation Council

February: Jordan's foreign debt default becomes public

April: Jordanian government begins to implement IMF programme

April: Riots break out in Maan, spreading to a number of towns

November (8th): Jordan holds free and fair elections; Islamists the winners

1990   August (2nd): Iraq invades Kuwait; King Hussein embarks on controversial 'mediatory' role

1991   January: Muslim Brotherhood join coalition government

June: National Charter adopted

October: Jordan takes part in Arab–Israeli peace summit in Madrid

1993   November: Jordan holds its first multi-party election since 1956

1994   October (26th): Israel and Jordan sign peace treaty

1995   August: King Hussein initially supports Saddam Hussein's defecting sons-in-law

October: Jordan hosts second of four regional economic conferences as part of its effort at normalisation

1997   September: Israeli agents bungle assassination of Hamas leader in Amman

1999   January: Month of high drama ends with King Hussein changing the succession from his brother Hasan to his eldest son Abdullah

February (7th): King Hussein dies; King Abdullah II succeeds; Hussein's second-youngest son, Hamzah, declared to be crown prince

2000   September: Second Palestinian uprising begins

2003   March–April: A US-dominated coalition precipitates regime change in Baghdad through war

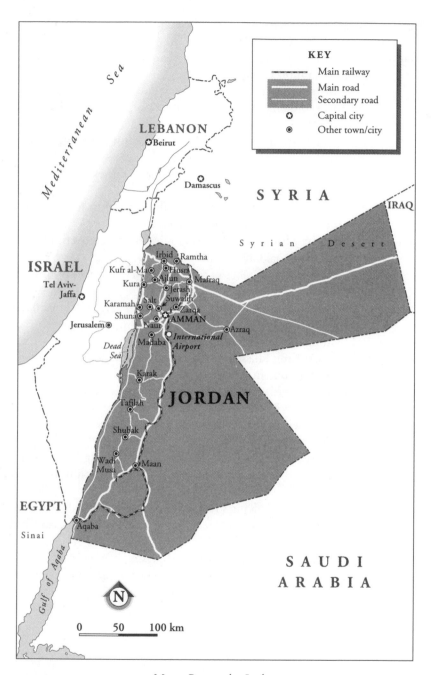

KEY

- - - - - Main railway
━━━━━━ Main road
─────── Secondary road
✪ Capital city
◉ Other town/city

Mediterranean Sea

LEBANON

◉ Beirut

✪ Damascus

SYRIA

IRAQ

Syrian Desert

ISRAEL

Tel Aviv-Jaffa ✪

Irbid ◉ ◉ Ramtha
Kufr al-Ma ◉ ◉ Husn
◉ Ajlun ◉ Mafraq
Kura ◉ ◉ Jerash
◉ Suwailih
Karamah ◉ ◉ Salt ◉ Zarqa
Shuna ◉ ✪ AMMAN
Jerusalem ◉ ◉ Naur
◉ Azraq
◉ Madaba ◉ *International Airport*

Dead Sea

◉ Karak

JORDAN

◉ Tafilah

◉ Shubak

Wadi Musa ◉ ◉ Maan

EGYPT

Sinai

◉ Aqaba

Gulf of Aqaba

SAUDI ARABIA

N

0   50   100 km

Map 1. Present-day Jordan

Introduction

The modern history of Jordan is the story of the creation of a state and the attempt to mould a political community that would render allegiance to that state, and it forms the subject matter of this book. Arguably such stories are never completed, though in Jordan's case the first is considerably more advanced some 80 years after its commencement than the second. The existence of Amman as an economic and political power centre, and the elaboration of a formal set of sophisticated structures and processes can, at one level, make the Jordanian state seem a convincing entity. However, a turbulent region, the relative strength of its neighbours, lingering concerns about its own economic viability (not least its habitual reliance on external rents) and an informal political culture sometimes at odds with the trappings of the modern state give one pause for thought. As for the creation of a political community there are more, perhaps many more chapters to be written in the story. The task of reconciling Palestinian and Transjordanian, Islamist and liberal, the tribal and the post-tribal among others continues to challenge the Jordanian body politic.

There have been three broad phases in the state-building project in Jordan. The first spans the period from the post-First World War settlement to the post-Second World War settlement. The riddle it addressed was how to forge a modern state from what was a dusty, under-populated, under-developed and impoverished periphery. The project was essentially an external, neo-colonial one, led by a small band of British officials on the ground and the dependent administrative elite they introduced from outside. Increasingly, people from the new entity of Transjordan were drawn into the project. However, this gentle venture, characterised as it was by a growing partnership between the British, the Hashemites and local leaderships, was plunged into a precarious uncertainty with the emergence of the Arab–Israeli conflict.

The second phase spans the end of the 1940s through to the beginning of the 1970s. This turbulent period was one that was not without its

I

opportunities, as the determined Hashemite pursuit of viability through ter-ritorial expansion demonstrates; the West Bank was consequently acquired in 1950. Nevertheless, the storms of 1950s Nasserism and the viciousness of Israeli cross-border retaliation against non-state actors were to expose the vulnerabilities of the new state, and the West Bank was subsequently lost in the 1967 war. In the end, only retrenchment behind a national security state saved Hashemite Jordan in the late 1950s and the early 1970s. The state survived, but against virtually all expectations.

The third phase spans the early 1970s through to the late 1980s. It was indisputably the era of oil, and, in Jordan's case, the secondary benefits of oil wealth recycled in the form of Arab aid and remittances. With monarch and state acting as the conduits for the distribution of much of this rent, both appeared to grow stronger, with public institutions, administrative and economic, proliferating. However, declining income in the 1980s left both increasingly exposed, with the amassing of foreign debt postponing what became the economic crash landing of the late 1980s.

It was at this point that a new stage of state-building began. But how to characterise it? The fourth phase as the period of liberalisation and democratic reform foundered in 1993, as King Hussein prepared to make a historic peace with Israel; the fourth phase as participation in supra-state cooperation and integration, Shimon Peres' 'new Middle East', foundered with the collapse of comprehensive Arab–Israeli peacemaking in 2000. What this fourth phase will look like it is simply too early to tell.

The threefold staged project of state-building was to some extent mir-rored by three distinct attempts to turn the people in Jordan into a Jordanian political community. The first came with the incorporation of the social-cum-spatial periphery into the physical and normative domain of the state. By the 1930s this cause was progressing well, but based on what one might call a two-way colonisation. Jordan remained a British colonial possession under the thin guise of the League of Nations mandate system, but increas-ingly it was the political culture of the people in Jordan that coloured the nature and *modus operandi* of state politics. Though hardly yet a Jordanian nation state, by 1946 it could be claimed that there now existed a kingdom incorporating a Jordanian state nation.

For the political community project the late 1940s were even more pro-foundly disruptive than for that of state-building. Onto a predominantly tribal, stable, rural and marginal population in Transjordan was grafted a people ('the Palestinians') who were more differentiated economically and socially, but who were also better educated, more prosperous and, in large part, damaged, that is to say psychologically if not physically, and materially dispossessed. New cleavages emerged: between political and economic elites from the two banks; between the rural and the urban; between Amman and Jerusalem as potentially competing centres of gravity. Tension was exacerbated by growing impoverishment, the spread of radical ideas, and a static governing elite. But in spite of fluctuating tensions the diverging tendencies in terms of political community were ameliorated, ironically, by two, very different ideas. On the one hand, it could be claimed that the people in Jordan were one people, based on a common Arab and predominantly Muslim identity (Caucasian and Christian millets respectively notwithstanding); at the same time, the subjective viability of Jordan was aided by the existence within one state of two lands (the East and West Banks), within which the aspirations and identities of the two peoples did at least have some room to breathe, thereby facilitating mutual coexistence.

Consequently, the third and much more problematic phase aimed at reconciling the notion of political community came after 1967, or more specifically after it became clear that there would be no speedy restoration of the West Bank. Jordan now became one land, the territory of the East Bank, but with a population that was increasingly Transjordanian or, after the transformation of the PLO, Palestinian, with a consequent marginalisation of over-arching political identities. A bloody conflict for the political soul of the remaining territory took place in 1970 and 1971, though the expulsion of the armed units of the PLO and the consequent oil-induced prosperity soothed the rawness of conflicting identity and interests. But in spite of the outcome of the Jordanian civil war it remained the case that a substantial part of the (notably urban) population of the country was Palestinian. A de facto arrangement whereby Palestinians dominated the private sector, Transjordanians the public sector, and politeness otherwise prevailed, began to unravel in the late 1980s to mid-1990s. An increasingly impoverished state, a formal peace treaty with Israel, regional recession and growing unemployment have created a sense of injustice on all sides, and the language of ethnic politics no longer lies securely under wraps. Once again social cohesion and political stability in Jordan cannot be taken for granted.

If the period spanning the existence of these state and political community-building projects forms the historical focus of this book, its point of departure comes several decades before that. In order to understand the dynamics of the modern state in Jordan one must understand the social dynamics that existed prior to the state's creation. In addition, one must understand earlier experiences of politics and state-building, in the Jordanian case the extension of Ottoman authority into the area from the 1860s onwards. Too often in the past commentators and scholars have begun the story of Jordan with the British and the Hashemites, ignoring both the Ottoman experience and indeed the people of Jordan.

CHAPTER I

On the Edge of Empire

Prior to the First World War, the potential for the emergence of a state from the lands beyond the River Jordan was almost non-existent. There was no significant urban concentration to act as an embryonic power centre around which political and economic power might coalesce; indeed, Amman was a deserted village until the 1870s. Neither was there much sustainable prosperity in the area from which an economic surplus capable of supporting the complex structures of a modern state might be drawn. Moreover, there was little sense of a collective community on which the ideology of a state might be built.

That is not to say that the people who lived in Transjordan prior to the Great War had no experience at all of 'stateness'. Since 1867, a substantial part of the territory had come into contact with an increasingly assertive Ottoman state: as a tax extractor (from the peasantry); as a resource distributor (to certain bedouin tribes); as a provider of arterial security; and, latterly, as an initiator of economic projects like the Hijaz Railway, which linked Damascus and Medina from 1908. The people of Transjordan, though relatively impoverished and with little formal education, had a shrewd view of the benefits and costs of interacting with a centralised state. Mobility was an important factor in deciding the degree to which sections of Transjordanian society could avoid the negative aspects of the Ottoman state.

For all their geographical and economic marginality, the lands of Transjordan were neither unsophisticated nor rule-free. The area beyond Ottoman control may have been anarchic in the literal sense of there being no over-arching government, but a complex and knowable ethical code or tribal law existed by which disputes could be addressed and resolved. Life was certainly dynamic in Transjordan during this time, not least owing to the vagaries of the climate and the logic of tribal interaction, with its emphasis on exploiting opportunities provided by the fluctuating ecology. There was a shifting relationship between the growing profile of the Ottoman state and the largely unregulated activities of the semi-nomadic tribes, with the agrarian peasantry and trade reflecting the dynamic. This dynamic would re-emerge in the 1920s as the British replaced the Ottomans and attempted to create a state based on the lands across the Jordan, where only the edge of empire had prevailed before.

Little detail is known about Transjordan between the seventeenth century, when it fell out of direct rule by the Ottoman Empire, and the belated attempt to reincorporate it practically, as opposed to nominally, into the empire, in the final three decades of the nineteenth century. The reasons for this Jordanian 'dark age' were twofold. First, the climatic and economic marginality of the area, with its long stretches eastwards and southwards of arid desert: until 1867 and the reimposition of an Ottoman control system there was little reason why anyone should venture that far, either for political or commercial reasons. Second, Transjordan clearly generated no special priority for the Ottoman state itself, with its attentions firmly fixed on its European not its Middle Eastern provinces, and, as far as the latter were concerned, its essentially urban and arterial focus. If its nominal rulers could summon little enthusiasm for the place then why should anyone else? A good illustration of this is linguistic in that the world came to know Transjordan as what it was not: a land conceived of as being literally 'across (and hence beyond) the River Jordan'. With few foreign travellers, little by way of Ottoman records, and an oral as opposed to a written culture predominating among its inhabitants, there is little of a recorded nature about the deep history of the area.

The skeletal corpus of surviving information that we have about the 50 years or so up to the Ottoman reassertion is overwhelmingly based on the recorded impressions and experiences of a relatively small number of European travellers. Their conceptions of the area were inevitably skewed according to their own preconceptions and preoccupations. A good example of this is the fact that their concern with 'Transjordan', with its strong biblical associations, would have had little currency either as a geographical or a cultural description for either the Ottomans or the local population. For the Ottomans, the preoccupation was much more with the administrative units of Greater Syria, of which a truncated Transjordan was soon to become a part. For the inhabitants of the area the focus of identity was either more precise – membership of kin-group or village – or more general, notably part of a loose but distinct religious entity. This disparity in conception was neither new nor unusual. For Europeans had long conceived of the

Ottoman Empire, a multi-ethnic organisation cemented by a predominant ideology of Islam, in specifically ethnic terms as a 'Turkish' state.

It is hardly surprising that the relatively small number of Europeans who ventured across the Jordan during the 1800s had difficulties in conceptualising its nature. First, the area contained a relatively small population, which suffered poor health and low life expectancy, thereby restricting the potential for demographic growth. Second, the harshness and unpredictability of the climatic conditions, with the arid nature of the overwhelmingly desert conditions and the precariousness of the rain-fed uplands agriculture, resulted fundamentally in a subsistence economy, thereby restricting the potential for human development. Third, the economic activity of the area reflected its ecology, with a relatively small area of sustainable agriculture around Ajlun in the north, more fluctuating agrarian fortunes along the upland spine running vertically to the centre of the country, and livestock herding based on the search for pastureland on the edge of the desert.

The climate and topography of the area determined the socio-economic division of labour that typified Transjordan. In Ajlun, the Ottoman administrative unit covering the north of the country, where economic activity was as certain as it could be and the hilly uplands provided a degree of protection against bedouin expropriation unavailable on the plains, a relatively settled peasantry was to be found. These peasant communities clustered around villages, which became associated with dominant clans. Examples include: the Shraidah in Kufr al-Ma; the Nusayrat in al-Husn; the Khasawnah in al-Nu'aymah. In spite of the sedentary nature of these people, tribal norms dominated the culture of the area, with the emphasis on the *noblesse oblige* of the shaikhly head of the dominant clan as strong as among the semi-nomadic tribal population of the area.[1]

Bedouin tribes engaged in pastoral nomadism dominated the livestock herding activities, with the range and regularity of movement of such people depending on the land and water resources under their control. For the more formidable of the tribal confederations, such as the Bani Sakhr in the central area and the Huwaitat in the south, extra income could be earned from merchants and even the Ottoman state in protecting (for which read 'undertaking not to raid') the movement of convoys of predominantly commodities and pilgrims. Such symbiotic relations were not unchanging. The Ottoman decision to construct the Hijaz Railway appeared to threaten the material interests of the larger tribes, as pilgrimage and other traffic by rail would have less need of their assistance, either in the form of transportation or protection.

The third and smallest of the socio-economic groupings in Transjordan at this time was that of the artisan-trader, who was to be found in the handful of settlements in Transjordan, but who was often obliged to be mobile in order to render his services. The more significant among this group also acted as an economic bridge between the peasants and nomads on the one hand and the external economy on the other. In what was often an economic interaction based on barter trade, the narrow range of agricultural products produced locally – notably wheat, on the part of farmers, which the social historian of the time, Raouf Abujaber, called 'the king of all cereals';[2] camels and sheep, wool and dried yoghurt on the part of livestock herders – were exchanged for staples like tea and sugar or basic consumer goods, such as textiles and utensils.

THE OTTOMAN STATE AND ITS IMPACT[3]

The Ottoman attempt at imperial self-rejuvenation began in the 1830s with the *Tanzimat* reforms.[4] In addition to the modernisation of administrative practice, the raft of reforms included a movement for the incorporation of the imperial peripheries, especially after the politically disruptive occupation of the Levant by the renegade forces of Muhammad Ali to 1841. Through the unprecedented level of centralisation of empire, this incorporation was to be executed more effectively than had been the case over the preceding three centuries.

As befitting such marginal lands, the move to incorporate Transjordan took place relatively late in the process of reform and in what were to be the last decades of the existence of the Ottoman state. Even here the experience was to be one of a fitful, and in some respects incremental extension of authority, with some false starts and a geographical limitation which hardly saw the process extend much to the south of Karak, that is to say beyond the northern half of what would eventually become the territory of the state of Jordan.[5] Even when the incorporation of Transjordan was in full swing there was a limit to its scope and style, with a further centralising impetus only coming after the Young Turk Revolution in Istanbul in 1908.

There were good reasons for this. While the pacification of the north-western areas of Transjordan was important to the development of trade and to the extension southwards and eastwards of an administrative net, there was less economic incentive to push that line further south. Moreover, the Ottomans, as befitting an imperial regime that had based an empire on rule through local elites, no doubt instinctively felt that the new strategy of reform was likely to be more successful, not to mention cost-effective, if it incorporated significant local players than if it was predicated on military domination. Such means were not required in Ajlun and Salt, where a symbiotic relationship was increasingly forged based on the provision of security in exchange for the receipt of taxes. However, the Ottomans were not above the use of more brutal methods, when openly opposed. It is no coincidence that the main example of a more punitive approach occurred in response to the Karak revolt in 1911, raised in the name of resisting taxation and conscription, Karak being an area where the reciprocity of state–periphery relations was far less well established.

The transitional period of incorporation was an extended and untidy one, both administratively and socio-economically. After a number of false starts, a stable administrative structure was established in Ajlun and Salt in the late 1860s. The former was placed under the reorganised administration of the Hawran to the north, while the latter became part of a new administrative unit based on Nablus to the west. The central area of Karak was also made part of the Nablus district, but only nominally so, while the Red Sea port of Aqaba was never considered to be part of 'Transjordan' at all. With the Ottomans now looking to expand southwards, a further reorganisation followed in 1893 in which Karak became an administrative district in its own right under the provincial government in Damascus, and had Salt attached to it.

The extension of the active implementation of Ottoman authority in Transjordan soon ran up against the semi-nomadic tribes that instinctively resisted the imposition of a rival basis for authority. However, once the tribal leaders discovered that there were gains to be made from the arrangement, important local interests and power groups were happy to explore the unfolding new relationship with the Ottoman state. At the forefront was the interaction between the Ottomans and a number of the most powerful semi-nomadic tribes, most notably the Bani Sakhr. With both tribe and state being essentially a security-oriented collective, with goals of defence and economic security in mind, it would have seemed that in the Transjordanian case, as in others, the two sides would have been pitted in a zero-sum struggle; a fight for supremacy and autonomy respectively. This would have been problematic for both sides: the tribes because of the notional resources at the disposal of the state which they could never hope to match; the state, in the absence of aircraft and four-wheel-drive vehicles, because of the rapid mobility of the tribes in the arid areas outside its physical grasp.

In the Transjordanian case, the experience of Ottoman imperialism was not one of a life and death struggle, but rather one of emerging accommodation. The tribes were increasingly incorporated into the state-inspired security regime. This meant that they lost the opportunity themselves to extract a security tax, or *khuwa*,[6] from the peasantry of the north, who now paid their taxes to the Ottoman state. Instead, the tribes benefited directly through the payments they received from the state for assuring the pacification of trade and communications routes, and indirectly through an increase in trade, from which they were in part the beneficiaries. A broader atmosphere of security through land registration, combined with a boom in European cereals prices, enabled the tribes to develop the lands they controlled for agriculture, with trade again enhancing the economic potential of such activity. As Eugene Rogan has succinctly put it: 'While [Ottoman] direct rule was imposed by force, it was maintained by persuasion.'[7]

A measure of the increase in security in the northern heartland of Transjordan was the growth in settlement and production across the area. According to Rogan there were three distinct waves of village settlement in Transjordan between 1867 and 1910. Each of these was a function of the deliberate policy of the Ottomans, and aimed at populating lands between administrative centres with cultivators, 'with title to land employed strategically'.[8] These three waves comprised: local peasants, who radiated out from existing settlements to create new villages; the Ottoman settlement of refugee communities; sharecroppers settled in plantation villages by bedouin tribes, fearful of the encroachment of the state.

For commentators of a romantic persuasion, the favourite story told relates to the second wave, and the introduction of refugees from the expansion of the Russian Empire in the Transcaucasus. Communities of Circassians and Chechens were, as Conder put it at the time, 'planted'[9] in Transjordan from 1878 onwards in a handful of sites, predominantly in the Amman–Suwailah–Na'ur triangle. Initially, it was the Ottoman intention that these hardy people would defy the semi-nomadic tribesmen of the area by expanding a chain of settlements, extending the areas of cultivation and bolstering the cause of sedentary preoccupations. After the early hardships of conflict and disease, these communities emulated their Ottoman patrons and made their peace with the tribes. Today, they have been assimilated into Jordanian society, though with distinctive cultural and political features.

The arrival of larger numbers of increasingly more prosperous merchants, in particular from the north and west, was a less alluring but probably more important illustration of the growing areas of settlement as a function of the extension of security. There had long been movement and interaction on vertical and lateral axes, notably trading relations with Damascus. The growing security from 1870 onwards, the increasing demand for wheat as a result of demographic growth in Palestine, and higher world wheat prices all served to help boost production. This in turn stimulated labour migration, as people from Palestine crossed the river to try their hand as sharecroppers and agricultural workers in the growing area under cultivation, especially those run by bedouin shaikhs such as the al-Fayez of the Bani Sakhr, and the number of villages grew. Nevertheless, even by the beginning of the twentieth century, it was only 'a primitive economy' of predominantly small family farming units that existed in Transjordan.[10]

Increased production also afforded more opportunities for merchants and traders, especially those based in Nablus and Damascus. Some gravitated to Transjordan, bolstering the numbers in the country's only real town of note, Salt, but also settling in smaller numbers in other towns such as Irbid. Indeed, Lars Wahlin, a Swedish scholarly expert on Salt, has referred to Nablus as Salt's 'sister-town' based on the demographic movements of this time, with more intensive contacts taking place to the west in Palestine even than with other parts of Transjordan to the north or south.[11]

Though Salt was still the largest population centre, its fortunes were on the wane relative to Amman, which was still a settlement dominated by Circassians, by 1903. The reason for this shift in fortunes, which was soon resented in Salt, was the extension southwards of the Hijaz Railway. Increasingly, businesspeople would relocate to Amman in order to profit from the commercial opportunities the railroad provided. A leading family to benefit from this new trend was the Khair family, that had arrived from Salt, having originated in Damascus. Its leading member, Sa'id Khair, quickly established himself, marrying a Circassian and exploiting his Arab identity to have himself elected as mayor. As ever with an eye to the political main chance, he subsequently married one of his daughters to a leading shaikh of the Bani Sakhr.

This trend was speeded up during the Great War. As was the case with the British during the Second World War, conflict provided a qualitative opportunity for such merchants from outside to increase profits by supplying the Ottoman war effort. Between 1916 and 1918, the Ottomans were obliged to fight on a new front to meet the emerging challenge from the British in Egypt, backed by limited support from the 'Great Arab Revolt' of Hashemite myth-making.[12] Amman was established as the headquarters of the Ottoman army in Transjordan. It commissioned a handful of the most prominent merchants of the day, such as Sa'id Khair and Seydu Ali Kurdi, to procure essential supplies, such as wheat, barley and legumes, for the military. These merchants used their contacts in Damascus, from which the supplies were sent, to ensure that Amman was well stocked. Opportunities for speculation resulting from successive failures of the cereals harvest during wartime further boosted the income generated. The war effort enabled these small merchants to amass great wealth, for instance with Kurdi purchasing some 10,000 dunums of land with some of the proceeds.[13]

The defeat of the Ottomans at the hands of the British General Edmund Allenby and the subsequent collapse of the empire suddenly robbed Transjordan of the framework of security that had since the 1870s been externally inspired. It was under these circumstances that the successes of the indigenous state-building potential of these years could now be judged.

Tellingly, the initial attempt at forging a regional state disregarded any claims to an exclusive existence that Transjordan might have had. An Arab government under the Hashemite Amir Faisal bin Hussain was established in Damascus after October 1918. This development had been fostered by British wartime encouragement to the Hashemite dynasty based in the Hijaz in a series of letters between its patriarch, the Sharif of Mecca, and a Cairo-based British official, known as the Hussain–McMahon correspondence. It was on this understanding that the Hashemites had joined the British war effort against the Ottomans, capturing Aqaba but little else, and now claimed their territorial spoils of war. Throughout this short process, it was assumed that Transjordan would simply continue to function as the southern extension of Damascus' natural hinterland. In an echo of the Ottomans, the Damascus government ran Transjordan through a mixture of reactivating the practices of the former administration and co-opting the traditional local elites.[14] The latter had no role to play in decision-making in Damascus, however.

But international politics eventually caught up with the dynamics on the ground. The San Remo conference of 18–26 April 1920 at last set about formalising a new map of the Near East. It did so in fulfilment of Anglo-French secret diplomacy during the war, enshrined in the Sykes–Picot accord, under which Transjordan would be part of Britain's post-war sphere of influence. The post-war international political context made it a straightforward proposition for the two dominant imperial powers to implement their accord. Consequently, at San Remo France claimed mandate responsibility for Lebanon and Syria,[15] and Britain assumed responsibility for Iraq and Palestine. Any specific mention of Transjordan was omitted, a reflection of its relative unimportance, though it was assumed to be covered by the jurisdiction of Palestine. With San Remo proving to be pivotal in the emerging politics of the region, the celebrated though somewhat chaotic administration in Damascus would only continue briefly until the French precipitated its collapse in July 1920 through military intervention. As the international asserted itself over the regional as far as the unfolding history of the Near East was concerned, so the administrative apparatus in Transjordan began to corrode. With the failure to recreate a state based on *bilad al-sham* (the ancient notion of 'the land of Damascus'), and with French colonial intervention robbing Transjordan of its centre of political gravity to the north, the focus shifted to the future of the area itself.

The uncertainty of the situation in Transjordan was exacerbated by the fact that Sharifian administration from Damascus had eroded its connections with Palestine, which had in any case not been clear-cut at San Remo. Moreover, political convulsions had seized central Arabia, where an alliance of the al-Saud dynasty and Unitarian (or Wahhabi) religious puritans was conquering territory in all directions. Britain therefore soon realised that it could not permit a political vacuum in Transjordan for fear that it would soon be filled by others in what was still a highly dynamic, post-conflict regional context. With the spectre of French expansionism from the north and Wahhabi tribal-cum-religious expansionism from the Arabian interior to the south-east, Britain could not allow an alien wedge to disrupt its lateral territorial connection between its two newly acquired strategic possessions of Palestine and Iraq. From its very inception as an entity Transjordan's value, not for its own sake but as a buffer and a bridge among lands of inestimably greater importance, was recognised.

For the British, the dilemma was what sort of authority to introduce on the ground. Policy became an arena of departmental contest involving the Foreign Office, the War Office and the newly established mandatory authority in Jerusalem. The British were unwilling and unable to take over the role that the Ottomans had been playing since the 1870s. War had been an exhausting experience and there was neither manpower nor treasure to spare. Unlike France in Syria, therefore, no troops would be sent to occupy Transjordan. The British authorities consequently undertook no more than a holding operation, pending a time when political will could be galvanised to decide on the new arrangements for the area.

British reaction to finding themselves in possession of the lands east of the Jordan was in one respect comparable to that of the Ottomans: they decided to try to work with the existing local elites. The British High Commissioner for Palestine, Sir Herbert Samuel, famously travelled to Salt in August 1920 and met with a large group of local dignitaries. He announced that Britain would establish a number of autonomous administrations, and that just a handful of officers, some rather young, would be assigned to them. As if to

Fig. 1. The market place in the town of Salt, c. 1920s (JEM, 6.10)

underline Britain's aversion to an expensive embroilment in Transjordan, the civil secretary in Palestine, Sir Wyndham Deedes, wrote of these men that their 'only weapon' was to be 'influence' and 'advice'.[16] Transjordan's brief but chaotic flirtation with local self-government had begun.

Initially, three administrations were established, one in each of Ajlun, Salt and Karak, the last also being the site of the rather grandiosely entitled 'National Government of Moab'. The local councils consisted of leading notables and dignitaries, the vanity of position making the administrations popular among such traditional leaderships, but also encouraging their counterparts of a lesser stature to seek their own platforms. It is noteworthy that the fledgling settlement of Amman was still not considered sufficiently large or significant enough to be worthy of its own administration, three representatives of it taking part in the *majlis al-shura* or consultative council based in Salt.

The results of these developments were almost immediately discouraging. The administration in Ajlun soon fragmented into four (Irbid, Ajlun, Mazar, Jarash) along traditional lines. The town of Tafilah demanded autonomy from Karak, establishing the trappings of administration even though the substance was lacking,[17] as subsequently did Wadi Musa. The fortuitous sale of a mineral concession for £1,000, the forerunner of rent-seeking in Transjordan, did fleetingly provide the government with precious resources with which to give credibility to its intent. With the powerful tribal confederations of the hinterland beginning to reassert themselves, the reach of the Karak government was by mid-November limited to the town itself.

It is no surprise that the limited success that was achieved during this seven-month experiment took place in the area of Salt. The larger, settled and more commercially minded population of this town understood the benefits that both security and centralised government could bring, and attempted to maintain the same structures and processes that had existed before. They further appreciated that the key to the creation of a functioning gendarmerie was the collection of taxes, though it was the insufficiency of the tax base that, even here, doomed the venture. However, the local governments had already become unsettled by the arrival on 21 November 1920 of Amir Faisal's elder brother, Abdullah, at Maan in the south. With the political fortunes of Transjordan once more in a state of flux why should anyone agree to pay taxes?

The experience of the self-governing administrations in Transjordan may have been brief but it was also telling. The members of the elite involved in them were not Europeans with a history of experience in state-building according to a rational–legal model and therefore it would be unfair to expect them to have used such an opportunity in such a pursuit. More importantly, the experience indicated how relatively lacking Transjordan was in what one might call the raw material of statehood, namely an emerging power centre capable of penetrating and subjugating a hinterland, a reliable economic surplus capable of sustaining the structures and institutions of a state, and an ideology in the name of which a state could be established and sustained. Only after the effective collapse of the local governments would the state-building project get properly underway in Transjordan.

CHAPTER 2

Founding State and Regime

The decade of the 1920s was crucial in terms of the emergence of both state and regime in Transjordan. A defining moment came with the British decision to separate the mandates of Palestine and Transjordan; at last the periphery was to become a centre in its own right. From then onwards, state-building took on a logic of its own. The establishment of public agencies and military forces created an administrative and coercive core. The resulting construction boom acted as an economic magnet and began to create vested interests for the existence of the state. Amman, once established as the capital, rapidly eclipsed other provincial centres as the focus of the emerging national politics. The British provided the international personality for the new Transjordanian entity.

The forging of a regime to preside over the newly emerging state in Transjordan was more uncertain. In the absence of any alternative indigenous formula, the British authorities embraced Abdullah's tentative, slow-motion *fait accompli* and installed him as the country's amir in 1921. But in spite of this apparently smooth investiture, Abdullah's fortunes would fluctuate over the next three years, as a function of his handling of domestic politics and his sponsorship of the residue of the Syrian nationalist movement. Abdullah's appeasement of the more powerful tribes precipitated challenges from their traditional enemies, while his nationalist allies caused regional problems with the French mandate authorities in Damascus. In both cases Abdullah's contempt for the apparently unviable state of Transjordan was palpable. Although he may have come close to being ousted by the British, in the end Abdullah survived two periods of probation. He made a Hobson's choice of pragmatism by ending his sponsorship of the national movement in 1923 and accepting a greater administrative role for the British in 1924, which ultimately reconciled him with his mandate overlord.

With the British taking responsibility for the creation of the framework of a modern administration, and introducing a ready-made executive elite from outside Transjordan, a formula for governance had been forged that would last for a generation. Abdullah provided the titular Arab leadership, and increasingly managed the vicissitudes of local politics; British overseers and their appointees took responsibility for the commanding heights of the state, especially in its coercive and financial embodiments; rent, in the form of an enduring subsidy paid by Britain, helped to build up the infrastructure of the state, and forged the beginnings of what was to become an enduring political economy for the state's survival.

ABDULLAH'S CONSOLATION PRIZE

Abdullah's move from Mecca to Maan in November 1920 with a retinue of some 300 men (and in possession of six machine guns)[1] marks the beginning of the forging of a political regime in Transjordan. The move should be viewed in two ways. First, as a strategic Hashemite counter-move to arrest dynastic fortunes in decline, especially in the wake of the reversal in Damascus. It is unlikely that Abdullah would have embarked upon the enterprise without patriarchal endorsement, and Sharif Hussain did indeed write letters to Transjordanian notables preparing the way.[2] Second, as a very personal move by Abdullah aimed at projecting his own ambition and reasserting his own status within the Hashemite clan. As a vain and self-centred man racked by sibling rivalry, Abdullah had become increasingly put out by the higher political profile enjoyed by his younger brother Faisal, especially in dealings with the British. It would not have been lost on Abdullah that whatever the British eventually decided for Transjordan, the future of Iraq also stood in the balance.

The move to Maan was undoubtedly a shrewd one, judged with two political audiences in mind. It clearly embodied a symbolic restatement of Hashemite political ambitions in greater Syria and beyond, there being little sign of a more limited, exclusive interest in Transjordan, the size and nature of Abdullah's entourage being seen by local eyes as giving weight to his authority. But it was also a measured one, designed not to antagonise the British, the size of his immediate following being insufficiently large or well armed to constitute an army in British eyes. For while the British had established themselves at Karak and points further north, Maan remained a twilight territory in terms of sovereign jurisdiction; Aqaba, of course, continued to be viewed as territory entirely within the orbit of the Hijaz. The shrewdness of Abdullah's push northwards could be seen in the British response, that was in effect to make no response at all.[3] Ultimately, Abdullah's move was an attempt to bring himself back to the attention of the British, from whose favour he would have hoped to benefit. With little

Fig. 2. Amir Abdullah (front left), Sir Herbert Samuel (centre), Sharif Shakir (front right)
in Amman, 1921 (JEM, 6.209)

money and memories of his brother's recent battlefield defeat at the hands
of the French, he had no realistic alternative.

Once ensconced at Maan, Abdullah set about consolidating his position.
He established his diwan and played the role of the Hashemite prince,
a role at which he could be very good when he wanted to be. He sent
some of his closest Hijazi retainers northwards to act as emissaries for his
cause, Sharif Shaker bin Zaid being the most prominent. With the political
arrangements for Transjordan still somewhat in a state of flux, it was hardly
surprising that so many tribal leaders and political activists accepted his
invitation to visit; for them, it was at very least an exercise in the hedging
of political and economic bets. In turn, nothing succeeded like success.
The more Abdullah's camp became a magnet for tribal and ideologically
inspired delegations, the less it could be ignored by other leading figures,[4]
and the more he would grow in credibility in the eyes of Jerusalem and
London.

British inertia on the ground in the face of Abdullah's move to Maan increasingly took on the appearance of policy, as growing numbers of Transjordan's traditional elites assumed that Britain was at very least passively conniving in Abdullah's ambitions. That this was not the case can best be inferred from Abdullah's own relative inactivity. He remained in Maan for more than three months, resisting the urgings of followers to move further northwards for fear of antagonising the British. Abdullah's caution was vindicated, since his presence helped to undermine the brittle local governments, while demonstrating that, in the absence of any viable alternative on the ground, he represented a reasonable bet for an indigenous administration. It was then in February 1921 that Abdullah eventually resumed his journey northwards into the heartland of Transjordan, to present the British with what had effectively become a slow-motion *fait accompli*.

Abdullah's timing was impeccable. His move preceded by ten days the culmination of a British grand review of policy towards the region to be held in Cairo. The Cairo conference represented an added moment of opportunity, as it also offered the possibility of the emergence of a coherent British policy. The bureaucratic reorganisation in London that preceded it, which centralised policymaking in the Colonial Office (CO), meant that policy towards the eastern Arab world would no longer be fought over by the more entrenched interests of the Foreign and India Offices. Finally, the CO was to be led by the strong-willed Winston Churchill, who was keen to resolve the uncertainties that had recently dogged Transjordan as well as Iraq. Yet, if this was a time of bureaucratic and titular change, there were also strong continuities running through British policymaking circles at the time, especially at the less formal level. This was particularly the case in terms of ideas and advice, with a clutch of Middle Eastern experts and Arabists, of whom T. E. Lawrence was to be the most influential over Churchill, having been at the centre of policy since 1918. Their overwhelming preference for a Sharifian Solution established the cognitive backdrop for Cairo.

Cairo did not disappoint. It was a crucial meeting in deciding the way ahead. Unfortunately for Abdullah it confirmed Faisal as the future political leader of Iraq, reflecting his closer ties with and greater credibility in the eyes of British officials. Abdullah emerged with the consolation prize of Transjordan, an acknowledgement of the success of his Maan strategy. Churchill met Abdullah in Jerusalem at the end of March, soon after the end of the conference, and, concluding the meeting with a handshake, anointed Abdullah as Britain's man.

Abdullah had thus been given tangible political responsibilities over a territory and demography, promoting his fortunes from those of merely an aspirant notable. Yet the Cairo outcome proved to be a high point in relations with the British over the next three years, which turned out to be increasingly tumultuous. The simple fact was that once the cordial meetings between Abdullah and Churchill were over, the realities of the situation began to assert themselves. At the heart of these were the practical needs of state-building and of the political incorporation of the people living in what was now the emirate of Transjordan.

These realities, which would have contained their own challenges at the best of times, were compounded by one very basic difference between the British and Abdullah. While the British were increasingly concerned with the mission of building a state according to the classical Western, European model in the distinctive and discrete entity of Transjordan, Abdullah viewed his new base purely as a territorial point of departure from which to expand the Hashemite domains. More personally, with his younger brother Faisal now established on a throne in the far more substantial territories of Iraq, Abdullah was determined to have parity. It was this basic difference that was to be responsible for the tension at the centre of British relations with Abdullah through to 1924.

Objectively, Abdullah had done well from the Cairo meeting. Chiefly concerned with the broader sweep of regional relations, Britain insisted only that Transjordan be pacified in order not to become a destabilising influence either on their much more important mandate of Palestine or on French-controlled Syria, difficulties with which would cause problems for Britain with its prickly European ally. Otherwise, Britain was agnostic on the means and form of government in Transjordan, which would become Abdullah's responsibility as amir. Indeed, London was to be generally lackadaisical in its approach to the actual status of Transjordan. At this initial stage Britain only insisted that there should be a review of the situation after six months: Abdullah, therefore, had control of his fief only on approval.

Although Abdullah cheerfully agreed to such an understanding, it after all having been the fulfilment of his Maan gambit, he had not the least intention of carrying it out. For Abdullah was nothing if not a revisionist; someone for whom subverting the existing order in either Palestine or Syria (or preferably both) was a *sine qua non* of his dynastic and personal ambitions. By contrast, Transjordan, in his eyes, was nothing, and hence worthy of little other than his contempt. In taking this view Abdullah failed to grasp either British imperial motivations, or the personal perspective of a new generation of British officials now responsible for Transjordan, whether in London, Jerusalem, or on the ground. He failed fully to appreciate that his half-year evaluation would be made against two criteria: his contribution to state-building; and the extent to which Transjordan was bothersome to the new administrations to the north and west.

It did not take six months for this contradiction to rise to the surface. By June 1921, with less than half of Abdullah's probationary period expired, the historian Uriel Dann notes that: 'the Colonial Office were practically unanimous that Abdullah should leave – if possible, with due regard for his dignity; if not, then without'.[5] The charges that were made against him in a stream of invective from the chief political officer in Amman, Albert Abramson, were a mixture of the professional and the personal. Abdullah was roundly criticised for presiding over a loose administration, operating with insufficient financial control and for being unable to impose security in the emirate. At the same time, Abdullah was accused of being lazy, feckless and a spendthrift.

While Abramson's report reflects a mismatch of policy priorities and conceptions of what a state should be, it is also suggestive of poor personal chemistry between Abdullah and Abramson. Although Abdullah was encountering little more than had been the norm since the defeat of the Ottomans as far as the security situation was concerned, some of his actions clearly did not help his cause. The appointment of his first chief adviser was a good case in point. Abdullah turned to Rashid Tali'ah, a Lebanese-born member of the Arab independence movement, or the *istiqlalists*, in a clear demonstration of where his political priorities lay. Abdullah's fondness for the *istiqlalists*, with their large Lebanese and Syrian membership, was rational in that it was these territories over which his ambitions ranged and not Transjordan; they were to be the political constituency that would, in Abdullah's eyes, sell the idea of his future rule in Damascus. But Abdullah could not have been less diplomatic in his choice, Tali'ah having been sentenced to death *in absentia* by the French for his political activities.

Although Tali'ah was soon dispensed with there was plenty else to perplex Abramson. Tali'ah's replacement, Mazhur Raslan, was also a nationalist, though a less controversial figure,[6] while the great majority of senior appointees, whether as advisers or as field officials, were nationalists from outside Transjordan. Likewise, there were no constraints placed on the comings and goings of nationalist activists. The recklessness of Abdullah's approach was underlined in June 1921 when a French soldier was killed in an assassination attempt on the French high commissioner for Lebanon and Syria, General Gouraud, by *istiqlalists* operating out of the sanctuary of Transjordan. With protracted wrangling over the extradition of the perpetrators, the incident hung like a pall over bilateral relations for the next two years. The amir had rashly allowed the development of exactly the sort of tension between Britain and France that he had been specifically warned against in London's original two conditions.

In spite of the widespread antipathy towards Abdullah that was emerging among British officialdom in Amman, Jerusalem and London, he was nevertheless to survive the six-month review. If his installation as amir had in the first place owed much to Lawrence as Churchill's *éminence grise*, Abdullah was doubly in his debt in retaining his position. In the face of so much negative advice from his department, Churchill sent Lawrence out to Transjordan for an independent assessment. Lawrence recommended that Abdullah should stay, dwelling in his report on Britain's shortcomings in supporting the administration. Lawrence made his report palatable by stating that Abdullah should remain *in situ* 'to give him more rope to hang his reputation' in order that union with Palestine could be engineered voluntarily.[7] In spite of the presentation of the argument the substance was clear.

This was not, however, to be the end of the matter between Abdullah and the British over the Syrian nationalists, although their importance in Transjordan was already waning as a result of amnesties in Syria and Iraq, and a shrewd appreciation on the part of many of their number that the new states were here to stay. Nevertheless, the issue of the *istiqlalist* presence was to drag on until February 1924, with efforts to weed out their number circumscribed by concerns about their influence within Transjordan's recently established Reserve Force, the Arab Legion. Although a British officer, Frederick Peake, had been appointed to build up the force, his role was limited due to *istiqlalist* control of the budget. A deterioration in morale and potentially discipline too as a result of the non-payment of wages provided a volatile backdrop but also an opportunity for action. It was in such a context that the British succeeded in ousting three nationalist figures who had reinvented themselves as senior officers. Together with two prominent nationalist politicians they were expelled from the country, while *istiqlalists* were removed from senior administrative positions. Still others, like Ibrahim Hashim, would choose Abdullah's way,[8] placing the certainty of political position in the emirate ahead of an uncertain existence outside. Hashim would loyally serve the country in senior positions until his ill-fated death at the hands of Iraqi putschists while on an official visit to Baghdad in 1958.

REGIME POLITICS: INCORPORATING SOCIAL GROUPS

If it was the presence and role of the *istiqlalists* that would dominate the worlds of diplomacy and domestic political chatter between spring 1921 and early 1924, it was the relationship between state and regime and key social groups that would be of more enduring importance. Of central importance was the relationship between the major social groups spanning the Transjordanian socio-economic continuum from the settled peasantry, notably in the north of the country around Ajlun, at one end to the semi-nomadic pastoralist tribal confederations, such as the Bani Sakhr and the Huwaitat, at the other. Spread along this continuum were many other tribes and groups of tribes, such as those, like the Adwan in the Balqa, who were formerly semi-nomadic but which had become more sedentary during the years of relative economic and physical security during the late Ottoman period. With the beginnings of a new state authority being introduced against a backdrop of the administrative confusion that had emerged since the collapse of the Ottoman Empire, a period of fluctuating and occasionally combustible fortunes could be expected as new political relationships were established, tested, and finally consolidated.

Churchill having given him extensive authority for Transjordan's internal affairs, along with a generous subsidy, Abdullah had responsibility for setting the tone of these early interactions. But Abdullah's lack of interest in the fortunes of the emirate itself, together with that of his *istiqlal*-dominated early administrations, meant there was little lead from the new political centre towards the building of a modern, and hence essentially liberal, state. Abdullah's instinctive initial course was one of expediency: appease the larger, well-organised tribal groupings in order to harness or at least neutralise the powerful; ignore or tax the weaker, socially inferior, more sedentary communities in order to expand the income base with the purchase of influence in Syria in mind. It was such an approach that helps to explain the critical evaluation of his first six months, in particular by Abramson and Peake on the ground.

The first challenge to the new political centre came as early as June 1921 with the Kura 'revolt' in the north. Villagers refused to pay the animal tax on the grounds that they had already paid it to the autonomous administration that had only recently become defunct. A contingent of the gendarmerie was dispatched to the area and sheep were seized in lieu of the tax, thereby identifying the police and the northern administration at Irbid as little more than pillaging marauders in the eyes of the local peasantry, who retaliated by ambushing and killing 20 gendarmes. Suddenly an incident, with which

Fig. 3. Jordanian peasant couple, 1933 (Stark, MF 129 D5)

the British had some sympathy, had been transformed in their eyes into a challenge to law and order and to the embryonic authority of the state. Consequently, British aircraft were deployed to overfly the area, an act that concentrated the minds of the villagers on conciliation, and established the atmosphere for a subsequent compromise with the political centre.

A similar though potentially more serious event occurred in 1923, with the different actors taking similar roles to those witnessed at Kura. In this case, the Adwan tribe led what Jordanian court historian Suleiman Mousa has called a 'taxes movement' (*harakat al-dara'ib*) against central government, which was not only vigorously levying existing dues but was also trying to recover funds outstanding from the 1918–20 period. Again, there was some sympathy on the part of the British towards the sufferings of the Adwan, especially as its traditional rivals, the Bani Sakhr, were, at Abdullah's indulgence, effectively exempt from taxes. The relative impoverishment of the Adwan, together with their symbolic diminution in status, threatened their traditional role as the paramount clan in the Balqa tribal confederacy. In spite of the apparent justice of their case, the Adwan too made the mistake in the autumn of taking up arms, their proximity to the capital and the extent of their notional tribal support base making their potential challenge considerably more serious than that at Kura.

The response to this most serious of challenges involved a de facto division of labour. As before, the mandate authorities found themselves with no alternative but to defend both state and regime. The deployment of armoured cars, regardless of the role they actually played in the eventual skirmishing, demonstrated both new military technology and imperial resolve in equal measure, as the RAF had previously done in Kura. In complement to the British, Abdullah's reaction to the challenge was to rally traditional support. At the forefront of the amir's supporters were those that had benefited from his selective rule and those whose tribal rivalry with the Adwan was most acute, like the Bani Sakhr. With neutral and even some of the Balqa tribes, like the Hadid,[9] gravitating to the strongest side, the Adwan and their supporters were easily put to flight, only to be reconciled, albeit on inferior terms, some six months later. In quick order the externally established state had seen off what was to be its greatest direct challenge prior to independence, a subsequent challenge in Wadi Musa in February 1926 collapsing immediately in the face of the deployment of a 450-strong predominantly Arab Legion force, supported by two armoured cars.

Although Abdullah's cultivation of the Bani Sakhr was a source of some resentment, as the Adwan 'rebellion' illustrates, it would be wrong to interpret it as a matter of caprice. Rather, his appeasement of the grouping was prompted by two factors: his own relative weakness in Transjordan, and growing concerns at vulnerability from external attack. Both factors necessitated that the new amir search for political allies. The first of these elements was in many ways a product of Abdullah's own making. His Syrian ambitions meant that meagre finances were diverted to the cultivation of political figures to the north, rather than being used to consolidate his rule in Transjordan. In turn, Abdullah proved to be too weak to employ force of personality to compensate for the absence of funds with which to co-opt such tribes as the Bani Sakhr. Consequently, his only option remained fiscal indulgence and partisanship in adjudicating land and inter-tribal disputes, the like of which brought stinging and repeated criticism from British officials on the ground and simmering resentment among those who were the losers in such cases.

If Abdullah's conduct of domestic politics was less than impressive during his first three years at the head of Transjordan, his sensitivity to regional dynamics, as one might expect of a Hashemite, was sharper. Although his main preoccupation in 1921 may have been with the political fate of Palestine and Syria, by 1922 he was concerned with the external domain less as a matter of opportunity than of dynastic survival. Parallel to emerging Hashemite dynastic ambitions in the early part of the twentieth century had been those of the al-Saud clan, based in the Nejd in central Arabia. By the early 1920s, the latest leader of the clan, Abdul Aziz ibn Saud, had re-established Saudi power within the Nejd and was threatening the Hashemite base of Hijaz, as part of a series of expansionist wars that would see the territorial establishment of present-day Saudi Arabia in the late 1920s.

The year 1922 witnessed the first major raid into the new emirate by the bedouin shock troops of ibn Saud, the *ikhwan*, penetrating as close as 12 miles short of Amman. A second major attack followed exactly two years later in August 1924, with the strategic struggle between the Hashemite and al-Saud dynasties reaching its climax. Although the second *ikhwan* raid was also seen off, it had played its part in putting Abdullah on the defensive and isolating Mecca and the Hijaz, which fell to the Saudis in October 1924; the Hashemites had been dispossessed of their longest-held and most prized territorial and cultural base.

It was Bani Sakhr lands to the south-east of Amman that bore the brunt of these two incursions into Transjordan by the *ikhwan*. Had the Bani Sakhr joined the *ikhwan*, and there were signs that leaders of the Huwaitat further south contemplated such a defection, it could have spelt disaster for the emirate. Yoav Alon has shown the importance for Abdullah of retaining the loyalty of the tribal confederation if Saudi expansionism was to be resisted, and has gone so far as to label the Bani Sakhr the 'de facto armed forces [of Transjordan] during the early 1920s'.[10] It was, however, the efforts of the RAF, with its ability to neutralise the bedouin's speed across the desert, that put the *ikhwan* to flight on the second occasion. The British thus ensured that Saudi expansionism would be confined in the west to the Hijaz.

An international treaty, the Hadda agreement, followed in November 1925 between the emerging states of Saudi Arabia and Transjordan. Its aim was the strategic goal of ensuring that the Saudi state did not have grievance to justify threatening Transjordan again. In order to secure such a goal the British made a number of concessions at the expense of the Transjordan-based tribes, notably the ceding of Kaf, which contained the winter grazing land of the Bani Sakhr and the Sirhan tribe, and the fact that Transjordan retained only 15 out of 60 permanent wells in Wadi Sirhan. Although it did not eliminate unsupervised bedouin traffic across the border, the treaty marked the end of the dynastic challenge of the al-Saud to the Hashemites. While they had not defended the Hashemites in the Hijaz, the British had ensured their dynastic survival in Transjordan.

BRITAIN AND THE FATE OF TRANSJORDAN

Abdullah survived his first six months; Abramson did not. He was replaced in November 1921 as chief British representative by the controversial and opinionated Harry St John Philby.[11] Philby's maverick life has attracted considerable attention, both because of his controversial career, which saw his later, expedient conversion to Islam, and because he fathered the Communist traitor Kim Philby. However, his short stay in Transjordan, between November 1921 and April 1924, was not especially notable, and he was withdrawn from his position after a breakdown in personal relations with Abdullah: a case of the emirate not being big enough for two vain and overweening egos.

The one notable achievement of this period, though one in which Philby was not an important player, was Britain's decision to recognise Transjordan's separate status from Palestine,[12] and to pronounce that it would not be included in the territory set aside for the establishment of a Jewish national home.[13] Initially, the prospects of an independent existence for Transjordan separate from Palestine had not seemed great once the Balfour Declaration of November 1917 had been made. Yet the inclusion of Transjordan in Faisal's Arab government based in Damascus had established the precedent for the separation of the two territories.

Nevertheless, the situation continued to fluctuate. As already noted, Britain's position on the possible linkage of Palestine and Transjordan had become more ambivalent during the San Remo conference in April 1920. Meanwhile, concern on the ground that the separation might prove fleeting was real enough, when, after the fall of the Sharifian government in Damascus in August 1920, Sir Herbert Samuel, the British High Commissioner in Jerusalem, went to address Transjordanian notables at Salt on new arrangements for the territory. Although Samuel was a strong believer in the full political incorporation of Transjordan into the Palestine mandate, for ideological as well as bureaucratic reasons, the message he delivered at Salt was altogether different. He was obliged to state that Transjordan would not come under the administration in Palestine. But this statement only seemed good for as long as the resulting local governments remained in place in Transjordan. With their collapse, the arrival of Abdullah and the uncertainty of his longer-term prospects, the situation seemed once again to be in a state of flux.

While the fate of Transjordan seemed uncertain, the leaders of the Zionist movement were vigorous in their efforts. They wished to see Transjordan incorporated into Palestine, certainly as far as eligibility for Jewish immigration was concerned. Ironically, they received some encouragement from no less a person than Abdullah. Surprisingly perhaps, given subsequent events, Abdullah was somewhat ambivalent towards the issue, casting his covetous eyes westwards. He therefore refrained from pushing the British hard for the formalisation of the division of Palestine and Transjordan. Neither were the British authorities quick in clarifying the position, especially with their collective equivocation towards the amir.

The lingering uncertainty dragged on until 1923 when, in response to Abdullah's promptings as to his standing in Transjordan, Britain finally took a stride in the direction of recognising his status. During negotiations towards the end of the previous year Abdullah was, in the view of his biographer Mary Wilson, 'met half-way'.[14] Choosing its words very carefully, Britain gave a written 'assurance' that it 'will recognise' an independent government in Transjordan under the rule of Abdullah, provided that it is constitutional, and permits Britain to fulfil its international obligations. With the independent dimension of the arrangement relating to the relationship between the emirate and Palestine (rather than the nature of Britain's political jurisdiction), further subtleties followed to confirm the incremental emergence of Transjordan's free-standing nature. In dealing with Abdullah the high commissioner in Jerusalem was now to act as

the representative of the mandatory power rather than as the head of the
Palestine administration. In 1924, Her Britannic Majesty's Government re-
ported to the League of Nations on 'the Administration under Mandate of
Palestine and Transjordan' rather than submitting a 'Report on Palestine
Administration', as had been the case in 1923.[15]

While Philby was colourful, his successor, Henry Cox, was not, and hence
has been little written about.[16] Yet Cox was to be the far more influential
as far as state-building was concerned. Arriving as Philby left, Cox would
remain as the senior British figure in Amman for almost 15 years. Again, if it
was John Glubb who would become famous in the 1930s for incorporating
the semi-nomadic tribal periphery into the state of Transjordan, it was Cox
who was most responsible for creating a solid core capable of doing the
incorporating in the first place.

Cox arrived at a time when the British authorities were becoming
increasingly frustrated with the nature of administration in Transjordan,
especially as it related to financial control. Indeed, the appointment of Cox,
as a dedicated and unsentimental colonial official, was a reflection of this
frustration, and he arrived with a no-nonsense mandate for reform. The
British government had made sizable annual subventions as Grant-in-Aid
since the establishment of the emirate in 1921, the beginnings of the practice of strategic rent transfers that Jordan has benefited from throughout
virtually its entire existence. Given the economic hardship in Britain, and
a drive to save money, Abdullah's perceived spendthrift nature had gone
down increasingly badly in Britain. The amir treated the national budget
as his private purse and his Arab ministers were unwilling and unable to
curb his spending. Thus, Abdullah was estimated to have spent in excess
of his civil list allowance for 1923 during the first seven months of the
year.[17]

The British approach to Abdullah began to change in late summer 1923,
with the introduction of a new system for the dispersal of the Grant-in-Aid.
From then onwards the British representative was not to release funds if

Table 2.1 *British Grant-in-Aid allocated to Transjordan (£)*

1921/22	1922/23*	1923/24	1924/25
180,000	100,000	150,000	80,000

* £10,000 subsequently deducted
Source: British official reports.[18]

the conditions on which they had been allocated were not observed. Subsequently, the British parliament voted to route the Grant-in-Aid through
Jerusalem, making the High Commissioner in Palestine responsible for its
dispersal. Against this new atmosphere of greater supervision, Cox, at the
prompting of Jerusalem, proved instantly to be more interventionist than
his predecessor. This new interventionism extended well beyond the financial and the administrative, with, for example, Cox using the dispersal of
funds as leverage against political appointments by the amir. Abdullah's
grudging appointment of Ali Rida al-Rikabi as chief minister at Cox's be-
hest in May 1924 proved to be a harbinger of things to come, and marks
the start of the second and final crisis in relations between Abdullah and
the British.

Although Abdullah accepted the imposition of Rikabi, he fought hard
against the introduction of a new system of financial supervision. He tried
to head off the new arrangement by taking a voluntary reduction in the
civil list, although Cox saw through his ruse. Abdullah then attempted to
fight the new regulations, but with Cox acting at the instigation of the
chief secretary to the Palestine government, Sir Gilbert Clayton, the amir's
ability to play off the hierarchy of the British authorities was curtailed.
During this struggle of wills Cox maintained that there were two options:
'either enforcing the submission of the Amir to adequate financial control
or disregarding him altogether and relegating him to the position of a
figure-head in so far as the administration of the country is concerned'.[19]
Although Cox dispassionately rejected the latter because of the danger of
its exploitation by those opposed to central government, he did entertain
the possibility of the replacement of Abdullah by his youngest brother,
Zaid.

Cox's assessment was accepted in Jerusalem and Clayton drafted an Ultimatum to Abdullah. In addition to requiring the amir to accept a new
system of financial regulation, familiar British grievances resurfaced in the
form of an insistence on the expulsion of political undesirables, the conclusion of an extradition agreement with the French in Syria, and the abolition
of the Department of Tribal Administration. The Ultimatum ended with
portentous words: 'I trust that Your Highness' definite acceptance of the
above conditions will render it unnecessary for His Majesty's Government
to reconsider the whole position of Transjordan.'[20] Abdullah well understood the implicit threat at the end. With no local base of support, the
influence of the *istiqlalists* having already been mortally wounded, and a
dependence on the British heightened by the *ikhwan* attacks, Abdullah

realised that he had no choice but to sign, which he did with resignation on 20 August 1924.

Although the Ultimatum was a public embarrassment and an apparent reverse for the amir, it proved in the longer term to be a blessing in disguise. The tighter administrative supervision would appreciably enhance the process of state-building in Transjordan, to the eventual benefit of Abdullah and his successors. The removal of the charge of financial mismanagement, coming on top of the waning of the *istiqlalists*, would remove all major bones of contention between the amir and the key British figures in Amman, thereby allowing the creation of a common partnership based on an increasing division of political labour; even Abdullah and Cox and Peake would eventually warm to one another. Moreover, the Ultimatum was a watershed in Transjordanian politics in that never again would the British seriously contemplate reconsidering their 1921 decision to install Abdullah at the head of the emirate; with the British now unequivocally supporting Abdullah, for local leaders all roads increasingly led to his door.

TOWARDS ADMINISTRATIVE CONSOLIDATION

The growing involvement of the British in the administration of Transjordan and the consequent elaboration of the state began to raise new questions about who would participate in the project. Such an issue had perplexed the British since 1920 and the first attempts to raise a Mobile Force in Transjordan. On that occasion the officer responsible, Captain Brunton, had sought to enlist a combined force drawn from both Arabs and the Circassian community, who had been introduced into the area by the Ottomans, and was still in many ways a distinct group. Although not ill-disposed towards the British, on this occasion the Circassian community declined, concerned that their small size and perennial association with external state force could leave them exposed, especially in the event of an early British withdrawal. Although Brunton's role in state-building in Transjordan was fleeting, it did re-establish the age-old strategy of using external communities unassociated with local political constituencies, interests and tensions to regulate indigenous peoples. The efficacy of such an approach was underlined from within during the momentary existence of the Transjordanian local governments, when a force of 50 gendarmes was recruited from Palestine by the Karak administration to collect fines and taxes and apprehend criminals,[21] an activity they discharged to great effect until overwhelmed by the size of the task.

The impetus to recruit important cadres of the new state from outside its territories grew during the first months of its existence. Peake, who had replaced Brunton, found it difficult to raise manpower for his Mobile Force, especially in the aftermath of the Kura affair, which had exacerbated the suspicions of the sedentary peoples about organised force. Consequently, as Vatikiotis points out, he 'resorted to Arabs who had served in the Ottoman armies', many of whom were from Syria, Palestine,[22] Egypt and Sudan.[23] The expulsion of the *istiqlalists* from the force in 1923 and an increasing willingness of villagers, whose recruitment Peake favoured, to join it began to change its composition. Nevertheless, by the end of 1928 nearly 36% of the force was still drawn from men from outside Transjordan, with 156 of its number coming from Palestine alone. The force was commanded by five British officers,[24] who had virtual total control over recruitment, training, internal discipline, promotions and strategy within the force. The Arab Legion, as it became known, also contained a disproportionately large number of Christians,[25] which again suggests that recruitment policy contained a self-conscious minority dimension to it.[26]

By 1926 the Arab Legion had succeeded in completely pacifying the populated and sedentary areas of Transjordan. But security was at best patchy in the geographical periphery of the state, which contained many of the traditional grounds of the semi-nomadic tribes, and there were no Arab Legion posts east of the Hijaz Railway. In order to incorporate these areas and to harden the international borders that had been created by the likes of the Hadda agreement, the British moved to establish the misnamed Transjordan Frontier Force (TJFF), which, inauspiciously, came into existence on 1 April 1926. The force was to be much less of a Transjordanian force than had been even the Arab Legion at its inception. It was to be part of the imperial forces in Palestine and hence under the control of the War Office, though primarily financed through the High Commission in Jerusalem. The majority of the TJFF's 1,000 men were drawn from Palestine, Syria and Lebanon.[27] The only notable 'Transjordanian' component was the Circassian, now reassured as to the long-term commitment of the British, which is believed to have made up 25% of its strength.[28]

Although the component of men drawn from beyond the territories of Transjordan was significant in the military, it was to be of more profound importance in the administration of the new state. The logic of statehood had gained momentum through the 1920s, with the establishment of the mandate; the creation of the early institutions; the growing normative consensus on the role and goals of the state after 1924; and with the formal, institutional grounding of the state after 1928. With this forging of statehood no longer contested, at least in the settled areas, procedures accelerated for the elaboration of state institutions and the creation of internal networks through the building up of a field administration.

After Abdullah's acceptance of the Ultimatum in 1924 a new clutch of British officials was appointed to the decision-making positions of the state. At first this took the form of the appointment of British officials to policymaking positions, notably Alan Kirkbride's arrival as Financial Secretary in January 1926. However, increasingly the British preference was for the appointment of less high-profile, though no less influential, personnel to be 'advisers' to areas of important existing administrative activity, such as justice and later finance, and directors of departments in such fields as customs and forestry. With Britain controlling the purse strings there was never any doubt that failure to follow 'advice' from the appropriate British official could result in restrictions on the dispersal of funds. Neither was the prominence of British officials a passing one, related to the emirate's administrative ability to govern itself. By 1936 there were 20 such senior officials in place.[29]

It was not only the British who populated the senior administrative stratum, but also an imported cadre seconded from the mandate administration in Palestine. Beginning with the direction of the Department of Public Works in February 1925, by early 1929 there were eight such senior appointments from Palestine. There was also extensive recruitment from outside Transjordan lower down the administrative scale. The motivation for this was the absence of sufficient numbers of educated and experienced figures from Transjordan to staff the emerging civil service. The British and the Palace had a penchant for such recruitment, both because of the dependent loyalty of such outsiders and, in the case of Abdullah, because their presence kept alive his pretensions to playing a wider role as an Arab leader. In 1936, nearly 32% of government servants had been born outside of the emirate.[30]

Many of these outsiders chose to make their permanent homes as well as their careers in Transjordan, attracted by the ease of opportunity not on offer in Palestine. Their long-term rights were safeguarded as they were formally incorporated into the population of the new state through the adoption of such legal provisions as the 1927 Aliens Law. A handful of these officials went on over the next three decades to become some of the country's best-known political figures, such as Samir al-Rifai and Tawfiq Abu al-Huda. Ironically, the presence of this Arab external elite caused more resentment among Transjordans than did the presence of the British. It helped to precipitate the first stirrings of a Transjordanian nationalism, defined by the presence of a predominantly Palestinian 'other', the impact of which would be felt especially in the late 1920s and early 1930s, as Abdullah and Britain proceeded with the cautious beginnings of institution-building in the country.

CHAPTER 3

The Long Road to Independence

By the late 1920s there was no longer any dispute about the existence of either state or regime in Transjordan. Britain was the mandate overlord in the emirate; Prince Abdullah was the titular head of the regime; a combination of British officials and a largely imported administrative class presided over the government of the country; and Amman was established as the growing power centre of the state.[1] Peace and order prevailed in the settled part of the country, if not in the majority of its territory.

Yet if the existential uncertainties of the early and mid-1920s were behind Transjordan there were still many question marks about the long-term nature of politics and society. What sort of political institutions should the country have? How would relations between the colonial power, the Hashemite ruler, and the various local elites evolve now that the big issues relating to the country had been settled? What would the implications be of the growing resentment of the indigenous Transjordanians at the privileged position occupied by administrators and traders from outside? And what of the marginal areas of the country: would Transjordan ever succeed in incorporating the more nomadic areas of Jordan into the new state?

The preoccupations of the country in the late 1920s were not, however, exclusively domestic. If Transjordanian politics was taking on an increasingly parochial form it was doing so against a backdrop of fluctuating regional tension. In Palestine, Jewish immigration was exacerbating tensions with the local Arab population, one which British officialdom was finding increasingly difficult to manage, let alone reconcile. In Syria, the French mandate authorities were having their own problems in terms of implementing a 'divide and rule' strategy thinly veiled as political development, with unrest having swept the south of the country. Though ructions in both Palestine and Syria were at one level disconcerting for Transjordan, for Abdullah, ever the Hashemite Arab prince, they presented opportunities for personal aggrandisement, and the possibility of graduating from his dusty backwater.

35

CREATING POLITICAL INSTITUTIONS

The acceptance of the Ultimatum in 1924 and the implementation of its provisions helped to clear the path for institutional development in Transjordan. Under the terms of the mandate for Transjordan, Britain was obliged to administer its mandates in accordance with Article 22 of the Covenant of the League of Nations. According to this Britain was responsible for the oversight of and progress towards political development in the emirate, and had to report on an annual basis on its progress towards this objective to the Permanent Mandates Commission in Geneva. Britain had indicated in its 1923 Assurance that constitutional government should be introduced. But up to 1928 the only institutional development of note had been the creation of the Executive Council, an early version of cabinet government. Though the hand of the League of Nations was a light one as far as the mandatory powers were concerned, the formal provisions had nevertheless to be complied with.

At the conclusion of the six months probation at the end of 1921, with no formal conclusion as to either the issue of sovereign authority or governorship in Transjordan, Abdullah had to some extent been suspended in a political limbo. Discussions on a draft treaty that would clearly set out the status and obligations of the parties had begun as early as 1922, but the initial drafts simply referred to 'an Arab Emir' rather than to Abdullah by name. The friction between Abdullah and the British over the *istiqlalists* did not provide an auspicious atmosphere for further work on the document. The replacement of Herbert Samuel by Lord Plumer as High Commissioner in Jerusalem in early 1925 caused further delay. It was not until March 1926 that a new working draft was produced.

On 20 February 1928, a formal agreement between His Britannic Majesty and the Emir of Transjordan[2] (subsequently amended twice) was finally signed. It is a document that reflects the power disparities between Abdullah and the British, and there was 'strong opposition'[3] to it locally.[4] At every turn the agreement emphasised the ultimate authority of His Britannic Majesty, with local powers being subordinate and conditional. The articles of the agreement reflected the British preoccupations with Transjordan hitherto, with strategic issues (especially related to military matters) and Britain's relentless pursuit of efficient and effective governance (notably in fiscal matters) to the fore. For his part Abdullah repeatedly agreed to be 'guided by the advice' (Article 5) or 'refer for the advice' (Article 6) of the British authorities. Transjordan's colonial status was thereby formalised.[5] Though parallels were drawn with the 1922 Anglo-Iraqi

Treaty, the British authorities were keen to emphasise that the substance of the agreement was 'not comparable' to the 'rapid progress' being made in Iraq.[6]

For Abdullah, the main benefit of the agreement was that it recognised the existence of a government 'under the rule of His Highness the Amir of Transjordan'. With the Hashemites having been chased out of the Hijaz in December 1925, this additional legal ballast was reassuring to Abdullah. Other benefits flowed from this fealty. Britain further incrementally bolstered the standing of Transjordan, with its immediate adjustment from a *mantaqa* (district) to an *amara* (emirate). London also agreed to meet the excess expenses of the administration, including that of the military. This codified the principle of an annual subvention from the colonial power, and recognised that Transjordan was insufficiently economically developed to support the infrastructure of a modern state. The formalisation of such rents would help to routinise the practice of reliance on external transfers. The agreement was also beneficial from a local political perspective because of the way in which it formalised the principles of political practice. As Kamal Salibi, in an authorised version of the history of Jordan, states: 'they [stipulations regarding the relationship with Britain] set the rules of the game; and, as in any game with set rules, the room for manoeuvre, no matter how narrow, remains open'.[7]

Ultimately, the agreement also proved a point of departure from which incremental progress towards an independence of sorts could be contemplated. This was certainly the view of the British authorities in Amman, and so also of the Colonial Office. Within three years of the agreement even the Foreign Office was persuaded of the wisdom of detaching Amman from its dependence on Jerusalem.[8] Progress in the direction of greater independence would be made more sure-footedly once the more flexible Alec Kirkbride had taken over from Cox as the British Resident.

The concluding of this agreement was accompanied by the forging of an Organic Law, generally referred to as a constitution, which was promulgated in April 1928[9] (subsequently amended in 1938). Its main innovation was the creation of a 21-member Legislative Council, with a three-year term.[10] The composition of the Council made it susceptible to executive control. The presence of seven appointed members (five of whom were from the Executive Council),[11] the fact that the chief minister also acted as Council chair, and the over-representation of minorities (three would be Christians and two Circassians) all mitigated against independent action.[12] Moreover, the Council would only sit in ordinary session for three months a year, it could be dissolved or prorogued on the whim of the amir, while only the

Fig. 4. The Parliament House in Amman, 1933 (Stark, MF133 B6)

chief minister or a departmental head had the power to introduce bills for consideration by the Council.

Though the body was to have limited powers,[13] its creation marked a sizable step forward in terms of the development of the emirate's formal institutions. During its early days the Council was also the focus of some considerable political controversy, as the pent-up frustrations of a decade with only limited channels of political protest now overflowed. Indeed, the Legislative Council reached its high watermark of controversy soon after, when it refused to pass the 1931 budget. Much of this political activism was funnelled into the Transjordan National Congress (TNC), arguably the country's first real political movement with a strong base in Transjordanian civil society, the creation of which shadowed the increase in institutional development.

There were to be six meetings of the TNC before its collapse, the first taking place on 25 July 1928. Its creation was supported by elements from most of the major tribal clans in Transjordan.[14] The motivation for the emergence of the TNC was twofold. First, an increasing alarm and frustration on the part of rural Transjordan, both tribes and small towns alike, at their continuing economic marginality, especially as the main urban centres of the state grew increasingly prosperous. This was not merely the politics of envy. It was also driven by an absolute deterioration in the economic circumstances of the periphery, principally as a result of poor rainfall and a run of bad harvests between 1927 and 1933, and locust infestation in the early 1930s.[15]

The second driver of the TNC was the growing resentment at the emergence of the external administrative elite introduced by the British to man the new structures of the state in Amman, as the slogan raised at the latter four congresses, 'Transjordan for the Transjordanians', well illustrates. Resentment against the prominence and disdain of the outsider, sentiments that had been acute during the brief period of *istiqlalist* government, was now transferred to the predominantly Palestinian members of Britain's colonial apparatus. The opposition attempted to use the Legislative Council to block the appointment of more seconded officials from Palestine.[16] An Aliens Law was adopted in 1927 in recognition of the need to clarify the demographic base of the emerging political community.[17] This resentment was exacerbated by the growing gap in wealth between the centre and the periphery, both as a result of the consolidation of the state and the impoverishment of the rural areas. This period thus marks the emergence of political cleavages that would recur at various stages during the subsequent history of Jordan. The heyday of the TNC was to be the forerunner of a specifically Transjordanian nationalism, also defined against the Palestinian 'other', which has been explicit and enduring since the civil war of 1970–71. It also marked an early example of the fluctuating tension between town and country, which was most pronounced during the swirling unrest of the 1950s, and which would underlie the eruption in social discord in Jordan in 1989.

In spite of the early furore, the first years of the Council were a misleading guide to its potential for disruption. The Council remained a focus for political activity in Transjordan. But this was more because electoral success was regarded as a reflection of the status of its members, in turn helping to bolster their standing in the eyes of their supporters. Because of the profile and contentiousness of these early sessions of the Council all sides increasingly resorted to whatever means lay at hand for effecting a favourable outcome at election time, no matter how unedifying. Accusations of vote buying became commonplace,[18] exacerbated by the two-round voting system, the latter of which, with its restricted electorate, being the most vulnerable to skulduggery. The executive was also not above such grubby practices. It used measures such as banning orders and even arrest to try to disrupt the campaigns of those candidates it perceived as hostile to its cause.[19]

After a sticky first couple of years, successive governments soon learnt how to handle the Council. For example, chief ministers adopted the practice of appointing elected members to the Executive Council as a way of incentivising cooperative behaviour. Hasan Khalid Abu al-Huda set the precedent by appointing three members, Ala al-Din Tuqan (Salt, Muslim), Awda Qasus (Karak, Christian) and Sa'id al-Mufti (Amman, Circassian) as ministers in 1929. By 1933 the number of opposition members on the Council had been reduced to two, hence facilitating the transaction of business,[20] apparently with Abdullah's encouragement.

Arguably, the real contribution of the Legislative Council was in fact twofold. Firstly, as a political safety valve. This was more important with regard to the further co-option of the Transjordanian elite than to purely ideological matters. The Council became a focus in particular for those who were born in Transjordan, as other formal avenues for political activism were difficult to break into, not least owing to the low educational attainment levels, even among members of the social elite. In the first elections for the Legislative Council, for example, only one of the 14 elected members, Muhammad al-Unsi (Balqa, Muslim), was not a Transjordanian by birth.[21] As the practice of appointing Legislative Council members to the executive became entrenched even more became at stake for such aspiring politicians. As Mary Wilson has noted, 'the Legislative Council proved to be an entree for native-born Transjordanians to the Executive Council'.[22]

The second enduring contribution of the Legislative Council was as a forum at which the competing interests between the state and the leading socio-economic actors could be aired, managed, negotiated and ameliorated. Key issues related to taxation and nationality occupied much of its deliberations during the 1930s. In March 1933, a consolidated land tax law was adopted by the Council in modified form owing to the 'strong opposition' of landowning interests within the Council,[23] an earlier, less accommodating bill having failed the year before. The compromise struck imposed a cap on the amount of tax that could be levied in excess of the burden of the previous three taxes.[24]

INCORPORATING THE TRIBAL PERIPHERY

The growing disparities in income levels between the centre and periphery of the new state and the activism of the TNC drew attention to what had been an enduring challenge since the establishment of the Transjordanian entity. This was how to incorporate those who were naturally sceptical and suspicious of the state for both cultural and material reasons. In other words, how to establish the largely symbiotic relationship between the tribes and the state that had been such a success of the late Ottoman period.

Initially, British officialdom had perceived the semi-nomadic tribal confederations with great suspicion. These tribesmen were regarded as lawless marauders, whose brigandage was a threat to the principle of the rule of law, and specifically to the peaceable and hard-working peasants of the country's marginal, cultivable areas. It was therefore to the peasantry of the country that Frederick Peake went when he first arrived in order to build up the coercive capacity of the state. As the job of state-building became the central mission of the British personnel on the ground, so the nomadic tribesmen acquired an even less fortunate reputation: they came to be seen as a force for preventing the consolidation of the state, and hence as an enemy of modernisation itself.

This frustration for a handful of British figures took on a wider significance in the late 1920s, with the continued concerns at Wahhabi expansionism from the Arabian interior. The British sought to pacify the tribal periphery in south-eastern Transjordan, the domains of the Bani Sakhr and Huwaitat, in order to remove any reason for cross-border raids from the emerging Saudi state. This they envisaged as an adjunct to the 1925 Hadda agreement, which had formally ended hostilities between the two entities. However, the premise on which the British strategy was based ignored the fact that mobility was an essential feature of the semi-nomadic, tribal economy, and that international boundary demarcation had paid little attention to the traditional use of space for seasonal grazing and the utilisation of water resources. In short, tribal clans that traditionally moved across what had become an international border, whether they were aware of it or not, were disinclined to change their traditional practices.

The creation of the Transjordan Frontier Force (TJFF) by the British represented a typically conventional attempt at a solution to a most unconventional problem. With its own difficulties of operating in a hostile desert environment, the deployment of the TJFF was not an operational success. Nor was it successful in binding the tribes into the state, as the overriding philosophy was to act against the interests of Transjordanian tribesmen, even though the majority of the aggressive raiding emanated from the *ikhwan*. Initially, however, the inclination of Whitehall was to act more coercively in order to try to make the policy work, and consequently, the RAF was pressed into service on behalf of the TJFF. A tribunal was established to arbitrate on issues of the ownership of booty. In one notorious case the TJFF prevented part of the Huwaitat from pursuing across the newly negotiated international border tribal raiders who had just seized some of their livestock; the logic of the territorial demarcation of states had trumped the justice of the case.

By 1930, in view of this frustratingly limited success, the British once again changed strategy. While still concerned at Wahhabi raiding, they now sought to co-opt the badia tribes. They entrusted with the task a British army major, John Glubb, who had already achieved considerable success in moulding bedouin recruits into an effective force in Iraq. Glubb was quickly a success, with raiding effectively brought to an end by 1932, and the Transjordanian section of the Iraq Petroleum Company oil pipeline, the construction of which was completed in 1935, made secure.[25] Soon after, Glubb became the chief arbiter of tribal law, displacing Abdullah's envoy to the tribes, Sharif Shaker bin Zayed. By the middle of the decade Glubb could claim a complete turnaround: that 'public security in the desert is better than in the cities'.[26] Riccardo Bocco and Tariq Tell have concluded that Glubb's approach 'had brought a degree of authority the tribes had not known since Umayyad times'.[27] Glubb had quickly established himself as one of the heroes of the state-building project in Transjordan. Thus was created a relationship that would endure for some 25 years, the success of 'Glubb Pasha' being so great that he would run the army in Jordan long after his presence in the country had become an anachronism.

Glubb began by establishing a Desert Mobile Force with about 130 men and six armoured cars in November 1930. From the beginning, there were two areas in which he excelled and which were pivotal to his success: his recruitment policy and his role as benefactor. His first characteristic success was in persuading the leading shaikhs of the tribes to allow their sons to join the force. This was something that they were well disposed to do, partly for cultural reasons, because of the honourable nature of its militaristic activities, and partly due to economic necessity, reflected in successive years of impoverishment. By such an approach to recruitment, Glubb literally absorbed the tribes into the state, giving the nomads an instant identification with and material stake in arguably its most important institution.

In doing so, he did not act either as a romantic, like Lawrence, or a maverick, like Philby. While in general sympathetic towards the tribesmen, Glubb's approach was essentially an instrumental one. In order to maintain his own authority within the new body, Glubb made sure that no single tribal confederation was over-represented in the force.[28] He also

Fig. 5. Members of Glubb's Desert Patrol, 1935 (Glubb, Film 1, No. 25)

manipulated internal rivalries in the larger tribes in order to encourage rival figures to compete for his favour, an approach that King Hussein would later use with equal success. Thus, in winning them over, Glubb did not require that the new recruits disavow their tribal identities, and members of the force still identified themselves by their tribal affiliation.[29]

Ironically, in view of the overall British preoccupation with state demarcation, Glubb also recruited from tribes outside the territory of Transjordan, notably from Iraq. This was a way of letting it be known that such a force would be built up whether or not local sections contributed to it. As Glubb himself wrote in *The Story of the Arab Legion*: 'If the Huwaitat did not enlist the result would be that their country would be policed by men of other tribes, not, as they hoped, that it would not be policed at all.'[30] This then was not an exclusively Jordanian army but truly an Arab Legion. The presence of such a mercenary element, which routinely comprised between 20% and 30% of the overall military strength through the 1930s and 1940s, also gave Glubb an insurance policy. It meant that he could rely upon the unswerving personal loyalty of a kernel of tribesmen-turned-soldiers should his relationship with the Transjordanian tribes deteriorate. As a British officer who worked with Glubb in Jordan observed of this external contingent, 'Such men are above politics and their loyalty to Jordan is unquestionable.'[31]

The second reason for Glubb's success was that once he had established an initial link with his constituency he then went on to play a role as a benefactor of the tribes. He did this, for example, by dispensing much-needed provisions to the poverty-stricken tribes through his access to state finances. The head of the Bani Hasan Relief Committee, formed in 1934 to alleviate the poverty of one of Jordan's largest tribes, was one of Glubb's British officers in the Arab Legion.[32] Glubb also paid for sick tribesmen to use hospital facilities in the towns and was the inspiration behind the creation of the Desert Mobile Medical Unit in 1937. Other British-controlled state institutions noted and followed Glubb's example, with the Iraq Petroleum Company financing the recruitment of a force in order to patrol its pipeline and guard it against sabotage.

In other words, Glubb set himself up as the principal intermediary between tribes and the state, thereby giving himself considerable leverage with the former against their non-compliance with his policies. The creation of such a two-way relationship helps to explain Glubb's indispensability, and hence his longevity, as well as the personal loyalty that accrued to him and that would still be manifest in the mid-1950s. In encouraging such reciprocity between state and tribe, Glubb had transcended the narrowly rational-legal notion of stateness of his national origins. While himself an Englishman imbued with a Western state perspective, Glubb had recognised the importance of instilling the state with the values, norms and identities of the society in which it was being built.

POLITICAL AFFAIRS IN THE EMIRATE

The incorporation of the tribal periphery into the state removed the last major socio-economic obstacle to the consolidation of the state in Transjordan. Though the economic hardships of the late 1920s and early 1930s were to continue for some of the decade, the 1930s were a relatively quiet time when state and tribe worked increasingly closely together and without friction. The amelioration of these economic problems by the extension of the state's field administration removed the political edge from the TNC, which had arguably been most animated on the subject of poverty and hardship in the countryside. Less than a decade-and-a-half after its creation, Transjordan had become an entity at peace with itself.

This does not mean that politics withered away during the 1930s. On the contrary, bile, controversy and intrigue were no strangers to the emirate during this time. However, the hurly-burly of politics, Transjordan-style, had already acquired its distinctive features. First, the cut and thrust of domestic politics had been largely contained and channelled by the state. Geographically, most meaningful political interaction took place in Amman, which after 1924 was the seat of the amir, and which contained the institutions of power, from the nascent ministries to the office of the British Resident. A key institution in terms of the channelling of such political activity was the Legislative Council, which was often the scene of impassioned speech-making and grandstanding by the opposition.

Second, the high politics of Transjordan as it was rapidly emerging in the 1930s was, as it was elsewhere in the Arab world at the time, very much one of elite politics or the politics of the notables. Abdullah was high-born. The elected representatives (and in the case of the badia figures also) returned to the Legislative Council were notables and shaikhs, with large land-holdings.[33] The clan names that would grace the Legislative Councils of the 1930s would be many of the names that would crop up repeatedly through the elite political dealings of successive decades: Hindawi from Ajlun; Tall from Irbid; Majali from Karak; Shraidah from Kura; Hmud and Kayid from Salt; and bin Jazi from the badia areas. Political communication from this small and rarefied stratum moved vertically downwards through a differentiated, though not unchanging, hierarchy of men of status.

With little by way of advanced education available within the emirate, opportunities for accelerated, meritocratic-based change were at first few. Neither were there significant political movements in the urban areas, which were still comparatively small towns.[34] It would be the 1950s before the emergence of a strong, urban-based ideological politics would sweep through the country. There was the beginning of an interest group politics, notably among the merchants, with the establishment of the Amman Chamber of Commerce in 1923. Even here, hierarchies of birth and wealth would soon establish themselves, with families of Syrian merchants like the Tabaa and the Bdeir, and Palestinian merchants like the Asfour, Mango and Qattan families set to dominate such institutions until the 1950s.[35]

Third, the style of local (as opposed to mandate) politics at the very centre of power was highly personalised, parochial and self-regarding, dominated by tactical considerations of self-advancement. Again, the *dramatis personae* was a short one. There was the British Resident, and those officials who were close to him, whose involvement in local politics was limited but whose potential influence on the appointment of cabinet members could be decisive; gaining his ear and favour was a passport to accelerated success in the emirate. Members of the Christian community in Transjordan, for example, approached the British representative in 1939 to persuade him to intercede on their behalf after the recall of some Palestinian Christian seconded officials had lowered the proportion of Christians in the administration.[36] On this occasion, he refused on the grounds that Christians were still over-represented as a proportion of their demographic profile.

There was the amir, who increasingly presided over local politics in the aftermath of the ultimatum, but who was limited in his broader govern-mental powers especially in foreign policy; for him local tensions were a useful way of exacting strategic concessions from the British. Abdullah as a rule would try to influence the appointment of the individual members of the Executive Council.[37] He tried to head off domestic criticism by spon-soring a court faction, the People's Party, which was established in 1927, and which included such figures as Sami Hijazi and Qasim Hindawi, both Transjordan-born. The party acted as a counterweight to the TNC, and helped to sanitise the political impact of the Legislative Council when it was in the ascendant, winning elections in 1931 and September–October 1934.

There were the politicians themselves: a decade after the first Legislative Council elections it was observed that the keen interest in elections 'rep-resented the widespread personal interest taken in candidates rather than any awakening of political consciousness'.[38] The politicians divided into two groups. One consisted of local notables with their local constituency as a base of support and indeed their local enmities. It was, for example, no coincidence that the Majali clan, as leaders of the western alliance covering the town of Karak and its hinterland, became firm supporters of Abdullah and members of the People's Party, as their great rivals and heads of the east-ern alliance, the Tarawnah, led the opposition TNC.[39] The predominance of personal over ideological politics meant that excursions into formal, organised politics, such as the establishment of the Solidarity Party (*hizb al-tadamun*) in 1933 by Mithqal al-Fayiz of the Bani Sakhr, were in fact purely self-serving, designed to bolster the standing and influence of their founders.

The second group of politicians consisted of the more ambitious mem-bers of the British-inspired external elite, men like Tawfiq Abu al-Huda, Ibrahim Hashim and latterly Samir al-Rifa'i who thrived on their politi-cal wits and their exclusive loyalty to the political centre, whether British and/or Hashemite. Such figures were on the whole more competent ad-ministrators and more adroit politicians than the first group, since they did not achieve prominence as a function of high birth. Nevertheless, they too were potentially insecure as politicians. Their vulnerability, however, came from their lack of a political base of support in Transjordan, which made them susceptible to being removed from office on an emiri whim. There is no doubt that Tawfiq Abu al-Huda was the dean of this group. He would go on to demonstrate his fundamental loyalty to the throne through the role that he played as the leading member of the 'King's men' in the Regency Council in the early 1950s, which helped to shore up a double Hashemite succession.

RISKS AND OPPORTUNITIES IN THE REGION

Underlying Prince Abdullah's move to Maan in 1920 was an ambition to assume power in either Baghdad or Damascus. With his brother Faisal installed as king in Iraq, his attention focused squarely on Syria, as his sponsorship of the *istiqlalists* had shown. However, by 1924, though he was reluctant ever fully to accept such realities, Abdullah's Syrian ambitions were in terminal decline, with the ousting of the *istiqlalists* and the consolidation of French rule. That is not to say that Syria, unlike Transjordan, began to settle into an orderly existence. It was the periodic eruptions in Syria, many self-inflicted by the mandate power, that helped to keep Abdullah's illusions alive. This close interest in Syrian affairs was maintained by the significant size of the merchant and trader community in Jordan of Syrian origin, vertical lines of trade helping to maintain and nurture such relations and hence foster continuing political ambitions.

The first of the big political ructions in Syria came with the Druze rebellion in southern Syria in 1925–27. This unsettled northern Jordan, not least because of the significant refugee inflows that helped provide cover for Druze military operations across the border. Though martial law was declared in the oasis of Azraq, some 80 kilometres (50 miles) east of Amman,[40] the danger soon passed. Abdullah, having learnt a painful lesson in 1921 on the importance of good Anglo-French relations to Britain, did not seek to exploit the opportunity, fearful of jeopardising his improving position. Abdullah's stance towards Syria was, however, never entirely benign, as is illustrated by his appointment of the brother of the leader of the Druze revolt, Zaid al-Atrash, as an honorary *aide de camp*. In spring 1936 Abdullah was quicker to try to take advantage of the situation in Syria, by prompting some of his closest supporters 'to advertise his qualifications for the throne in Syria both in official and nationalist circles',[41] invariably to little avail.

The most opportune time for revisiting the Syrian political succession came in 1941, after the installation of the Vichy regime. Abdullah, who was never one to take no for an answer, repeatedly called for unity between Transjordan and Syria in 1941, 1942 and 1944. Britain's reply was unenthusiastic, stating that it would agree to such a measure if it were supported broadly in the Arab world. Such a formulation was effectively a negative, in view of the growing political rivalries between and among both the leading personalities and also the leading power centres of the Arab world. Ironically, Hashemite Iraq as well as monarchical Egypt emerged at this time as the main vetoing states of Abdullah's dreams, as Nuri al-Said and Nahas Pasha respectively began from 1942 onwards to push their own variants of Arab union. The conclusion of the Alexandria Protocol in September 1944, with British encouragement, opened the way for the establishment of the Arab League in 1945, with Syrian membership as well as Iraq, Egypt, Lebanon and Transjordan as founding members. The chance for Syria to be gifted to Abdullah, as the Sanjak of Alexandretta, formerly a part of Syria, had effectively been given to Turkey in 1938 by the mandate power France, had passed.

If Abdullah's pretensions in Syria were increasingly forlorn, much more promising appeared to be the emerging situation in Palestine. Abdullah, with his Hashemite opportunist's eye for the acquisition of new territory, had always been interested in Palestine. When he met Churchill in Jerusalem in March 1921, he mentioned the idea of uniting Palestine and Transjordan under a single Arab ruler on at least four occasions, even though the plan had met nothing but discouragement. Abdullah had been distracted from regional politics by the necessities of domestic consolidation through much of the second half of the 1920s. By the end of the decade, with the agreement in place, he was once more looking beyond his immediate borders and it was Palestine that caught the eye.[42] As much as with Syria, Abdullah's westwards curiosity was maintained and fuelled by the significant population of Palestinian origin in Transjordan, many of them merchants moving laterally to expedite their trade.

In doing so Abdullah was thoroughly pragmatic, being prepared to cultivate Palestinian Arabs and Zionist organisations alike, depending on whoever might be willing to do business with him and be able to deliver. Abdullah's relationship with the Arab political activists of Palestine was complex and uneasy. It was at its most antagonistic in the competition that existed over political leadership with the Grand Mufti of Jerusalem, Haj Amin al-Hussaini. In general, it was a relationship that was choppy more often than it was not, with activists in Palestine exploiting the conditions in Transjordan to attack Abdullah's rule as undemocratic and subordinate to the British. Abdullah complained ceaselessly at the stream of hostile nationalist propaganda from Palestine made possible by Britain's tolerant approach. Relations never reached breaking point with the nationalists, and at times the two sides could work together; indeed, two of the leading activists travelled with Abdullah to Baghdad for the funeral of his brother, King Faisal I, in 1933. But neither were they cordial, and such moments of cooperation were invariably transitory.

Abdullah's approach towards the Jews was the easy attitude of the patrician. Joseph Nevo observes that, for the amir, in a reference to their semi-separate status as a 'nation' under the Ottoman Empire, the Jews were 'simply a modern millet',[43] one which could be immensely valuable, especially given their European political connections, but which nevertheless could not be taken very seriously other than as a minority group within the broad sweep of Muslim, Arab lands. At times of heightened tension and conflict in Palestine, such as the 1929 Western Wall riots, Abdullah invariably sided with his core constituency, condemnations of Zionist policy peppering his public diplomacy. This, however, proved to be no barrier to the pursuit of pragmatic politics, and Abdullah's contacts with Zionist organisations became a major area of criticism for Arab nationalists in Palestine. By the early 1930s, Abdullah and the Yishuv (the Jewish community in Palestine) had become 'natural allies',[44] based on a common enmity to the Arab national movement in Palestine, led by the Mufti.

The emergence of major and continuing discontent over the issue of Jewish immigration to Palestine did not leave Transjordan itself unaffected. If the political balance had decisively favoured the colonial power through the middle of the 1920s, this began to change with the increasingly acute nature of the Palestine situation. It was the need to insulate Transjordan against such destabilising factors that helped to increase the importance of Amir Abdullah to the British authorities. Meanwhile, for Abdullah, maintaining peace at home was a way both of pleasing the British, and hence of trying to win over more power from Cox and Peake, while also indicating his own ability to manage the emerging problem in Palestine: if he could preserve the peace at home could he not do so in Palestine itself? The British mandate authorities were of course happy at Abdullah's cooperation, and concluded that early stirrings in Transjordan were contained in 1928 'due mainly to the attitude taken up by the Amir and his Government'.[45] This limited gratitude, however, never made it likely that they would consider a bigger stage for Abdullah.

Pragmatic cooperation between Abdullah and the Zionist movement prior to the establishment of the state of Israel reached its zenith during the early to mid-1930s over the issue of land transactions. The issue arose in the aftermath of the 1930 White Paper that limited the sale of land in historic Palestine. The potential of land sales east of the Jordan increased when the British mandate authorities took the view that such sales were entirely a matter for the government in Amman. For Abdullah, who invariably lacked a supply of funds commensurate with his status and ambitions, and had been given personal title to land endorsed by the Legislative Council,[46] land leases seemed to offer a way of generating significant levels of cash, and a lease was duly concluded.[47] Moreover, the spectre of Jewish settlement that it seemed to offer would confirm that the amir was capable of ruling over Jew and Arab alike. The leaders of the main shaikhly families of Transjordan, notably the leaders of the Bani Sakhr and the Majali and Tarawnah clans based in Karak, also supported Abdullah in considering such land sales. For the increasingly impoverished rural Transjordan, where land was the only asset but buyers were few, this interest seemed to offer a ready-made solution to the deep economic problems of the moment.

In the end, however, no sales were actually made, let alone Jewish settlements established. The issue gave Arab nationalists based in Palestine, like Nabih al-Azmah, ammunition with which to attack Abdullah, and agitation increased, especially in the towns. The Trans-Jordan Congress of June 1933 vigorously opposed the idea, and sought 'to prohibit strictly the sale of lands to Jews and their dealing with Trans-Jordan in any shape or manner and to prevent the permanent stay of any Jew in Trans-Jordan'.[48] The fact that a Transjordanian solidarity delegation attended Arab demonstrations in Palestine in 1933 indicated the combustibility of the issue at home, should the amir and rural elites have chosen to pursue the idea, and the British now flinched at the prospect. In the end the British settled the matter by steering through a Nationalities Law that proscribed the sale of land to non-nationals.

This did not prevent almost continuous low-key contacts taking place between Abdullah and principally the Jewish Agency throughout much of the 1930s, as the amir attempted to persuade the latter of the utility of a bi-communal state of Arabs and Jews under his leadership. Nor did it prevent the Jewish Agency from paying Abdullah a substantial yearly subvention in the form of an option on a land lease that was improbably continued right through until 1939. By this stage, of course, the annual option was no longer either about leasing land or Jewish settlement, but, as Avi Shlaim has noted, 'the perceived need to secure the backing of an Arab ruler as a counterweight to Palestinian antagonism'.[49] While much of Transjordanian society was not unsympathetic towards the Palestinians and felt suspicion towards the rising tide of Jewish immigration, this was only 'a second-hand dislike'.[50] It did, however, cost Abdullah increasingly dear among the Arab mainstream in Palestine and beyond, especially after the death of his brother. As Mary Wilson has concluded, Abdullah's 'attempts

Fig. 6. The town of Amman, 1933 (Stark, MF 133 C2)

to strike a pose of regional leadership [following Faisal's death] on the heels of his recent transaction with the Jewish Agency were at best not taken seriously and at worst suspected of masking treachery'.[51]

The revolt in Palestine between 1936 and 1939 elicited some considerable initial concern in Transjordan. The authorities placed a premium on a law enforcement-oriented response. The police were drilled in mob control in anticipation of unrest; demonstrations in the capital were banned;[52] the size of the Arab Legion was temporarily expanded to keep Amman in good order. Transjordan experienced a few isolated acts of violence, especially against the Iraqi oil pipeline; later there were reports of gun-running and rebel incursions. Some 50 or so Transjordanians were reported as having gone to Palestine to fight with the Arab side.[53]

On the whole, however, unrest in Transjordan was never more than patchy and fleeting, and never amounted to a serious challenge to the state. This was not least because of improvements in the Transjordanian economy. The end to the run of bad harvests produced relative abundance in 1937 and 1938. This was supplemented by higher wages for those involved in its gathering, as seasonal labour flows were restricted by the conflict.[54] Moreover, there was more work than usual because of the construction of the Baghdad–Haifa highway,[55] the most eye-catching example of an ambitious road-building policy introduced in 1936. By the time of the end of the unrest in Palestine, the people of Transjordan were able 'to congratulate themselves on the peace and relative prosperity which they are enjoying at a time when all their neighbouring territories are far from happy'.[56] But if those presiding over the fortunes of Transjordan thought that they had manoeuvred through the worst of the Palestinian problem they had another think coming. Within a decade the issue of Palestine would engulf the emirate, and change the nature of its society and politics forever.

THE SECOND WORLD WAR

By the time of the outbreak of hostilities in the Second World War, Abdullah had been based in Transjordan for 18 years. In spite of his continuing ambivalence towards the place, and undaunted ambition to preside over a wider, more plausible state, he had become the recognised face of an emirate that was by now itself an emerging state. Though his initial days in the emirate had been most inauspicious, for the last decade or so his relationship with the British had been changing. He was no longer disdained as an ineffectual, peevish and selfish figurehead. As the situation in Palestine had deteriorated, he was regarded with increasing favour as a moderate partner capable of delivering stable government. As Ron Pundik has written the year 1939 saw 'the end of the tutelage period and the beginning of partnership, even if it was an unequal one'.[57] By the end of the 1930s Abdullah and the British were very much a team.

This complementary relationship was to thrive over the following decade as a result of key British personnel changes on the ground. In 1939 Glubb had taken over as the commander of the Arab Legion from Peake, who had been happy to maintain it as a police and gendarmerie force. However, it was the change in the British Residency that was to establish the chemistry that would make the relationship work most smoothly. In the same year Cox finally left, his best work as a state-builder having been long completed between 1926 and 1931, his somewhat dour and rigid approach ill-suited to a more cordial and collegiate relationship with the amir. Cox was replaced by Alec Kirkbride, who as a young officer had first found himself in Transjordan during the period of the local governments in 1920, and who then had faced a political dilemma of how to deal with Abdullah's march northwards from Maan.[58] The relaxed, easy-going and positive manner that had governed his instinctive response to that political contingency would be ideal for his new position; meanwhile, Abdullah well remembered the helpfulness of the young British officer of nearly two decades earlier.

If the British had come to value Abdullah during trouble and conflict in Palestine, their appreciation would grow during the Second World War. Britain's declaration of war on Nazi Germany was quickly followed by a raft of measures aimed at shoring up the emirate. German residents were taken into custody, censorship was introduced, it was made an offence to trade with the enemy, and currency and price controls were introduced. Such was the easy relationship between the British and Transjordan that all was accepted, as Kirkbride noted, 'with surprisingly little complaint'.[59] There was relatively little hoarding and profiteering. Notables and tribal shaikhs offered their services to the mandate power. This was indeed the period of the phoney war.

The mood subsequently changed within Transjordan as a consequence of wider developments in the war, with the continental victories of the Germans, and the abject collapse of France in summer 1940, which saw the quisling Vichy authority extend to the very boundaries of the emirate in Syria. The borders of Transjordan, as ever, were porous to enemy propaganda, and German disinformation permeated the country. Abdullah became quite depressed at the direction that the war had taken, and feared that he had backed the wrong horse, not least because his great rival, Haj

Amin al-Hussaini in Palestine, now attended to by Transjordan's leading dissident, Subhi Abu Ghanimah, had taken up the cause of the Axis.

The main real political test of the relationship between Britain and Transjordan came in April 1941, following the short-lived coup d'etat by Rashid Ali al-Kailani in Baghdad, especially once Kailani had sought help from the Axis powers. For much of Transjordan, including, Kirkbride relates, 'many' of the officers of the Arab Legion, the coup destroyed any hope of an Allied victory, and indicated, with typical tribal pragmatism, that it was 'high time to get in touch with the new conquerors and to make terms'.[60] Kirkbride further indicates that the situation in Transjordan was of an existential gravity for the British, and unless the situation in Iraq was restored quickly 'our position in Jordan would become untenable'.[61]

The British moved an Arab Legion contingent into Iraq, as part of a general effort to undermine the putschists, a strategy that would result in the collapse of the coup after some two months. In the meantime, it appeared fleetingly as if pressure across the Jordan border might not prove possible to exert. A mechanised squadron of the TJFF, which joined the Legionnaires at the H-4 pumping station on the Iraq Petroleum Company pipeline, were, in Glubb's words, in 'a disaffected condition', and hence had to be withdrawn.[62] There was also an attempt to foment rebellion in the Arab Legion, though this was more a function of intra-tribal competition, notably within the Bani Sakhr, than ideological principle. While some members of the Legion also went home prematurely, a force drawn from the Desert Patrol continued to Iraq,[63] thereby vindicating Glubb's approach of recruiting tribesmen from beyond the boundaries of Transjordan. It was these contingents that provided the majority of the Arab Legion that continued to move on Baghdad.[64]

With the Legion having proved itself in Iraq, the way was opened for its expansion under Glubb and for it to play an enhanced role. Admittedly this did not extend to the initial British invasion of Vichy-controlled Syria, Abdullah suffering the discourtesy of only being told about it on the day of its commencement. Nevertheless, the value of the Arab Legion to the British war effort can be seen in the fact that financial subventions were increased to allow the expansion of the force to some 8,000 men, some four times its pre-war strength. By the end of hostilities most of its number were serving outside the emirate in support of the British cause, especially in Syria, where the Legion's most notable success was the capture of the eastern town of Sukhna.

The increased funds used to finance the expansion of the Arab Legion ensured that unprecedented levels of resources flowed into the areas of the tribal periphery during the war, with Glubb's patronage at its height. This was not the only positive impact on the badia economy. The bedouin lands received a further boost from British policy during the war, with the initiation of an extensive programme of public works in the south of the country. During the winter of 1941 between 5,000 and 8,000 tribesmen worked on rail and road-building schemes in the Aqaba area alone, with the logic of Glubb's original recruitment policy now common practice on the part of the British. Bedouin tribesmen also benefited in other ways during the wartime boom, ranging from a resurgence in demand for traditional forms of transportation to the smuggling of goods in order to take advantage of differential and rising prices across borders. Large tribal landowners, together with settled smallholders, also benefited during the 1940s from the growth in economic infrastructure, with its positive impact on the fortunes of the agriculture sector.[65]

The other socio-economic group to benefit from the policies of the mandate power during the war was a segment of the merchant stratum in Amman, which was either Syrian or Palestinian in origin. These merchants benefited from the trade and procurement policies of the British war effort in the Middle East and their market implications. Key to this prosperity was the creation of the Middle East Supply Centre (MESC) in 1941, which sought to control trade, and in particular the supply of foodstuffs.[66] In spite of the MESC's best efforts to regulate prices and prevent shortages there were many loopholes in its own regulations, which meant that the Levant was characterised by wild fluctuations in price and supply, and from which quick-witted merchants could easily make substantial profits. Those relatively few to make huge profits did so because of their ability to gain trade quotas, which they did as a result of a combination of factors, including the favouritism of Amir Abdullah and a handful of mandate officials, and their own financial standing. As Abla Amawi concludes, this 'quota coterie' of up to 31 merchants emerged as an elite at the top of the hierarchy of merchants in the emirate.[67] As one observer of the day has recalled: 'If you had a quota, you had a fortune in your hands.'[68]

There were other, even less salubrious ways, to make a wartime fortune. These included hoarding and speculation, especially in grain, which was rampant. Smuggling, ranging from fuel to livestock to staples like rice and cooking oil, was widespread given the differential pricing that existed across the region, with Transjordanians fully exploiting their long and porous borders. In general, the MESC encouraged poachers rather than game-keepers. For example, merchants who had been entrusted with the operation of a grain-extraction scheme, whereby consumer goods would be made available

Fig. 7. A street scene in the northern town of Ajlun, 1943 (Stark, MF 133 B3)

to grain producers in order to keep cereals supply within a regulated system, simply moved them illegally to the most lucrative regional markets. Local merchants also discovered that they could benefit from enhanced demand in the local market, especially for building materials, inputs for transport infrastructure expansion and for the rise in the demand for motor vehicles. For example, in 1937 the Arab Legion had only 27 motor vehicles; by 1943 this figure had shot up to 600.[69]

The happy convergence of the establishment of the MESC, Transjordanian loyalty to London in the dark days of war, and the efficient military contribution of the Arab Legion in the field, also resulted in other benefits accruing to Amman from Britain. Most eye-catching among these came in 1942 when the British Treasury advanced a loan of £50,000 for the development of the Red Sea port of Aqaba.

INDEPENDENCE, AT LAST

Amir Abdullah benefited from the creation of a new world order at the end of the Second World War, as he had done at the end of the First. On this occasion too he was the beneficiary of evolving thinking on the part of the British. On this occasion too the benefit was not as good as it at first had seemed. But then Abdullah knew the British well enough to take what was on offer and then appeal to their sense of pragmatism in the pursuit of the incremental improvement of his position.

The British authorities were certainly minded to bolster the standing of Transjordan and its amir. They did so in recognition of the fact that the world was fast changing and the decolonisation bandwaggon was on the roll. Indeed, the British had used just such normative considerations in calling for the independence of Lebanon and Syria in 1941, as a way of expediently weakening Vichy. They had fended off Abdullah's insistent requests for independence then only on the grounds of impracticability while the war still raged. By 1945 the status of Transjordan was becoming anomalous, Transjordan being alone at the Cairo conference among the five founding members of the Arab League not to enjoy an independent existence. By withholding such a status Britain was effectively retarding and undermining its closest friend in the region. The move to grant Transjordan independence was also the product of a new realism on the part of the recently elected Labour government and of its Foreign Secretary, Ernest Bevin, in particular. It was clear that the efforts of the war had reduced Britain as a superpower and it was no longer capable of acting as the hegemon of the Middle East. London's decision-making with respect to Transjordan was rendered easier by the confidence that both state and leader were proven allies.

Against such a backdrop, a new Anglo-Transjordanian treaty was concluded, that superseded the 1928 agreement. It formally terminated the mandate and created an 'independent' state. Consequently, the Hashemite Kingdom of Transjordan was formally declared in May 1946 when Abdullah was crowned king. Though officially independent, the substance of the relationship was more one of continuity than change. As Elizabeth Monroe has written delicately the treaty was of a 'pre-war pattern'.[70] The kingdom, as the emirate before, remained dependent on the British for its annual subsidy. Britain was permitted to station its troops in the kingdom for the next 25 years. British officers continued to command the Jordanian army. Kirkbride, whose title had changed but little else, continued to occupy a privileged position as senior adviser to the king, although that was as much a reflection of personal chemistry as of neo-colonial obligation.

Even in those areas where change did take place it fell well short of a robust sovereignty, being riddled with equivocation. British control of the finances and administration was to be 'relaxed'. King Abdullah was to be permitted to appoint consuls to some neighbouring Arab states, provided they confined themselves to consular activities. Palestinian secondees in the administration were to be replaced by Transjordanians if possible. Such shortcomings gave the Soviet Union the pretext to veto Transjordanian membership of the UN, a veto that would stand, embarrassingly, as late as 1955. Even the US dawdled in its recognition of the kingdom, influenced by a Jewish lobby that had still not come fully to terms with Transjordan's organic separation from Palestine. It would not be until as late as 1949 that the US would establish full diplomatic relations with Amman. It was then little wonder that the leaders of competitor states in the Arab world, such as King Faruq in Egypt and King Abdul Aziz ibn Saud of Saudi Arabia, belittled the kingdom and its head of state. Stung by such inadequacies, King Abdullah lobbied behind the scene for further powers, a request that was granted with the amendments to the treaty of 1948.

CHAPTER 4

Loss of Innocence

The year 1946 was the apex of achievement for Transjordan, soon to be rebranded as the Hashemite Kingdom of Jordan. The slow but steady construction of a state, which characterised the 1920s and 1930s, had been accelerated during wartime. Unimagined levels of prosperity had flowed as a result of British procurement and trade policy in the region. Amman was unquestionably the hub of the emerging state. King Abdullah, now a senior statesman among regional leaders, real and aspirant, gave the entity prestige above its station, a position that was enhanced by formal if not quite substantive independence. The makers and shakers of San Remo could look with pride on the achievement of Transjordan, as it emerged some 25 years after their conference created the mandate system. Though the relative absence of truly independent institutions meant that Transjordan did not quite conform to the model end-product League of Nations mandate, it was undoubtedly its leading success. Perhaps even more than its successes at state-building, Transjordan had emerged with a political community that, while far from homogeneous, shared a widespread consensus about the new state's existence and its overall political direction. In short, Transjordan was not yet racked by the existential, legitimacy problems that were to blight most emerging Arab states at the time.

The year 1946 was of course in many ways a misleading barometer of the health of the new Transjordanian entity. Its economic achievements would in any case have ebbed, following a return to post-war normality. The new political context of rapid decolonisation would have created political challenges for a country with an enduring over-reliance on influential British officials. Jordan would also have had to face the uncertainties of a political succession at some stage, with disharmony lurking within the Amman branch of the Hashemite family. It was, however, the looming prospect of war and dispossession in Palestine that gives 1946 a special poignancy for Transjordan. Within a short time a turbulent series of events would ensure that Transjordan would never be the same again, with its carefully constructed and maturing political community the major casualty.

The next five years would see Transjordan play a leading role in what has become known as the first Arab-Israeli war. More than 50 years later it remains one of the most controversial periods in the history of Transjordan and of the Hashemite dynasty.[1] Transjordanian historiography reflects the controversial nature of this period. Important and contested questions still abound. What was the nature of the secret diplomacy between Abdullah and the Jewish Agency in 1946, 1947 and 1948? Did Abdullah sell the Arabs in Palestine short? How far was Transjordan responsible for the collective failure of the Arab side in the war? Was there a popular mandate for the incorporation of the West Bank into the Transjordanian state? Historical interpretation is in turn of contemporary political importance, especially regarding such issues as: the extent to which Hashemite dynastic and Transjordanian national interests, if one can speak of such a thing, coincide; the nature of the relationship between the Transjordanian state and Israel; and ultimately, the fitness of the Hashemite dynasty to preside over an Arab state.

By 1950 it might appear that Abdullah had done well, given the precariousness of the situation. The Arab Legion had fought with distinction, especially in Jerusalem; Transjordan had taken the West Bank, much of the territory designated by the United Nations for an Arab state in Palestine; though perennially thought of as small and weak, Transjordan had emerged both diplomatically and militarily as the most effective of all the Arab states, in contrast to the shambles that were the supposed regional power centres of Baghdad, Cairo and Damascus. In the words of one contemporary commentator 'Jordan's strength has increased over the last three years in a diplomatic, a military and a "prestige" sense.'[2] Yet, such apparent gains were to be quickly exposed as the largely irrelevant residue of a dying age. For Transjordan, the era of innocence, if it had not ended in 1948, died with King Abdullah's assassination in Jerusalem on 20 July 1951.[3]

THE ONSET OF STRIFE

The end of the Second World War formed a catalytic backdrop to conflict in the territory of historic Palestine. The future of the British presence had been undermined by a combination of economic and social exhaustion at home and the new international norms that frowned upon imperial enterprises, even if partially disguised. Jewish immigration had accelerated exponentially as a result of the trauma of Nazi persecution and genocide in Europe. Local Arab opposition was implacable, though its effectiveness had been undermined by the exertions of the 1936–39 Arab revolt in Palestine. The United Nations was disposed to be involved in the problem, but was itself newly created, thereby lacking the robust institutions, will and focus to play a decisive role. The scene was set for power politics to decide the future of Palestine.

Conflict was not, however, immediate. It was to be 29 November 1947 before the General Assembly of the UN, with US and Soviet backing, though voluble Arab opposition, would pass its partition plan for Palestine, the moment at which conflict became inevitable. It was not until 15 May 1948 that the British terminated the mandate, and the establishment of the state of Israel was declared, to be followed by an inter-state war. In the meantime, there was wave upon wave of diplomacy, some of it secret, some of it visible only in form, aimed at trying to manage the outcome of the fast-moving events.

During this period the issue of partition was the crucial subject. The British Royal Commission, led by Lord Peel, in its report published in 1937, had advocated partition as a solution to the growing ethnic tensions in the area, the first major body to do so. While Abdullah would have preferred the simple union of Palestine and Transjordan under his own leadership, he immediately welcomed the partition idea as one that provided immediate, practical opportunities for substantial territorial acquisition, a view for which he was castigated in the Arab world. From here on in Abdullah's expectation would be that he would inherit the area in Palestine designated for the Arab population.

The Jewish Agency, that had so assiduously cultivated Abdullah during the 1930s, sought him out again soon after the end of the war. Two meetings were held in King Abdullah's house at Shuna in the Jordan Valley in August 1946. Rather than an act of betrayal, Abdullah would have regarded a dialogue with the third of the three main protagonists on the ground as nothing new, and indeed eminently sensible. The secrecy of the meetings indicates that he knew that others would view it differently. It was unfortunate that Abdullah's sense of his own manifest destiny should have become focused by the opportunities of the moment on the sliver of the Arab world that was soon to become the benchmark of Arab honour and principle.

The Shuna meetings went very much as the representatives of the Yishuv would have expected. Both parties agreed in principle on the issue of territorial partition. Abdullah would preside over the Arab territory, which would be incorporated into his newly established kingdom, preferably without conflict. Cementing the convergence of interests of Abdullah and the Yishuv was their mutual antipathy towards the Mufti of Jerusalem, Haj Amin al-Husseini, with whom both had become implacable enemies over the course of the preceding two decades. Neither wanted to see an independent Arab state in Palestine established under his leadership.

If partition was Abdullah's preferred policy, confirmed by both a consistency stretching back to Peel, and fully in keeping with his Hashemite dynastic ideology of expansion and incorporation, his public diplomacy in the aftermath of the Shuna meetings was considerably less clear-cut. Hemmed in by the Arab consensus, articulated and standardised by the recently established Arab League, and concerned about the propaganda of Arab nationalists in Palestine, Abdullah felt it expedient formally to deny the principle of partition. Evidence of this tactical dissimulation abounds. At the London Conference of Jews and Arabs in autumn 1946, for example, he instructed his representative, Samir al-Rifai, not to break ranks with the other Arab participants. While welcoming the visit of the United Nations Special Committee on Palestine (UNSCOP) to Transjordan, in contrast to its boycott by Arabs in Palestine, Abdullah was again coy on the issue of partition. The political context in which Abdullah was manoeuvring also proved to be increasingly uncomfortable, as violence became more and more prevalent on the ground. Nevertheless, in spite of this unforthcoming public stance, Abdullah confirmed his original position in a new meeting with the increasingly anxious Jewish Agency, this time represented by Golda Meir, in November 1947.

Abdullah was also busy behind the scenes with the British authorities. London had not advocated partition after the end of the war for fear of undermining its precarious position in the Arab world, even though Transjordan was its 'only sure ally'.[4] The eventual majority recommendation of UNSCOP for partition gave Britain the justification for altering its position. London consequently fell into line on the formal issue of partition, though it abstained in the crucial General Assembly vote, and refused to accept responsibility for the implementation of the plan. Belatedly concerned that its evacuation should not be succeeded by chaos, the idea of Abdullah taking over the Arab-designated area was attractive to Britain, as was the assumed strengthening of a regional ally. What Abdullah needed to know was that Britain would not obstruct his move from the inside, either through the use of its financial leverage over his kingdom or through the presence of the 41 British officers commanding the Arab Legion.

Abdullah used the renegotiation of the Anglo-Transjordanian treaty in February 1948 as cover for detailed talks in London on post-mandate contingencies. King Abdullah was represented by his prime minister, Tawfiq Abu al-Huda, and his military chief, Glubb. Though initially having proceeded 'carefully and quietly',[5] by January 1948 it was clear that Britain would look kindly on the constructive use of the Arab Legion. That is to say Britain was well disposed towards the deployment of the force, provided that it was not sent into the areas reserved for the Jewish state. No less a person than the British Foreign Secretary, Ernest Bevin, the commanding figure in Britain's external affairs of the day, effectively confirmed the British position to Abu al-Huda during their February meeting. Meanwhile, the British government also resolved the anomaly of Glubb's position of still being a Colonial Office employee, insisting that after the May proclamation of the kingdom he should 'become a mercenary in the service of a monarch who was friendly to Britain'.[6] It was then just a question of handling the public diplomacy of the Legion's deployment.

While assiduous in his attention towards the British, King Abdullah had fewer bothers as far as his Palestine policy and the domestic arena was concerned. Mary Wilson has correctly observed that the nature of Transjordan 'allowed Abdullah to pursue his objectives in Palestine with less regard for popular opinion than any other Arab leader'.[7] The reasons for this are several, from the centrality of British power and the relative autonomy of a state based on foreign subventions and personnel, through Abdullah's autocratic tendencies to the hierarchical nature of socio-political relations inside the kingdom.

That is not to say that there was no opposition whatsoever. New ideological groupings, notably the Muslim Brotherhood, were indeed beginning to take root in Transjordan. A younger generation of urban-based intellectuals and political activists, personified by a future radical prime minister, Sulaiman Nabulsi, protege of the veteran Jordanian opposition politician and exile, Subhi Abu Ghanimah, was becoming a focus of debate and discussion. Such figures would rapidly move to prominence in the 1950s in the context of social turmoil and political radicalism for which the Palestine issue would be to a great extent responsible. As yet, though, these groupings and movements were located on the ideological and political periphery in Transjordan and hence were regarded as relatively unimportant. Consequently, Abdullah's expansionist strategy was not seriously scrutinised at a level of high politics, let alone effectively opposed. Little consideration was therefore given to the implications of the policy for politics and society in Transjordan, especially over the longer term.

A HASHEMITE DREAM

Once Abdullah had enlisted the effective support of the British for his ex-pansionist strategy there was little to do but to wait for the formalities to take their course. Wary of being accused of breaking Arab ranks and pur-suing his own ambitions at the expense of the Arabs of Palestine, Abdullah was careful to bide his time and keep a low profile, neither of which, as a politician, came naturally to him.

The massacre of a substantial number of unarmed villagers at Deir Yassin on 9 April 1948 by the extremist Jewish group the Irgun Zvi Leumi greatly aided Abdullah's position. First, the outrage sparked a refugee outflow, and increasingly impassioned appeals to Amman to intervene on behalf of the Arab population of Palestine. For Abdullah, the desperation of those on the ground meant that he was no longer the sole *demandeur* as far as Palestine was concerned. Second, it made military inaction among the neighbour-ing governments to Palestine much less tenable, and hence hastened the emergence of a full-blown, inter-state armed conflict. The principal Arab states were no longer able to get away simply with an indirect involvement in the dispute, through the sponsorship of the Arab League-administered small irregular force, the so-called Arab Liberation Army (ALA).

A combination of Abdullah's revulsion over Deir Yassin and the prox-imity of Amman obliged the king to take the lead. His message offering to save Palestine was accepted by the Arab League, in spite of the opposition of Syria and the shrill objections of the Mufti. The one condition attached to the green light was that Abdullah should liberate the whole of Palestine, an objective that he was neither free to pursue nor capable of realising. Abdullah's position was hindered by the fact that Britain insisted on the full withdrawal of all detachments of the Arab Legion already stationed in Palestine as a prelude to its use in occupying Arab-designated territory.

Meanwhile, Abdullah's understanding with the Zionist movement over the future of Palestine had also become less certain given the pressures of the moment. It seemed as though Abdullah felt that his best chance of fending off pressure from the Arab League was to deliver political successes beyond those offered to the Arab side in the partition. Consequently, his perennial ideas for the future of Palestine, of an Arab–Jewish federation under his rule and with Jewish autonomy, in the past dismissed as flights of fancy, now seemed to harden into policy. A further meeting with Golda Meir as late as 11 May in Amman saw her interpret this position as being put forward in the form of an ultimatum, compliance with which alone would be the *sine qua non* for the aversion of war.[8] The Zionist side responded defiantly, as, having come this far, the Jews were not to be deprived of statehood. In spite of the unsatisfactory outcome, such meetings did, however, increase Abdullah's political vulnerability to the charge that Israel and Transjordan were conniving at the partition of Palestine at the expense of the Palestinians.

In turn, King Abdullah had been only partially successful in his demand that Transjordan should take command of all forces mobilised under the banner of the Arab League, in addition to his own Arab Legion. The messy compromise that followed a flurry of rushed consultations as time ran out for the mandate was that each country contingent, comprising Egypt, Iraq, Lebanon and Syria, should fight under its own command structure, but that Abdullah should be given the title of supreme commander of the Arab forces. Though such an announcement was good for Abdullah's ego, and must have added to his sense of historic opportunity, it would quickly become a very visible liability in the event of anything short of a substantial victory. An ominous sign of things to come was that while the Arabs wrangled over such parochial matters, the Yishuv prepared for war, with a Jewish offensive against strategic positions in the Arab-designated territory commencing as early as March.

Finally, Abdullah had the thorny issue of Jerusalem to consider. The Old City, holy to the three monotheistic faiths, was obviously the biggest prize of all. Abdullah's Sharifian lineage, through which he claimed to be able to trace his origins back to the tribe of Prophet Muhammad, meant that he could hardly ignore the future of Jerusalem, especially as his claims to legitimacy as an Arab leader were partly founded on a religious base.[9] However, under the terms of the UN partition resolution the city of Jerusalem was to be denied to both sides, instead being given over to international jurisdiction.

The first stage of the conflict lasted for one month, with 35,000 Jewish regulars and irregulars and around 21,500 Arab troops taking the field.[10] Abdullah's forces, though at 6,000–7,000 (of whom some 4,500 were operational) smaller in size than the Egyptian contingent, were well organised, well led and experienced.[11] As such, they were always more likely to do well in a short and focused conflict than in a protracted and diffuse fight. However, they were insufficient to attempt to take over all of the territories designated for an Arab state under the partition. Consequently, the Arab Legion was not deployed to such areas as Gaza and western Galilee. Initially, the Arab Legion moved into Palestine to take up positions in Jenin, Nablus and Ramallah, but was immediately faced with a dilemma posed by a move by Jewish forces on Jerusalem. Abdullah hesitated owing to the formalities of the international legal position and then ordered the Legion to the city, the symbolic importance of Jerusalem being too great for him to ignore. Glubb, in turn, prevaricated for a further day for the same reason before obeying the order.

So it was that during the first phase of the war the Arab Legion fought mainly in Jerusalem and around Latrun, an area crucial to preventing Israeli supplies from entering the city. With the Jewish side's motives as much the product of ideology as Abdullah's, the fighting in Jerusalem was intense. The two sides were evenly matched, but the Arab Legion was successful in seizing the Jewish Quarter and eventually held the whole of the Old City. The Arab Legion also held the towns of Lydda and Ramle, designated for the Arab state in the UN plan, but only with a nominal presence for fear of spreading its forces too thinly. Though prudent enough from a military point of view, the longer-term political effects of the decision not to consolidate these positions were to be profoundly negative for Transjordan and its leadership. Elsewhere in the fighting, only the Egyptians had occupied a significant amount of territory in Palestine. Meanwhile, only Iraq had coordinated with Transjordan, an Iraqi contingent at Nablus freeing up Arab Legion units for its main effort. By the time of the cease-fire, the Jordanian side had done all the fighting it desired. As Mary Wilson has concluded, by June Abdullah's 'immediate goal of establishing a credible presence in Palestine had been more than achieved'.[12]

But for Transjordan the cost of its success had been considerable. The Legion had suffered nearly 20% casualties. It was running low on ordnance, but without hope of imminent resupply, owing to Britain's solitary rigorous, and hence unhelpful, implementation of a UN arms embargo on all the warring sides. Moreover, the initial bout of fighting had witnessed the beginning of a severe refugee problem, which by June would see up to 300,000 Arabs leaving their homes either as a result of Jewish military attack or the fear of being engulfed in fighting. As an inevitable by-product of geography the majority of these refugees gravitated to territory held by Jordan, thereby increasing the infrastructural and economic strains on the Jordanian state. For Transjordan the establishment of a credible and secure cease-fire was now likely to be crucial for its military prospects, the future of the refugees and hence its own political fortunes.

That one did not extend beyond the initial period of one month was due to a combination of prudent Israeli and imprudent Arab bellicosity. Egypt and Transjordan, the countries with the most exposed positions, favoured an extension to the cease-fire, not least because it was becoming clear that Israel had used the pause in hostilities significantly to improve its military capability. Those with less to lose, like Lebanon, Saudi Arabia and Syria, were the most truculent, as was the Arab side in general with its continuing misplaced assumptions of the certainty of victory. In an uncanny rehearsal of the lead-up to the 1967 war, Egypt soft-pedalled its opposition to a further bout of conflict for fear of being outflanked politically by Syria, while Transjordan again dared not oppose the Arab consensus. As it approached a renewed round of fighting, Transjordan had been able to mobilise some more men, but that was all. With no new operational aims, the renewal of conflict was deeply unpalatable for Amman. Against a situation already deteriorating alarmingly, hostilities were rejoined on 9 July 1948.

The second phase of the fighting, which lasted ten days, saw the Arab Legion hold onto its most important territory in Jerusalem and the associated areas of Latrun and Ramallah. However, it also saw one of the most contentious developments in the conflict, that is to say Glubb's order for a pre-emptive withdrawal from Lydda and Ramle, followed by Israel's occupation of the two towns. The act of retrenchment was the obvious corollary of their tactical takeover by the Legion in the first place, the towns being surrounded by Jewish settlements and, in the words of Glubb's biographer, James Lunt, 'clearly indefensible'.[13] Moreover, the withdrawal simply reflected what Glubb had been saying all along, namely that the cost of holding Jerusalem would be the necessity of relinquishing territory elsewhere. The passive nature of the strategy was testimony to the growing weakness of the Transjordanian forces in the field, especially regarding the matter of munitions. However, the appearance of the move, together with the Legion's strategy, what Glubb called 'passive defensive',[14] according to which no attempt to capture any new territory in the fighting was made due to the chronic shortage of ordnance, was less forgiving.

The military dimension of the withdrawal was accentuated by the human dimension of the decision. In what the Israeli writer Simha Flapan called 'one of the gravest episodes of this tragic story' the Israeli authorities expelled most of the Arab population of Lydda and Ramle,[15] resulting in long columns of hungry and angry refugees filing eastwards. Their pitiable flight helped to exacerbate an atmosphere of political disquiet emerging in Amman, and made political recriminations almost inevitable.

Stories soon began to circulate purporting that the Arab Legion's circumspection was a function of its British officers and their separate agenda, and that Abdullah was colluding with Israel to increase pressure on the Egyptian flank, a view that would be peddled with growing intensity by Cairo in the autumn. Abdullah's response was to deflect rather than to rebut, with the British as his lightning-rod. In one notable incident, the king upbraided

Glubb in front of the cabinet, in the sure knowledge that such an event would become the talk of the town, and sustain speculation of Glubb's imminent dismissal. His tactic seemed to work, with the demonstrations that subsequently took place at home being directed against Britain, and Glubb's car being stoned. That Abdullah kept Glubb on, however, was both an indicator as to his competence and a function of Abdullah's shrewd sense of self-interest.

The credibility of such anti-British speculation was fed by those who wished to cover up for their own failures. Though the second phase of the conflict had only lasted for ten days all of the Arab armies had lost ground to a militarily reinvigorated Israel, with losses in the Galilee especially serious. By the end of the round of fighting, Israel had seized the initiative and would retain it through to the end of the war.

As the relative gains on the ground for Transjordan *vis-à-vis* the other main Arab states started to become clear so Amman's rivals, Cairo in particular, began to feel more and more uncomfortable. Increasingly, it was Amman's success and their lack of it that came to dominate the thinking of the other Arab protagonists, rather than the overall direction of the war against Israel. Moreover, in a region of personalised regimes, relative success was given a special intensity by its articulation in terms of the standing of individual leaders. Attempts by rival Arab leaders to neutralise the political gains for King Abdullah took two principal forms. First, the Arab League adopted a number of resolutions through the summer that were clearly against the interests of Transjordan. The most important of these was the critical stance adopted against the peace plan of the Swedish UN mediator, Count Folke Bernadotte, Jordan being cajoled into joining the consensus position. Though hardly realistic, Bernadotte's deliberately vague proposal had appeared to favour Amman, envisaging the creation of an Israeli-Transjordanian political union in historic Palestine. Second, the Arab League threw its weight behind a nationalist political solution for the Arab area of Palestine, in order to countervail Abdullah's growing authority on the ground. The League encouraged Haj Amin al-Husseini to proceed with the establishment of an 'All-Palestine' government, as a tangible alternate pole of political gravity to Amman. The Mufti enthusiastically established his administration based in the Egyptian-held territory of Gaza, just prior to the next round of fighting. King Abdullah alone within the Arab League refused to recognise this rival administration.

A third and final round of fighting ensued as a result of an Israeli offensive on 15 October, a cease-fire only following on 7 January 1949. In planning an autumn attack, Israel's leaders had two choices. Either to attack the

Arab Legion and seek the capture of more of the West Bank, or attack Egypt and try to gain control of the Negev Desert and a foothold at the top of the Red Sea, Israeli forces hitherto not having ventured south of Beersheba. Each strategy had its supporters, with David Ben-Gurion, the political colossus during the early years of Israel's existence, agonising between the two options. Ben-Gurion had initially been tempted by a West Bank offensive against the 'big triangle', which he believed would result in victory. However, he eventually opted for accommodation rather than territorial expansion over the West Bank for composite reasons, including possible British involvement, the large Arab population that lived there (a potential hostile majority), and because he valued political relations with Abdullah.[16]

Instead, Israel attacked Egypt. Ben-Gurion guessed correctly that Abdullah would not risk his precariously held gains by coming to Cairo's assistance, as his grandson, King Hussein, by contrast, would subsequently do during the June 1967 war. With the Egyptian forces inferior in nature, in terms of size, equipment and leadership, Israel was successful in its maximal battlefield ambitions. Egypt reluctantly turned to Transjordan and Iraq for assistance, seeking diversionary attacks by the Arab Legion. All it got was a small deployment to Hebron to aid Egyptian forces that had been cut off from the main army. Even this move could be interpreted as simply strengthening Amman's hold on the West Bank. At the same time the Israelis also pushed a combination of ALA, Lebanese and Syrian troops out of most of northern Galilee.

As the leader of a separate state, concerned with his own territorial interests, the disinterested Abdullah and his army acted impeccably, ever judicious in view of its limited capacity. As the supposedly supreme commander of the Arab forces, in a region where Arab solidarity rivalled the state in its claims on loyalty, Abdullah's inaction was breathtaking in being so politically untenable. It is hardly surprising that the perception came to hold that, in the famous title of the book by Uri Bar-Joseph, Israel and Transjordan were during the 1948 war 'the best of enemies'.[17]

That Bar-Joseph overdid the hyperbole can be seen from the way in which Israel dealt with Transjordan in the course of the emergence of a general armistice agreement, which was signed on Rhodes on 3 April 1949. This was a victory for what Avi Shlaim has called Israel's 'coercive diplomacy',[18] with Transjordan being picked off, as Egypt had been picked off on the battlefield before. Though its territorial losses were not as great as the Egyptians in the Negev, its social-cum-economic costs were significant while its political costs were incalculable. Ironically, the negotiation itself had the potential to be politically cost-free for the king as a ground-breaking Israeli-Egyptian armistice had already preceded it. Moreover, Abdullah's choice of secret talks at Shuna as the preferred medium for substantive negotiation, rather than Rhodes itself, should have enabled him to use his personal relations with the Israeli leadership to the full. But, in spite of the long history of their relations, the Israelis had no intention of letting their erstwhile partner off lightly.

First, Transjordan was obliged to relinquish territory in the southern Negev, as a result of an Israeli violation of the cease-fire. Next, and more seriously, Amman was forced to vacate a 300-square-kilometre area in Wadi Ara, as the price for Israel allowing it to take over positions in the northern part of the West Bank that had been successfully defended by the Iraqis. The latter would result in 80,000 people, or 16,000 families, losing their livelihood, as rural dwellings were cut off from their farmland.[19] Again the symbolism was disastrous; here were two further examples of Transjordan yielding Arab land in Palestine, in contravention of its Arab League mandate, to set alongside the experiences of Lydda and Ramle. In contrast to the Negev reversal, the Wadi Ara deal was impossible either to hide or to spin. With its central location, prime agricultural land and sizable number of inhabitants, the Wadi Ara debacle was visible and tangible, and provoked further fury against Abdullah in the region, and even rioting in the West Bank. 'Utter perfidy on one side and utter stupidity on [the] other', was the judgement passed by one UN official on the Israeli-Jordanian armistice negotiations.[20]

The armistice and its reactions did not provide an auspicious context for the commencement of the administration of the West Bank by Transjordan. Not for the last time, Israel had used its preponderance of power against its basically not unfriendly Arab neighbour to the east, to the detriment of the long-term durability of that state, and hence, by extension, to its own interests and security. In spite of these reversals the armistice left Abdullah with most of his gains intact, and with a de facto Israeli recognition of his sovereignty over them. At last, after nearly three decades of politicking, Abdullah had finally succeeded in expanding his domains from merely those of the territory trans-Jordan, in realisation of a Hashemite dream.

UNITY ACROSS THE JORDAN

The military occupation of land allocated for an Arab state in Palestine gave Abdullah control on the ground, and, it was assumed, political authority. This assumption was unexpectedly challenged with the declaration of independence by the All-Palestine government, a body which, since its flight from Gaza to Cairo after the third round of hostilities, Abdullah had considered to be a spent force. The nature of the popular support for the declaration in the West Bank jolted Abdullah into the realisation that the subjugation of the territory could not be taken for granted. Consequently, the issue was raised anew as to how best to go about politically incorporating the territory into the new Kingdom of Transjordan. Moreover, the political conundrum for Abdullah was how to incorporate the territory in a way that would convey, if not popular support, then at least elite legitimacy for such a move. With tension, conflict and recrimination straddling 1948 and 1949, such an end was subject to fluctuation. On the other hand, the context was to a degree propitious, with control on the ground enabling Abdullah's men to use their patronage to undermine the All-Palestine government. With the other Arab states humiliated on the battlefield and with domestic problems afflicting Egypt and Iraq in particular, Abdullah clearly believed that as far as action was concerned it was a case of the sooner the better.

Abdullah's main objective, as the Middle East historian Joseph Nevo has demonstrated, was the creation of 'a "direct" appeal' from the Arab population in the occupied territories 'demanding their annexation to Transjordan'.[21] In other words, the eventual union of the two banks of the Jordan should appear, not as the acquisitive move of an ambitious dynast, but as a magnanimous gesture from the throne under pressure from an expectant populace. In the end it would take Abdullah two attempts and a significant delay in order to gain the outcome he desired.

The prototype for the manoeuvre was the first 'National Palestine Congress', which was held in Amman in October 1948. It was a large gathering made up of long-standing Hashemite supporters, bulked up by the presence of many refugees from all over Palestine. It was paid for and choreographed by the Amman government. It aimed at eclipsing its rival in Cairo as much as praising Abdullah's leadership.

Encouraged by the Amman gathering, a second major bid at such managed spontaneity was convened, this time with the venue switching to the West Bank town of Jericho. An eclectic attendance of between 2,000 and 3,000 took part in the gathering on 1 December 1948. A combination of the presence of Abdullah's supporters on the ground, the use of his fledgling administration and the control afforded by the Legion provided a context in which many leading personalities could be encouraged to attend. The event itself was stage-managed by Abdullah, notably through the medium of Shaikh Muhammad Ali al-Ja'bari, the mayor of Hebron and long-time supporter of Abdullah's, who presided over the conference.

Abdullah hoped that such a traditional gathering would generate a perception of popular backing in the West Bank. With the right atmospherics,
he hoped that union would follow swiftly and easily. Even such a benign
gathering as the Jericho conference did not go entirely according to plan.
Notables from Ramallah and Jerusalem in particular were reluctant to give
Abdullah a *carte blanche*. Though prepared to recognise him as monarch,
they were unwilling to give up their claim to the whole of Palestine and
refused to endorse his policy of consolidating the partition. Frustrated by
the outcome, Abdullah acted petulantly as the various delegations went to
meet him at Shuna at the culmination of the conference, their only real
sin ironically having been a desire to recognise Abdullah 'as King of all
Palestine'.

The Jericho conference produced a new surge of vituperation across the
region, especially from Egypt. But it was not this that stymied Abdullah's
plans, as back-biting and name-calling among the Arab regimes were nothing new even then, and, after all, Transjordan did control the situation on
the ground. The delay in the declaration of a political union was driven by
the fluctuating thinking in the capitals of the two most important external powers in the Middle East, Britain and the United States. Once again
Britain, with its interests spread across the region, not least in Egypt, urged
caution, for fear of a further backlash. Furthermore, Britain felt that annexation would be premature with fighting continuing on the ground and
the attendant uncertainties that that could bring. As for the US, it had even
refrained from recognising Jordan itself until the end of January 1949.

The hiatus in the status of the West Bank after the Jericho conference
at least had the utility of further weakening the All-Palestine government
on the ground. It also provided a breathing space for the Arabs in Palestine
to consider their position. As a result, many became resigned to the inevitability of rule by King Abdullah as part of a Transjordanian state. As
Mary Wilson has observed, most Palestinians regarded Abdullah with 'an
ominous ambivalence' during this time.[22] In the meantime, Abdullah encouraged this sense of inevitability through a whole raft of changes implemented periodically during 1949. These ranged from the offer of Jordanian
citizenship to all West Bank Arabs and the removal of all travel and customs
restrictions across the Jordan River, to the replacement of the military administration by a civilian one and the naming of three Palestinian ministers
to the cabinet. The air of oppressive inevitability grew in December 1949,
when King Abdullah assumed all powers previously vested in the mandatory power in Palestine. Even Britain's opposition to a union had faded,
now that hostilities were over, as Abdullah was told on a visit to London in

August 1949. The ground had been laid for a union that now only awaited elections in both parts of the kingdom.

Elections finally took place in April 1950 for the new 40-man Chamber of Deputies. Seats were divided equally between East and West Bank constituencies. The principle of equal representation was also adopted for the appointed 20-member upper house or Senate. However, this symbolic demonstration of equality masked the fact that the population of the West Bank was almost twice that of its eastern counterpart. What was to become a long tradition of representative bias in both Jordanian-elected and appointed institutions to the detriment of Palestinians and town-dwellers (often one and the same) had commenced.

The election took place in an atmosphere of regulation, with the Arab Legion still at its posts in the West Bank, and radical political groupings, like the emerging Ba'th Party, officially proscribed. In spite of these restrictions the sense of electricity in the air was conveyed by the election of two Ba'thists and three nationalist activists formerly loyal to the Hussainis. The majority of those elected from the West Bank were educated, urban professionals, while the East Bank representation – 12 landowners, five professionals (including two civil servants) and two merchants – was significantly different in composition.

On 25 April 1950, in a move worthy of the Jericho conference, a group of Palestinian deputies in the new Jordanian parliament introduced a motion proposing the unification of both banks of the Jordan. The motion was passed unanimously. Under the terms of the union the Arabs of the West Bank were immediately offered Jordanian citizenship, a gesture that was against the explicit instruction of the Arab League, which feared such a move might prejudice the possibility of the return of refugees. The majority of West Bankers accepted the union because, as the British writer on Arab affairs Peter Mansfield has observed, they were still in a state of political shock, and had little by way of an alternative.[23] Avi Plascow has gone so far as to conclude that 'annexation was quite popular among large numbers of Palestinians, although it was opposed by the radical intelligentsia who in reality had little influence'.[24] Britain recognised the move almost immediately. The Arab League obliged Abdullah to issue a statement saying that the unification was temporary until the whole of Palestine could be liberated, which he did, but stopped short of the expulsion of Transjordan.

All things considered, at the level of high politics, King Abdullah had done well to achieve his aim so painlessly. It was, however, an odd marriage that Abdullah had arranged, geographical contiguity notwithstanding. The old eastern part of the kingdom contained 94% of the territory, but only around one-third of the one-and-a-half million population. Levels of illiteracy were estimated at over 90%, and in 1938 there had been only 74 schools of all types in the country. The productive sectors of the economy were also chronically under-developed, with agricultural output subject to fluctuations and manufacturing virtually non-existent. In the new western part of the kingdom, economic and educational attainment were altogether much more impressive, with a considerably higher level of collective wealth. For example, half the West Bank labour force was engaged in agriculture. Though the eastern part of the country had formally taken over the western part under Hashemite leadership, the question could nevertheless be profitably posed as to which would stamp its mark most indelibly on the new state.

THE DEATH OF A KING

In the end, King Abdullah had less than 15 months to enjoy the fruits of almost a lifetime's political ambition. He was assassinated, aged 69, by a lone Palestinian gunman on 20 July 1951, the product of a grubby plot, possibly with wider connections to dissidents in the West and East Banks and even perhaps beyond.[25] Convicted with the handful of plotters was a distant relative of the Mufti, and a former close confidant of King Abdullah's, Abdullah al-Tall, who had been part of the secret armistice talks in Shuna and was subsequently the military governor of Jerusalem. He had already fled to Cairo. Truth to tell, the killing could have happened at any time, as there must have been many potential assassins among the Palestinian dispossessed who looked within for a scapegoat for their problems. As Kamal Salibi has written: 'every move he [Abdullah] made with respect to the Palestine question since 1929, and more particularly since 1947, was analysed down to the last detail and given the worst possible interpretation'.[26] Moreover, Abdullah's personal security was notoriously lax.

No doubt Abdullah died a more contented man than he had been when he first came to Transjordan as a restless young prince, with ambitions beyond his competence. Ruling in Amman and Jerusalem, he could claim a sort of parity of achievement with his great sibling, now long-deceased rival, Faisal. He had earned the affection if never quite the respect of the British. He had presided over, if he had not actually built, a state-in-the-making more stable and harmonious than most in the region. As to his death, it was the way a pious man like Abdullah would have liked to have gone: wearing his traditional robes and turban, at the entrance to the al-Aqsa

Mosque in Jerusalem, with the Quran being recited in the background, on a Friday morning, with his grandson and favourite, the future King Hussein, by his side. At the end, he could content himself that he had made of Transjordan something more than just an expanse of desert lying beyond all things important. The knowledge that Jordan would have been reduced to its original territorial space just 16 years later would, though, have distressed him. Abdullah's assumed final contentment is testimony to his inability to predict the turbulence of the coming two decades.

With the king dead it was necessary to hail a new king. That though was easier said than done. Though Abdullah had had three wives, he had only fathered two sons, Talal and Nayif. Given the Arab tradition of succession based on a combination of lineage and meritocracy, the European norm of primogeniture did not automatically apply. The simplicity of the choice meant that Jordan was not faced by the multiple possibilities of succession evident in a state like Saudi Arabia. Nevertheless, Jordan found itself wracked by another quandary: that neither man was really suitable for the job.

Since his birth in 1909, the prevailing assumption had been that Talal would accede. He was the eldest child born to Abdullah's first wife, herself of Hashemite stock. He was a serious boy, anxious to please. He attended Sandhurst, the culmination of three years in Britain. However, Talal's childhood also reflected the turbulence of the age. His education comprised an unsatisfactory patchwork of private tutors and teachers. He saw little of his father during his formative years. On his return from England in 1927 he had little to do, a series of invented jobs giving way to a frustration compounded by an emerging friction with his bullying father in the claustrophobic environment of the royal quarters. Talal's marriage to his cousin, Zain, and the birth of their first child, Hussein, in 1935, only partially ameliorated the atmosphere. At some stage during this difficult time the beginnings of schizophrenia began to manifest themselves, an affliction that would eventually oblige Talal to abdicate. With Abdullah's contempt for Talal perhaps surprisingly indulged by Kirkbride, the British Resident, and wearyingly accepted by more distant British officials, by 1941 a law of succession had been passed that would allow Abdullah to exclude Talal.[27]

The initial beneficiary of Talal's travails was his half-brother Nayif, who was five years younger. He was an unexceptional youth, who had the fortunate attribute of a personality more akin to his father's. His chief strength during this period was simply that he was not Talal. So it was that for most of

Fig. 8. Amir Talal, aged 13, 1922 (Philby, Misc. Tj 5)

the 1940s it was Nayif who appeared to be the monarch-in-waiting, though this period allowed political insiders to become resensitised to his limitations. It was therefore increasingly likely that, in the event of a succession, by way of compromise, Nayif would play the role of regent for an eventual Hussein accession. This sense of hierarchy was compounded by Talal's increasingly erratic behaviour, involving violence and heavy drinking, and a willingness openly to criticise the British. Indeed, Prince Talal was actually staying in Switzerland where he was receiving medical treatment, when he was belatedly given news of his father's death. There was, in any case, with the need to hold the political centre, little alternative but to name Nayif as regent immediately after the assassination.

There then followed an unsteady period of seven weeks when the political permutations for Jordan were many. The killing of Abdullah had momentarily thrown the kingdom out of kilter, with the dead king's bodyguard going on the rampage in Jerusalem and anti-Palestinian riots breaking out in Amman; this potential for spontaneous outbreaks of violence as an aspect of politics was a foretaste of the next few years to come. The vacuum at the centre also gave an opening to regional powers that would seek to exploit the situation for their own ends. In 1951 it was Hashemite Iraq that was best placed to take advantage, with a high-level Iraqi delegation, led by the Regent Prince Abdul Illah, flying to Amman ostensibly to pay their condolences. It was suddenly clear that Jordan's structural weaknesses had been exposed by the unexpected assassination. Devoid of Abdullah, the kingdom had ceased to punch above its regional weight; rather than being an active player in helping to determine the future of the region, Jordan had overnight become what it would largely remain, namely an object of the politics of others.

That Nayif did not inherit was due to a combination of his own poor judgement, providence in the shape of a moment of calm lucidity on the part of Talal, and the calculations of the main political players in Amman at the time. Nayif saw the uncertainties of the interregnum as the moment to advance personal ambitions that extended beyond being merely a regent for his nephew. However, he did so in a ham-fisted manner, displaying a diplomatic style inherited from his father. Nayif threatened not to confirm the death sentences against those already found guilty of the king's murder, and even mentioned resignation, with its attendant risk of political confusion, if his ambitions were not assuaged. Such a performance instantly alienated Kirkbride and members of the external elite, like Abu al-Huda, who were doing all they could to try to manage an orderly succession. News emanating from Switzerland that Talal was apparently sane and was on his way back gave the momentum back to Talal, whose popularity on the street did nothing to harm his cause. With his position rapidly deteriorating, Nayif flirted with the idea of a military coup, at which he proved marginally less proficient than at diplomacy. Easily stymied, Nayif's usefulness was almost expended. It was to a rousing and widely supported reception that Talal arrived home on 6 September, to be whisked off immediately to assume the throne.

CHAPTER 5

The Roaring Fifties

In just five years Jordan had been transformed by war, dynastic ambition and succession politics. It had left behind forever its quiet childhood years as a small, colonial possession. It had entered what would prove to be an increasingly turbulent adolescence. The kingdom would be buffeted by the turmoil of regional politics, with the rise of radicalism in the 1950s and the overbearing attentions of Nasser's Egypt. Simultaneously, it would be convulsed by a range of domestic factors, with the dispossession and destitution of the refugees combining with the new poverty of urban and rural Transjordanians, providing a combustible cocktail against which the machinations of elite politics would be played out. The instability would be compounded by leadership uncertainties that would not be resolved until 1957.

For many foreign commentators the Jordan of the 1950s was a state suffering from terminal illness.[1] Its origins were seen as anachronistic; its institutions brittle and vulnerable; its leadership inexperienced and uncertain; its internal political consensus lost forever. The prognosis was either for radical revolution or the swallowing-up of Jordan by a larger Arab entity, whether Egypt, Syria, Iraq or a combination thereof. Neither, of course, took place. The state, created and nurtured by the British, proved to be more resilient than anticipated, especially its coercive core. Glubb's Arab Legion transferred its personalised loyalty to the young King Hussein, who had inherited the steel of his great-uncle, Faisal, to go with the emotion of his grandfather, Abdullah. At the same time, the radicalism of the 1950s was soon seen for the ephemera that it was; a mere cloak for the ambitions of a disparate collection of individuals, as would be graphically illustrated after the overthrow of the Hashemites in Iraq in the bloody revolution of 1958. By the end of the 1950s, Hashemite Jordan had survived to grow to adulthood, the benevolent despotism of its political system illustrating just how far behind had been left the naïvete of its youth.

The swearing-in of King Talal ended the uncertainties of political succession, as the challenge from his half-brother Nayif faded away. The new monarch was serious and earnest in his desire to do well. He was popular in the country among those who cared about such things, from ministers to the mob. In Queen Zain he was supported by a determined and feisty consort. A future succession was secure through the presence of their three sons. The eldest, Hussein, had already shown himself to be a young man of substance, whose fearlessness and practical abilities made him the obvious choice for the title of crown prince.

King Talal's reign began auspiciously. Its major project was the reform of the 1946 constitution, a document that had emerged when Britain's influence had still been all-pervasive. In doing so, Talal was happy to consolidate his reputation as a liberal, though his motives were probably not as straightforward as they appeared. As Robert Satloff has written, 'Talal was wedded to the notion of reigning as a constitutional monarch, an idea that most likely grew as much out of his driving need to be what Abdullah was not as it did out of his liberal inclination.'[2] Whatever his motivation, Talal's move helped to nurture his reputation at home. Even some five decades later in Jordan, Talal is routinely referred to as a liberal and the 1952 constitution seen as his monument.[3]

Talal apparently found a ready partner for his reformist project in the prime minister that he inherited and, perhaps surprisingly, kept on, Tawfiq Abu al-Huda, and to whom the task now fell of drafting and steering through the new constitution. Though hardly himself a liberal by inclination or conviction, Abu al-Huda was capable of pragmatism in spite of his reputation as having the mentality of an accountant. On this occasion he proved to be especially wily. The cause of constitutional reform allowed him both to stay in office and to deflate from the inside the liberal opposition in the country, which had been finding its voice over the early months of the decade. To manufacture relevant credentials, he opted for the loss-leader of releasing political prisoners and lifting censorship.

The output of this incongruous *cohabitation* between Talal and Abu al-Huda was certainly a more liberal constitution than its predecessor, but one that was not as progressive as it at first appeared. As a declaration of values it was lofty, with its various guarantees of personal freedoms. It was also a significant improvement on what had gone before in terms of the separation of powers, and especially in circumscribing the role of the head of state. In substantive terms, however, a lot less was conceded than initially met the eye, with many of the new freedoms subject to the caveat of 'being in accordance with the provisions of the law'.[4] Moreover, the constitution contained provision for the declaration of martial law, a measure that would be invoked to shattering effect some five years later.

On issues of practical importance, notably the basis on which no-confidence motions could be adopted by parliament, a hardball negotiation took place. Invariably the experienced and adept Abu al-Huda drove a tough bargain, with, in this particular case, a clause eventually being adopted that required a two-thirds vote of the elected lower house for a no-confidence motion rather than a simple majority. Such clauses helped to maintain the pre-eminence of the executive over the legislature in Jordan ever after, in spite of the constitution's dogged insistence that Jordan's 'system of government is parliamentary'. Fifty years later, and in spite of the turbulent politics of the 1950s, only two governments had been voted out of office by parliament.

The adoption of the new constitution on New Year's Day 1952 was a misleading gauge as to the health of the Talal reign, or, more precisely, the health of its sovereign. Talal's mental health declined so precipitously during the first quarter of the year that by May the country was in crisis; by 11 August he had been deposed in a constitutional process that few if any had embraced with relish.

By the late spring, Talal's behaviour was increasingly violent as well as erratic. His refusal to accept treatment, along with the timidity of doctors and political figures alike in the kingdom,[5] made the situation extremely difficult to deal with. The role of two foreign doctors in recommending immediate treatment abroad inevitably accelerated loose talk of a political conspiracy to remove the monarch in order to stymie his liberal and anti-colonial inclinations. Political weakness at home inevitably prompted renewed interest in domestic Jordanian affairs from among regional states; in echoes of the aftermath of the assassination of King Abdullah, Hashemite Iraq was the most active, its motives, as before, unhealthy and self-serving. Even the king's half-brother, the indolent Prince Nayif, sniffed the chance of a comeback. A family holiday to Europe, which Talal had been persuaded to take as a half-baked compromise, simply resulted in his increasingly embarrassing behaviour becoming public knowledge across the continent. His absence also made the situation even more difficult to manage at home.

In Talal's absence, the cabinet formed a Throne Council to exercise the king's powers. The king's hospitalisation was again sought. Jordanian envoys, Hashemite family members and Iraqi interlopers zig-zagged across Europe in an undignified scramble to affect the outcome of an uncertain process that was thrown this way and that by Talal's frequent and sudden mood swings. The end, however, was quick. By 2 August Talal was refusing to countenance abdication, despite tentative efforts in this direction. Meanwhile, the situation had taken an alarming twist, with Talal the subject of political machinations from among a faction of army officers, such stirrings being then as unusual in Jordan as they had become run-of-the-mill in Iraq and Syria. Such a development set alarm bells ringing, coming as it did just days after the Free Officers' historic move that ousted the monarchy in Egypt. Concerned at the drift of events, Abu al-Huda finally decided to act decisively, as the only man capable of resolving the issue. He convened an extraordinary meeting of parliament, which unanimously voted for the deposition of the king on the grounds of insanity.

When the end came it must almost have been a relief for Talal, who accepted his fate with resignation. Ironically, it was his own constitution that had provided the process for his demise, fittingly though for a man who was uncomfortable with his inherited role as titular autocrat. Talal lived out most of the rest of his days until his death on 8 July 1972 in a private sanitarium overlooking the Bosphorus in the Ortaköy district of Istanbul, a tranquil setting for a troubled man. The end of the short, sad period of what Aqil Hyder Hasan Abidi has called 'the Talal interlude'[6] saw the beginning of the second of the two main periods of Jordanian history, the Hussein era.

NEW SOCIAL REALITIES

The kingdom that Hussein inherited was one that had been totally transformed by the conflict in Palestine, demographically, economically, sociologically and, by extension, politically. The population of the country had more or less tripled in size. There were over 458,000 refugees in the newly expanded state, nearly one-third of the new total population. The aggregate Palestinian Arab component of the population brought with it funds in excess of the total money supply of Transjordan. The administrative capacity of the state had been swamped.

The newly established refugee camps were made up mostly of displaced villagers, who tended to be disproportionately unskilled, illiterate and poor. Many of their number had become embittered by the experience of war, especially by the Arab Legion's failure to secure more of the territory of historic Palestine. The camps therefore became centres of suspicion and discontent. They were kept under close surveillance by the police, an institution dominated by East Bankers from traditional families, whose numbers were, in

Fig. 9. Jordanian Police with armed vehicle, 1961 (Stark, MF 134 A5)

response, greatly increased. Palestinians were to come to complain bitterly about discrimination against them by Transjordanians who dominated in the government, army and police.

However, Avi Plascow argues that in spite of the trauma of dispossession and dispersal there is little evidence that the refugees ever revolted 'or even played any prominent part in the mid-fifties disturbances' in Jordan, as claimed by many sources.[7] Initially, at least, this was because of the international relief effort that addressed the needs of their survival, a process that was institutionalised with the establishment of the United Nations Relief and Works Agency (UNRWA) in late 1949. The provision of basic staples for the refugees meant that they were better able to survive than their new, non-refugee neighbours, quickly coming, for example, to dominate the local employment market for unskilled labour by accepting wages lower than those that had applied hitherto.[8] This was an especially acute situation in the West Bank, where wage rates fell to as little as 50% of their previous levels.[9] Over time UNRWA also raised the quality of refugee labour through placement and vocational training schemes, thereby helping to create a manpower reserve that was later able to take advantage of growing oil-related employment possibilities in the wealthier Arab states. Between 1952 and 1961 there was little population growth in the West Bank primarily for this reason, with some 80% of the 63,000 Jordanians working abroad in 1961 originally from the West Bank.

Table 5.1 *Distribution of Refugees in Jordan, February 1952*

City	Camps	In houses	In barracks	In tents	Total
Amman	2	48,440	1,927	9,590	59,957
Irbid	1	27,837		1,700	29,537
Nablus	6	97,466	5,382	17,159	120,007
Jericho/Karamah	6	8,041	39,391	20,127	67,559
Bethlehem	4	25,640	548	4,729	30,917
Hebron	3	50,154		11,769	61,923
Ramallah	6	44,768	3,005	10,229	58,002
Jerusalem	1	25,866	4,482		30,348
Total	29	328,212	54,735	75,303	458,250

Source: UNRWA, reprinted in Georgiana G. Stevens, 'Arab Refugees: 1948–1952', in *Middle East Journal*, Vol. 6 (Summer 1952), pp. 281–290.

Not all of those on the move from Palestine were destitute or refugees. Many were Palestinians with either political or commercial ambitions, or even just semi-skilled workers seeking casual employment. A disproportionate number of these were bound for Amman, the centre of political and administrative power and an irresistible pole of attraction. For example, many of the businesses, including large, established organisations, such as the Arab Bank, that had previously established their headquarters in Jerusalem, now relocated them to Amman. So significant and sustained was the labour flow from the west that the per capita income of the East Bank stayed virtually constant during the years of the union in spite of sizable overall growth in its GDP.[10]

A major side-effect of this elite orientation on Amman was a fillip for the economy of the hub of the state. As Fawzi Gharaibeh has noted about the period: 'It can be safely said that the Amman region, the capital, has almost exclusively monopolized economic activity in Jordan, possibly to the detriment of other areas in the East as well as on the West Bank.'[11] This boost to the core economy of the state was deepened at the expense of the West Bank by other structural factors, such as a general reluctance to invest in the vicinity of what might become a focal point of future conflict, and the development of north–south lines of supply to Damascus and Beirut to replace lateral routes based previously on the ports of Jaffa and Haifa.

The growing centralisation of the expanded state saw a sharp increase in house rents in Amman. This in turn triggered a 'remarkable building boom', which saw between 1949 and 1952 more than four times the budget

Table 5.2 *Urban Growth in Major Cities of Jordan, 1952–1962*

City	Population 1952	Population 1962	% increase
Amman	190,647	296,358	55.4
Irbid	91,962	137,658	49.7
Jenin	40,519	86,731	114.1
Jerusalem	85,619	114,691	34.0
Nablus	53,509	182,994	242.0
Salt	41,299	68,188	65.1

Source: Statistical Yearbooks of Jordan, 1952, 1962, cited in Ishaq Y. Qutub, 'The impact of industrialization on social mobility in Jordan', in *Development and Change*, 1969–70, Vol. 1, No. 2, p. 41.

for development spending channelled into the construction sector.[12] This boom was particularly significant in its employment effects in helping to soak up some of the massive increase in casual labour that had been created by the refugee crisis.[13]

If Amman was to benefit as an economic and political power centre during the time that the West Bank was part of Jordan this was neither entirely inevitable nor purely the result of the social forces of centralisation. In part it was the product of regime policy,[14] concerned that the centre of gravity of the state should stay with Amman as an important instrument in the incorporation of the West Bank. For geographical and historical reasons Jerusalem was the obvious alternate pole in the new state, not least because it had been the seat of the British administration under the mandate. As Avi Plascow has put it: 'The [Jordanian] regime's general policy was to prevent Jerusalem from either gaining special status or becoming a symbolic focus for divisive West Bank–East Bank antagonism'.[15] The authorities in Amman set about the task with conviction.

Such a self-conscious approach helped to exacerbate the cleavage between the West Bank and the East Bank, notwithstanding the parochial and tribal divisions that existed within each side. For Transjordanians the influx of Palestinians resonated with the resentment of the 1920s and the 1930s over the importation of an external and primarily Palestinian administrative elite. The feelings of suspicion and disdain did not go unreciprocated. That the Palestinians moving to the east of Jordan instinctively looked to Jerusalem and down upon their new neighbours can be detected in a number of subtle ways, for example, through their disdain for the country's leading newspaper *al-Urdun*, and their overwhelming preference for the Jerusalem-based *Falastin* or *al-Difaa*.[16]

Fig. 10. The city of Amman, 1963 (JEM, 6.2)

A range of different devices was utilised in order to subdue the potential of Jerusalem, both administrative and infrastructural. Most importantly among these was the down-grading of the importance of Jerusalem as an administrative hub, with Jerusalem shorn of any administrative responsibility for the wider West Bank, and all district offices made responsible to the ministerial headquarters in Amman. Jerusalem was also deprived of prestige projects in such areas as infrastructure and industry, where otherwise considerable secondary benefits could flow. Thus, ideas for the establishment of an airport and a university in Jerusalem were denied. As part of the process of the diminution of the status of Jerusalem, rival urban and economic centres within the West Bank itself were built up, notably Nablus, the population of which tripled between 1952 and 1962, outstripping that of Jerusalem. Public sector industrial investments, notably a vegetable oil and a match factory, went to Nablus instead of Jerusalem. The throne seemed indirectly to encourage such a strategy. King Hussein was an infrequent visitor to Jerusalem during the period of union; it was not until 1963 that work began on a royal palace on the outskirts of the city, construction that had still not been completed by the outbreak of war in 1967.

Also benefiting was the immediate hinterland of Amman, which helped to entrench the impression that the East Bank was being built up at the expense of the West. Virtually all the big government-controlled industrial projects initiated during the time that the West Bank was part of Jordan, from the oil refinery at Zarqa to the cement factory at Fuheis, were located in the eastern part of the kingdom.[17] By 1965 the East Bank had been transformed from having virtually no industrial base in 1948 to being the source of three-quarters of the country's total industrial output.[18]

THE ACCESSION OF HUSSEIN

Talal was deposed in favour of his eldest son, Hussein, of whom much was expected. Though Hussein had learnt a lot from spending time with his grandfather, King Abdullah, in other respects he had not been especially well prepared for the job. His formal education had ended up a mess, as his father and grandfather, as ever in strident disagreement with one another, had tussled to stamp their mark on his upbringing. Moreover, much of the education that he did receive was spent outside the country and in the British public-school tradition, both at Victoria College, Alexandria, and then at Harrow. This dual cultural experience in his formative years was, however, to serve Hussein extremely well: throughout his life he would move easily between both an Arab and an Anglo-Saxon social milieu. At the same time, distance from family supervision had made it relatively easy for Hussein to indulge his two main fancies, women and fast cars.

In spite of his uncertain beginnings, Hussein was to rule over Jordan for some 47 years, before succumbing to cancer at the relatively young age of 63 in 1999. The longevity of his rule meant that during his last couple of decades on the throne, life in Jordan without him began to seem unimaginable. Jordanians increasingly came to revere him, not least because so few of them had ever known a Jordan without him. Regime myth-making was on hand to strengthen these perceptions of King Hussein as the father of the nation, and as the shaikh of the national tribe. As befitting a patrimonial system of politics, Jordanians came to see all good things, from promotions to wealth, as coming from the leadership, and from the person of Hussein. Apologists especially revered him for possessing *hilm*,[19] that is to say qualities of clemency, forbearance, patience and insight.

Many Western commentators, from diplomats to journalists to biographers, both wittingly and unwittingly, came to connive in the growing adulation. Over time, Americans and even Israelis showed themselves to be as romantically inclined as dewy-eyed Englishmen in their largely uncritical and even sentimental praise of the king. They hardly required the regime's myth-making machine to devise their own conjured image of 'the plucky little king', the acronym PLK coming to be used as a shorthand reference for Hussein. Thus King Hussein came to be seen as a brave and honourable man, a survivor against all the odds, a brilliant politician, a statesman. It is the image that filled the obituaries, and remains with us today.

As one cuts through the treacle, Hussein starts to emerge as a more complex character, replete with human frailties. Hussein was a man of action rather than a thinker, someone of considerable personal courage and nerve. He was also, as he grew older, a shaikhly figure, both in his apparently paternalistic concern for his people and in the adroit way he manipulated tribal dynamics. He was a man who blew hot and cold: at times hard-working, at times indolent; at times pro-Nasser's Egypt, at times hostile to it; at times a tireless advocate of the peace process, at times disillusioned and disengaged. He was a man who, though he liked his pleasures, was also quite highly strung, as the chainsmoking and the internalised stress-induced illnesses attest. He was a man of character, but also a man who could be dominated by strong personalities, from his mother, Queen Zain, to Nasser to Saddam Hussein. He was a man who was not always a good judge of character. He was a man who relied too heavily on small groups of often self-serving cronies, the alternating nature of their influence resulting in policy mood swings, especially in the realm of foreign affairs.

King Hussein was a man whose survival owed much to a dynamic personality but far more to good fortune and the actions of others, especially during the turbulent times of the 1950s; as Uriel Dann has perceptively written: 'Hussein survived because his most dangerous adversary, Gamal Abdul Nasser, lacked the singleness of purpose in wishing his destruction.'[20] Most importantly, Hussein survived because of the nature of the British-constructed state he had inherited; most fortuitously, he was lucky he acceded in Amman and not in Baghdad. He was a man whose political judgement, though often sound, was also prone to errors, some of them, like agreeing to the establishment of the PLO and entering the 1967 war, of major proportions. He was a man who, like his grandfather, was often surprisingly emotional in his decision-making and public statements; an Asad senior, cold and always calculating, he was not.

It was an altogether different political milieu that King Hussein found himself thrust into than was the gentler one that had been his grandfather's. From the Free Officers' coup d'etat in Egypt in July 1952 it seemed as if an inexorable tide of political radicalism was sweeping across the region. Nasser's stock as a regional leader rose soon after the consolidation of his rule in 1954 through a series of subsequent events of historic importance. Increasing cross-border attacks into Israel from Egyptian-controlled Gaza led to growing fears of war in 1955. Cairo's move to purchase Soviet arms through the conduit of Czechoslovakia in September 1955, the deal whereby Moscow agreed to finance the Aswan High Dam in 1955, the nationalisation of the Suez Canal in 1956 and Nasser's political victory during the Suez crisis of the same year served to ratchet up the external pressure on the West-leaning Jordanian regime. The Syrian experience of domestic turmoil and the emergence of 'radical' military leaders seemed to provide a model for the Jordanian politics of the future.

The main problems for Hussein at the outset of his reign, however, were his youthfulness and inexperience, special impediments in a traditional society that so values age, seniority and wisdom. Hussein had been only 15 when he saw his grandfather assassinated in Jerusalem in 1951. He was more than 15 months short of his eighteenth birthday when he acceded to the throne. Too young yet to assume his constitutional powers, Hussein remained in Britain to complete his studies and attend army college at Sandhurst. It was therefore left to the 'king's men', who had already seen the country through an assassination and an abdication, to provide the early continuity of his reign, until he was old enough to take over on 2 May 1953.[21]

The first five years of Hussein's reign can best be read as a frustrating struggle by an inexperienced and sensitive youth to assert himself in a volatile and uncertain political context. Hussein's first attempt to stamp his authority on the country came with the appointment of his first prime minister, Fawzi al-Mulqi, a move that was bold but flawed. In principle the idea was definitely right, in that Mulqi was a younger man, a new face and one who appeared to bring to an end government by a small group of yesterday's men, such as Tawfiq Abu al-Huda, Sa'id al-Mufti and Samir al-Rifai, men who, though unquestionably loyal, tended to patronise Hussein horribly.[22] And during his year in office, Mulqi did adopt a platform of reform, which, though often no more than symbolic, did deliver some concessions to parliament, notably the introduction of a simple majority rather than the two-thirds vote required hitherto to pass a no-confidence vote in the executive.

However, the man himself was a bad choice. Mulqi was an inexperienced politician, his Syrian origin cancelling the appeal that he was Jordan's first native-born premier, and of insufficient stature to cope with the growing turmoil all around. The suspicion was that Hussein, who was largely unfamiliar with the local political scene, had turned to him because of the way Mulqi had shamelessly cultivated the young Harrovian prince when serving as ambassador to Britain. Unfortunately, Mulqi's indifferent performance in office, together with his nominal reputation as a liberal, prompted the impressionable Hussein, over whom the queen's influence was strong, to make a second mistake: to retreat back to the more conservatively inclined old guard. Hussein had embarked upon the beginning of a zig-zag, which would typify his approach towards national politics through much of the 1950s.

The removal of Mulqi in May 1954 heralded a run of eight cabinets dominated by Abdullah's generation of politicians, who presided over government in Amman until October 1956. While Hussein's return to experience was understandable enough, as Jordan grappled with the rising pressures from outside, the old elite simply exacerbated the situation. First, a return to politicians whose careers were intimately associated with British influence in the country, and at a time when Glubb was still the head of the army, gave the impression of a political system harking back to a receding age, rather than bending with the radical winds of the moment.

Second, the *modus operandi* of these old guard politicians, whether the authoritarian tendencies of an Abu al-Huda, or the leisured patrician elitism of a Sa'id al-Mufti, was increasingly out of step with the participatory inclinations and relative political pluralism that was emerging in Jordan at the time. Perhaps the most egregious example of the period of short-sighted authoritarianism was Abu al-Huda's use of state interference in the 1954 general election. A range of government interventions at the time of the poll included signalling the pro-government candidates on the ballot papers of troops voting in the West Bank. A slew of illiberal legislation passed during this time appeared to confirm such a view. This included a new municipal law, in 1955, which gave the interior ministry extensive control over local government, while restricting the franchise for local elections in a way that would benefit the wealthy.

Third, and arguably the most significant, were the generational tensions that a return to the aging old guard presented.[23] For the younger generation of Jordanians, whether drawn from the relative sophistication of the West Bank or from among the increasingly educated well-to-do East Banker townsmen, such figures were a barrier to advancement. If Hussein's aim of a reversion to experience was to provide stability in national politics his strategy was a complete failure. The longest lasting of these governments survived for just seven months. The old guard politicians continued to play out their petty rivalries, regardless of the onset of the more profound systemic challenges from outside. The short-sightedness of these governments was to drive their more liberal opponents into the camp of the radicals, who became increasingly strident in their calls for systemic change. Frustrations grew quickly, especially among those borne along by the unfolding tableau of regional politics. The rapid rise of regional radicalism provided a multitude of temptations for the ambitious and impatient members of the political elite in Jordan.

THE BAGHDAD PACT AND THE OUSTING OF GLUBB

The most celebrated illustration of the unsustainability of maintaining an outmoded approach to the conduct of politics came with the issue of the Baghdad Pact. The Pact was a British-inspired alliance aimed at the containment of Soviet influence in the Middle East through the joining up of the NATO and CENTO security systems. It was itself a misconceived strategy that under-estimated the Arab nationalist preoccupation with the attainment of a full sovereign independence from the residue of European colonialism, especially in countries like Egypt and Algeria. It was also a somewhat transparent device through which Britain tried to maintain its sagging influence in the region in the face of post-war imperial decline. Britain quickly secured 'northern tier' participation in the alliance in the form of Turkey, Pakistan and Iran, with Iraqi membership exciting a flickering interest in the Arab world. With Hashemite Iraq on board, but Egypt already implacably opposed, Jordanian participation was the only, though risky, option for its extension into the Levant.

The young King Hussein's initial inclination was probably to join the Pact. Its British sponsorship, together with a package of military hardware that membership would unlock, appealed to both his instincts and his sense of tangible gain. The issue was also an opportunity for Hussein to assert himself as a leader at home and in the region. Nevertheless, sensitised to the rhythms of regional politics, and in particular Egyptian excoriation of Iraq's decision to join, Hussein spent much of 1955 reluctant to place the kingdom under more pressure, a tentativeness perhaps curiously shared by Britain for the same reason. Such caution helped the cause of the anti-Pact forces, with continuous Egyptian criticism winning over a decisive majority of the Jordanian public. Ham-fisted diplomacy by Menderes' Turkey helped to bring the matter to a head, with expectations at home and in the region focusing on an ill-advised visit to Amman by the chief of the British general staff, General Sir Gerald Templar.

The run-up to the visit saw Amman in a state of upheaval. The Egyptian embassy continued with its flagrant encouragement of the opposition, with money changing hands. Demonstrations were regular events, and the Arab Legion had to be deployed to keep order. Every ideologically oriented political party, from the Ba'th Party to the Muslim Brotherhood, all of which were united in their hostility to the residue of British power, openly campaigned against Jordanian membership. There were fears that the West Bank might secede in the event of Jordan joining the Pact,[24] a prospect that would have been especially alarming for a Hashemite. The loyal old guard politicians, whose cabinets now routinely included ministers of Palestinian origin, either lost their appetite for a fight, like Sa'id al-Mufti, or were overwhelmed by the enormity of the task, as was Hazza al-Majali. The latter's stance is particularly instructive. When the Mufti government fell after less than seven months in office the spirited Majali was appointed with the task of taking Jordan in come what may. The Majali government resigned with the country in uproar after just eight days, and the king finally backed off.

The Baghdad Pact debacle had been a very bad affair for the regime in Jordan. It had mobilised and radicalised much of the urban population, at a time when there was no shortage of radical parties on the political scene. It had shown how porous were Jordan's borders, and how impressionable its people to the exhortations of Nasser and Egypt. It had exposed the indecisiveness of Britain, Jordan's traditional sponsor, and had drawn attention to the growing limitations of its influence in the region. It had been a bruising experience for the country's political class, with the incentives to remain loyal to the centre diminishing at an alarming rate. Finally, the episode had unequivocally exposed the extent to which the fortunes of the regime were dependent on the loyalty of the army, and behind it the political economy of rural Transjordan. Though demonstrations ended and the country collectively drew breath after the failure of the Baghdad Pact mission, it was unlikely to be the end of Jordan's extended brush with radical politics. That second brush was to come soon enough, with the October 1956 general election in the kingdom and the installation of a radical government.

It is testimony to the fluctuating political atmosphere of the period in Jordan, and behind it the general volatility of Arab politics, that, before that next surge of radicalism, King Hussein fleetingly became a hero of Arab nationalist politics. The reason for his moment of glory was the announcement made on 1 March 1956 dismissing Glubb Pasha as chief of the general staff, together with his two British assistants, one of whom was director of general intelligence. The dismissal came as a bolt from the blue for the British authorities in London in particular, which had remained wedded to Glubb's continuing presence in spite of signs of unhappiness from the king. Glubb had been concerned at his relationship with the king for more than a year, but did not expect summary dismissal. In retrospect Glubb and others should not have been so sure of themselves. After all, May 1955 had seen the demise of what would prove to be the last administration of another stalwart from King Abdullah's reign, Tawfiq Abu al-Huda. That Glubb and his fellow officers were so oblivious to the impending move is surely strong evidence of the complacency that still pervaded the British presence in the kingdom.

There were two fundamental reasons why King Hussein made his move. The first was in essence personal, born of the generational divide that now separated Glubb from the king. Glubb had been close to Hussein's grandfather, King Abdullah, a working relationship that had been rendered more intimate by good personal chemistry. The relationship had been helped by the fact that Glubb was the younger man, there never being any doubt about the subtle hierarchy of authority. But after Hussein's accession Glubb was now the elder and by a considerable 37 years. Tensions were almost inevitable. This situation was intensified by King Hussein's very obvious dependence on Glubb's Legion during the rioting surrounding the Baghdad Pact. It was Glubb's error of judgement not to identify this as unhealthy and ultimately untenable. Instead, his demeanour was that of a clinging, over-anxious parent. His conduct towards the king was often condescending, both in his formulation of military tactics and in his management of some sensitive issues related to the promotion and dismissal of Arab army officers.[25] All served to increase the king's frustration and resentment at Glubb's patronising approach. Once Hussein had decided to dismiss Glubb, and circumstantial evidence suggests that the idea had crossed his mind at least once the year before, the move fitted nicely with the young king's attempts to curry favour with Nasser.

The second reason for Glubb's dismissal was political, the landscape of national and regional politics alike affecting the context and outcome.[26] In the short term, the dismissal of Glubb was a way for King Hussein to transform his political fortunes. The fact that he had taken other less successful palliative actions, from dissolving parliament to the appointment of the non-controversial Ibrahim Hashim as prime minister, suggests that Hussein was seeking gestures through which to turn around the political situation at home. That the ousting of Glubb was destined to be a success there can be no doubt. In a region still fixated with the symbols of political sovereignty, the dismissal of a British head of the military was an ace of trumps in the king's hand. Like discarding the Abdullah generation of politicians, it was in truth something that should have been done some time before.

In spite of the shock of the event, Glubb's dismissal caused little more than some temporary turbulence in the Anglo-Jordanian relationship. Glubb displayed maturity in advising strongly upon his return home against any retaliatory action. London was, in any case, hardly looking for more quarrels in the region. The dismissal was also helpful to Hussein's cause at the time of Suez, soon after, as it allowed the young monarch to deflect domestic pressure, a cause that was aided by his expressions of solidarity with Nasser during the crisis. In turn, the dismissal of Glubb helped prompt Britain to take a hard look at its relationship with Jordan and conclude that the 1948 Treaty of Alliance was a similar anachronism.[27] The king's difficulty, it was eventually concluded, had been with the presence and personality of one man, rather than the relationship as a whole. Hussein remained an Anglophile. He was happy to seek military assistance from Britain in 1958, in the aftermath of the downfall of his Hashemite cousin in Baghdad. Ultimately, the unceremonious ousting of Glubb made little impact on the Anglo-Jordanian special relationship.

THE RADICAL CHALLENGE FROM WITHIN

Gratified by his new-found street-level popularity and more in step with the politics of the region, King Hussein now appeared to walk with a confidence his leadership had up to then failed to display. Organisationally, he was propelled along by the momentum that his dismissal of Glubb had created. The younger generation of army officers predominantly from the urban areas of the East Bank, those that Glubb and his men had been trying to hold back, received accelerated promotions. The epitome of this process was the 'buccaneerish'[28] Ali Abu Nuwwar, the newly appointed chief of staff, who assumed the position in May 1956 while still only in his thirties. He had come to Hussein's attention during a period of de facto exile, when he served as military attaché to the Jordanian embassy in Paris. Hussein had fallen under the older man's spell during one of his European tours, the king sharing Abu Nuwwar's fondness for the good life.

In regional affairs too Hussein moved with greater assurance, and during the middle of the year could be seen to be tactically manoeuvring with the best of them. It was against such a backdrop of greater confidence that Hussein dissolved the lower house of parliament and opened the way for general elections.

Though the move to new elections may have seemed logical enough in the wake of the dismissal of Glubb, Hussein's mistake was to assume that he had acquired a decisive control over events, and hence that he could determine the atmosphere against which the poll would take place; in short, that his ace of trumps would win him more than one trick. Such naïvete was exposed in spades one month after the 26 June dissolution by Nasser's nationalisation of the Suez Canal. Thus, a series of events was set in train that would see a secret Anglo-French-Israeli conspiracy concluded on 12 October to oust Nasser, an Israeli invasion that temporarily resulted in the occupation of the Sinai Peninsula, and an Anglo-French invasion aimed at securing the Canal. The ambitious nature of the conspiracy would fall apart in early November under the impact of American pressure, leaving Nasser with a considerable political victory.

The timeframe of the Suez crisis was wholly infelicitous for Hussein, with elections scheduled for 21 October. Rather than seek their postponement on the grounds of *force majeure*, the king proceeded, apparently on the naïve expectation that the afterglow of the ousting of Glubb would carry him through and that consequently few radicals would be successful. In reality, the election campaign was totally dominated by the trial of strength over Suez. Tapping into the popular view of the Baghdad Pact, Jordanian public opinion, especially in the urban areas, was overwhelmingly in favour of Nasser. Candidates strove to outbid one another in their support for Cairo. While the election itself was the freest that Jordan had ever experienced, Saudi funds and Egyptian agitation helped to ensure that the playing field was far from level.

Candidates identified with the domestic opposition swept to victory in at least 22 seats of the 40-seat parliament, including three Communists, two

Ba'thists (who had campaigned under the slogan of 'from prison to parliament') and one member of the small, radical Islamist grouping, the Liberation Party. The biggest opposition winner, however, was the unfortunately named National Socialist Party (NSP) under Sulaiman Nabulsi, which returned 12 deputies and considerable moral authority, though Nabulsi himself narrowly failed to win a seat. Conservative loyalists, though on the defensive, still managed to occupy 16 seats in the new parliament. The Jordanian branch of the Muslim Brotherhood, an opposition party, but one with no love for Nasser, achieved four seats.

While the Islamists and the leftists came from relatively well-organised, ideological movements, the NSP was more a nationalist flag of convenience that enabled a number of younger, ambitious politicians to acquire a passport to prominence. At their head, Nabulsi was a professional man, an intellectual, who had long been involved in talking politics in the salons of Amman. Though in general terms a radical, Nabulsi was a man whose views bobbed up and down on the waves of the political seas of the moment. So, for example, he had already shown himself to be co-optable, serving as finance minister in the short-lived cabinet of Samir al-Rifai between December 1950 and July 1951. Soon after, though unconvincing as a revolutionary, Nabulsi had nevertheless drifted into more radical circles, notably with his support of a campaign against the regional arms race organised by the newly self-conscious Jordanian Communist Party in 1951.[29]

Behind Nabulsi stood a number of figures from leading families, such as Anwar al-Khatib, Hikmat al-Masri (who was quickly elected speaker), Saleh al-Muasher, Abdul Halim al-Nimr, and Salah Tuqan, whose posture as political radicals was singularly unconvincing. The presence of such patrician names in what purported to be a radical political movement was actually a reflection of a rather pragmatic response on the part of some of the established families in the kingdom in a context of uncertainty born of ideological contestation. As Yahya Haddad has stated: 'the more prescient families maintain membership of various political color and class so that in times of sudden political or class change the family will not necessarily lose its power position'.[30]

King Hussein responded to the outcome of the elections with both *sang froid* and a due regard for the spirit of the exercise. He therefore turned to Nabulsi, as the party leader, to form a government that was bound to reflect the NSP's showing. Not only was the new cabinet packed with Nabulsi's political allies, like Nimr and Muasher, but it also included the leading Ba'thist MP and firebrand orator, Abdullah Rimawi; trouble seemed to be in store. Nevertheless, in the immediate context of Suez this appeared to matter little. Hussein, still keen to show his Arab nationalist colours, had backed Nasser once war broke out and even argued for war against Israel, though, in a curious role reversal, he appeared to be reined in by Nabulsi.

Neither was the immediate aftermath of the crisis a moment of acute tension. Rather, the attention of the government turned to the future of the Anglo-Jordanian Treaty, the continuation of the British subsidy and ways of safeguarding budget security. The former was swiftly dispatched, with the treaty having few defenders, including Britain, which, in the words of Dann, now regarded it as 'an expensive bauble'.[31] Once Jordan had secured an alternative commitment to budget support, in the form of a tripartite pledge by Egypt, Saudi Arabia and Syria, the treaty was terminated. The Arab Solidarity Agreement was duly signed in Cairo in January 1957. It was another sign of Hussein's naïvete, not to mention the beginnings of a lifelong macro-economic illiteracy, that only the gesture, rather than the three countries' ability or willingness to pay, was taken into account. In the event, of the three, only Saudi Arabia met its first promised payment.

Though the transition from British alliance to Arab solidarity had been effected with a surprising degree of smoothness, it would prove to be a misleading gauge of the ability of palace, government and regional radicals to work together in the future. Indeed, less than three months after the Cairo signing the Nabulsi government would be summarily dismissed, and the start of a new, much less liberal chapter in the history of the kingdom begun. Specifically, contention would be focused on two things. First, Jordan's position in a developing world where bipolarity was spreading from the original theatre of Cold War tension. Second, how the kingdom fitted into a regional system where Nasser appeared to be the dominant actor. More profoundly the issue would be about who called the foreign policy shots in the kingdom: monarch or government.

Even as Jordan was getting ready to sign the Arab Solidarity Agreement, the United States was unveiling the Eisenhower Doctrine. A direct consequence of the Suez crisis, the doctrine nominally allowed the president to assist any state threatened by Communist aggression, through the use of both financial and military means. More generally it was understood to be a move aimed at limiting the expansion of Nasser's influence in the region, following the humiliation of the two former colonial powers. The announcement of the Eisenhower Doctrine seems immediately to have caught the king's eye, offering Hussein the chance to change his foreign policy orientation away from support for a has-been power and towards a superpower. Neither was the move entirely opportunistic. King Hussein was clearly impressed by the evenhandedness of President Eisenhower's leadership during the Suez crisis, and his no-nonsense willingness to order Israel's withdrawal from the Sinai.[32] King Hussein therefore soon made a bid for the existing modest levels of aid received from the US to be increased to around $30 million, commensurate with the magnitude of the subsidy he was losing from Britain.

Having warmed to the arrangement, King Hussein realised what was expected of him ideologically in the US. Soon after the first appearance of the Eisenhower Doctrine, the king began attacking Communism.[33] In turn, the security forces took their cue from their monarch, overseeing a swathe of measures aimed at clamping down on different manifestations of Communism, including closing down the Tass office in Amman and seizing party propaganda. In doing so, the king also wrong-footed the Nabulsi government that, though not perhaps instinctively sympathetic either to Communism or the USSR, had recently allowed the legal publication of a party weekly. Through his pointed attacks on political extremism, the king had identified Rimawi as both a key influence on the foreign policy of the government and one whose radical Arabism could easily be talked down as godless Communism. Hussein also covered his back by establishing a back channel with Cairo, Damascus and Riyadh through which he assured Jordan's awkward neighbours of a continuing relationship regardless of the fortunes of the government.

Rather than exerting a calming influence, Nabulsi looked increasingly like a hapless liberal caught in the political crossfire. He exerted little influence on the king's new gambit, while failing to contain Rimawi, who seemed emboldened by the emerging confrontation. Towards the end of March, Nabulsi, who tended towards flights of rhetorical fancy, announced that he intended to recognise Red China; on 3 April he declared his intention to establish full diplomatic relations with the Soviet Union. Borne along by the momentum of events and unsighted as to the dynamics of regional, inter-state politics, the radicals rushed towards confrontation, engineering the removal of trusted Hashemite retainers with, most notably, the cabinet retiring the king's director of security, Bahjat Tabaraa, an Abdullah loyalist of Lebanese origin. Also disconcerting for King Hussein was the news of 'Operation Hashim', an enigmatic night-time deployment by units led by East Bank townsmen officers or *hadari*.[34] Though ordered back to barracks by Hussein, the manoeuvre seemed to suggest that things were approaching a critical point, with military units now involved.

From a steady beginning, the two sides seemed destined for a head-on confrontation. Hussein realised that the removal of Tabaraa in particular was in danger of giving a decisive edge to the radicals, the neutralisation of the coercive apparatus of the state threatening to remove his ultimate veto power in domestic politics. The young monarch concluded that he could afford to indulge his liberal inclinations no longer. Faced with such naked power politics, the king rose to the challenge and dismissed the cabinet a day later on 10 April 1957. With the constitutional niceties out of the way the country braced itself to see what would be the outcome of the emerging power play.

A COUP FROM THE PALACE

The following three weeks have been labelled by Middle East historian Uriel Dann as 'the most crucial period in the history of the Hashemite monarchy'.[35] The centre-piece of this period was that of a military challenge, though the nature and extent of its direct threat are contested. The regime narrative has it that the monarchy was faced with an organised bid for power launched by a free officers' movement, with senior *hadari* figures, most notably Ali Abu Nuwwar, at its head. On the night of 13 April, King Hussein was informed of a commotion at the army base in Zarqa. He immediately set off for the camp with an increasingly uncomfortable Abu Nuwwar with him. On his arrival he found troops grappling with one another, bedouin against townsmen, many of the latter officers. Hussein plunged into their midst, rallying loyalists and facing down the traitors. Such prompt and fearless action ended the revolt. Abu Nuwwar, after pleading for mercy, was allowed to take flight to Syria and a period of exile, later to be rehabilitated when the threat had passed. Twenty-two men were put on trial, of whom five were acquitted and the rest sentenced to jail terms of between 10 and 15 years, nine of them *in absentia*.

Though the exact truth of what King Hussein in his autobiography called 'the Zerka uprising' is unknown and unknowable, it was clearly an important moment for the king and the future of the regime.[36] The Jordanian army contained genuine Nasserite sympathisers. Perhaps more importantly, it also contained ambitious and self-regarding figures, prepared to exploit the turbulent regional situation for their own personal ends. Moreover, the middle of April was a period of tremendous tension, when speculation was intense in the aftermath of the fall of Nabulsi. Whether it was more a pre-emptive strike by Hussein, and he would later describe it as 'the cleansing of a running sore',[37] or the exploitation of a chance dispute for political purposes, it was nevertheless a timely one. Either way, it provided a convenient opportunity to weed out those whose loyalty was suspect, and to bind those who remained into a personalised loyalty to him. Through a display of such steel, an attribute almost entirely absent in his cousin in Iraq, Hussein ensured that the events of July 1958 in Baghdad did not take place in Jordan. It left Hussein with a bedouin-dominated praetorian force that would be invaluable in later periods of crucial importance, whether the end of April 1957 or the civil war in 1970–71. It further assigned the guilt for extra-constitutional, coercive action to the opposition, thereby enabling the king to resort to such methods in the future but without having to bear a moral responsibility for so doing.

Though Nabulsi had been discarded and Abu Nuwwar and his confederates disgraced and exiled, the tussle between Hussein and the radicals in Jordan was not yet finished. On 22 April, a 'Patriotic Congress' was convened in Nablus, drawing together hard-core supporters from among the NSP, Ba'thists and Communists. It boldly challenged the political order through the issuing of a 'proclamation to the people', which called for federation with Egypt and Syria, the reinstatement of dismissed officers, the purging of loyalists and the unity of the people and the army. Its immediate tactics were to call for a general strike and popular demonstrations and to establish an executive committee of 16, which seemed to offer the prospect of a parallel government. Of the 77 signatories, 23 were serving members of parliament. In signing up to such a subversive agenda the NSP had irreconcilably aligned themselves with the extremists of the left.

Hussein and the army were not alone in facing such a renewed onslaught. The Muslim Brotherhood, which was implacably ideologically opposed to the Ba'th and Communists alike, had already gravitated towards the king's corner in alarm at the precarious position in which the country found itself. The organisation shared his alarm at the proclamation, mobilising its supporters to oppose those already taking to the streets, a move that led to clashes, notably in Jericho and Nablus. Also mobilising on the king's behalf were many among the tribes of Jordan, which, through the presence of their kinsmen in the army, formed virtually an auxiliary military. Adwan and Bani Sakhr tribesmen, sworn enemies from the 1920s and before, put aside their old frictions to converge on the capital, where they tore down posters of Nasser and surged towards the royal palace 'to reassure the King of their devotion to his person and their loyalty to the Throne'.[38] King Hussein allowed this brief breakdown in public order so as to justify his firm and overwhelming strike. On 25 April 1957, martial law was declared and bedouin troops mobilised. A temporary military government was introduced, with the country divided into seven military districts, and each newly appointed governor reporting to a military governor general. A system of military justice was set up. Several hundred people were arrested and imprisoned.

This decisive move would bring to an end the turbulent experience of pluralist politics in the kingdom. Political parties were dissolved and banned, publications closed down, and radical groups suppressed.[39] Eight MPs were arrested or chased away, and elected councils in the West Bank and some of the Palestinianised areas of the East Bank (notably Amman and Zarqa) closed down. It would be 1989 before political activity in any way reminiscent of the mid-1950s would re-emerge in the kingdom. It would take riots in the East Bank heartlands, near economic collapse and an arrogant and self-serving government in order to pressure King Hussein into restarting the experiment with liberal politics that he had dispensed with more than three decades before.

When in 1957 he made his decisive move, Hussein appeared unrestrained by sentiment or weakness. He had initiated a pre-emptive counter-revolution and did not flinch at following it through. State security institutions were reorganised and streamlined to facilitate such a move. It was to the country's civilian structures that the national security state now turned its attentions. The rise of radical politics had seen the recruitment and even the conversion of a large number of bright Jordanian townsmen, who were to be found in increasingly influential positions in a state whose institutions had expanded rapidly since the acquisition of the West Bank. One such figure was Hamad al-Farhan, whose accelerated rise in the recently created Ministry of National Economy allowed him to dominate its activities.[40] It was in part in order to wrest back control of the state from such figures that the counter-reformation was given such rein.

In having the freedom and the leeway to strike back at his opponents, Hussein was well served by newly emerging friendly states and the chaos and distraction of his potential enemies. The US was swift to demonstrate its support for the king by making a $10 million aid payment in the immediate aftermath of the extended crackdown and delivering a near guarantee against Soviet intervention. The revelation of this period was the Kingdom of Saudi Arabia, hitherto a dynastic rival of the Hashemites, their dispute harking back to the fate of the Hijaz in the 1920s, and nominally and incongruously still part of the nationalist regional camp. As had the Muslim Brotherhood, so the conservative Saudi regime also made a mature appraisal of the situation, concluding that its interests would overwhelmingly be served by the continuation of King Hussein in power in an independent, status quo-oriented Jordanian state. In addition to public support, Riyadh backed Hussein in practical terms by making the first of the transfers due under the Cairo Agreement. It also placed a military force at his disposal, thereby helping to deter an Egyptian-backed Syrian invasion, which fleetingly had looked to be a possibility. This clear statement of interest by the Saudi authorities marked the beginning of the emergence of a new cleavage in the Arab world between conservative and radical states. Thus, the emergence of what Malcolm Kerr came to call the Arab Cold War was beginning to take place.[41] King Hussein acknowledged the support of the Saudis by making a brief visit to the kingdom soon after; it would be the first of many such visits as Saudi Arabia would later emerge as a major donor to the Jordanian exchequer.

REBUILDING STABILITY

The successful completion of the pre-emptive, royalist putsch was not the last of the challenges that faced the kingdom during the roaring fifties. Though King Hussein had got a grip on domestic politics, albeit only through recourse to coercive force, he was relatively powerless to affect developments beyond his borders. It was these that were to make the remainder of the decade full of difficult tests.

The decision to establish the United Arab Republic (UAR), a union between Egypt and Syria, on 1 February 1958 was another of those chaotic and ad hoc developments that littered inter-Arab politics during the 1950s. That Cairo was bounced into the union by Syrian Ba'thists, anxious about the precariousness of their position in power in Damascus, and that Nasser then resolved to colonise the Syrian administration rather than observe the spirit of the union, underlines its unplanned and ultimately chaotic nature. It also helps to explain the collapse of the venture three years later. In its initial stages, however, the UAR was widely perceived to be something much more awesome: the first step in the practical realisation of Arab unity, leading to the revision of the colonially inspired Arab state system.

The rising premium placed on Arab unity in the aftermath of the UAR increased what Michael Barnett has coined as 'symbolic competition' and hence the risks of 'symbolic entrapment'.[42] At least for King Hussein, with his Hashemite background and pan-Arab sense of mission, the Arab unity goal could be pursued with a straight-faced conviction. Whether the popular perception would be to invest a unity scheme that was not based upon Nasser and Egypt with even a modicum of credibility was another matter. Hussein's first thoughts on a countervailing Arab community to the UAR turned to Saudi Arabia, only to be rebuffed by the inherent caution of King Saud and his ilk. He then looked to his Hashemite cousins in Baghdad,[43] a more realistic choice, in view of the essentially defensive reaction to the establishment of the UAR.

The first Iraqi response to King Hussein's enthusiastic proposal of the creation of a Hashemite federation was lukewarm, not least because of the sharpness of the competition that would inevitably ensue with the UAR. However, Baghdad appreciated the vulnerability of Amman, and warmed to Hussein's revised proposal that the presidency of the union permanently lie with the kings of Iraq, starting with the incumbent, Faisal II. Once the brief negotiation had allowed for Jordan to remain outside the scope of the Baghdad Pact, agreement was reached, allowing the Arab Federation of Iraq and Jordan to become manifest on 14 February. A federal government was established some three months later, with the Iraqi Nuri al-Said as prime minister and Jordan's Ibrahim Hashim as his deputy. The expectation was that in most matters, with the exception of foreign affairs and defence, the policy centre of gravity would remain within the respective capitals.

Though Nasser extended polite congratulation to the Arab Federation, the UAR media immediately got to work on defaming the new entity. The invective concluded that the federation was fated to disappear. They were right. It did so in the bloodshed of the palace in Baghdad on 13–14 July, in which King Faisal, the Crown Prince Abdul Illah and even Ibrahim Hashim were killed. Their nemesis was a free officers grouping in the Iraqi army, and its leader, Abdul Karim al-Qasim. Ironically, the opportunity for the coup in Baghdad was the deployment of military units to the Jordanian border for fear of a move against King Hussein, following the revelation of a well-planned coup attempt organised by the returning deputy head of the Jordanian mission to the US, Colonel Mahmud Rusan.

Angered by the slaughter of his relatives and injured by his dynasty's second historic defeat of the century, following the loss of the Hijaz, King Hussein's first inclination was to resist this reversal of fortunes. Declaring himself leader of the federation, Hussein momentarily resolved to invade Iraq, based on the erroneous premise that the putschists had not yet consolidated their hold across the country and in the vain hope that there might be defections from the army. With the faintly ludicrous image of little Jordan invading a regional power like Iraq, Hussein was obliged to stand down his troops and concentrate on holding his own position at home. In the event the situation was sufficiently serious to warrant turning Amman into 'an armed camp'.[44] King Hussein subsequently wrote that in 1958 he needed some help but 'not so much physical as moral help'.[45] That moral help arrived in the shape of a British military contingent comprising two battalions of paratroopers, together with support units in a division of labour that saw US forces move to Lebanon for similarly preventive purposes.

However, it was not quite true to say that Jordan's needs were not physical. Jordan was exposed as far as its strategic communications were concerned to the leverage of its more powerful neighbours. With hostile Arab powers on three sides, Jordan was particularly vulnerable because of its reliance on the port of Beirut for the main bulk of its imports, Jordan's own port of Aqaba not yet having been developed. With Syria's decision to close the border, depriving the kingdom of its oil supplies, the king was in even greater need of US support. Jordan was subsequently dependent for some four months on oil supplies flown in from Saudi Arabia, and, when that proved to be problematic, from Lebanon, using a flight path over Israel.

Moreover, Jordan remained under pressure from the UAR and the regional forces of radical revisionism, notably through a campaign of sabotage and political violence, aimed at demoralising the regime. For some two years to 1960 Jordan would sustain a series of bomb attacks on officials and foreign embassies, and attempts to disrupt the country's fragile infrastructure, with bridges, airports and telegraph lines the favoured targets. Those responsible for the campaign were widely believed to have infiltrated Jordan's border with Syria. Their most notable success was the assassination of the serving prime minister, Hazza al-Majali, in August 1960. This period of violent, external pressure dissipated with the collapse of the UAR in 1961.

CHAPTER 6

The Road to Disaster

By the early 1960s the chronic instability experienced by Jordan in the previous decade was at an end. The political domain was in the grip of a national security state, with the coercive capacity of the loyalist core of the army increasingly complemented by an emerging domestic intelligence apparatus. Against such a backdrop, the political realm in the kingdom was, in the absence of political parties, a sanitised one, with legal activity easily manipulated by an active political elite moving in orbit around the palace. The allure of radical Arab nationalism was in any case in decline after the collapse of the United Arab Republic in 1961. The growing struggle between conservative and radical forces in the region increasingly came to focus on Yemen after 1962, giving further respite to the kingdom, though regime change in Iraq and Syria in 1963 momentarily re-exposed Jordan's regional vulnerabilities.

With much of the chaos and incoherence of ideological politics cleansed from the landscape of legal politics in Jordan, it was more than ever up to the top to supply vision and strategy as far as the kingdom's future development was concerned. The path adopted was one of economic development and public planning in order to make best use of the country's meagre resources and to try to deliver rising levels of prosperity. The early 1960s saw the emergence of a new generation of predominantly technocratic politicians willing to engage upon such a mission. Of this new generation the most talented and most controversial was undoubtedly Wasfi al-Tall, a man whose legacy continues to be claimed by rival political currents within the kingdom long after his death.

Before the process of public sector planning could take root Jordan became sucked into the vortex that was the Arab–Israeli imbroglio in the 1960s. It was therefore 1967 and the disastrous June war that became the defining event for the kingdom in the 1960s, when King Hussein lost half a kingdom, including Jerusalem, and Jordan was again afflicted by the large-scale displacement of Palestinians as a result of war. Again, controversy surrounds the event. Why did Hussein throw in his lot with the Egyptians? Could he have stayed out of the war, retaining the West Bank, but without losing his throne? Was he really convinced of the unrelenting enmity of the Israelis?

The latter part of the decade saw hardly any less of an existential crisis than had been the case in the mid-1950s. On this occasion it was the presence of the Palestinian guerrillas, and the existence of a PLO entity within a Jordanian state that presented the challenge, coming as it did against a backdrop of a fluctuating low-level conflict with Israel and the renewed attentions of an often hostile Arab diplomatic milieu. In spite of countless negotiations and arrangements, the fluctuating tensions between Jordan and the PLO would continue, coming to a head in 1970. Only through recourse to the bedouin units of the army would the counter-military of the PLO be defeated and expelled, thereby once again securing the Jordanian state.

WASFI AL-TALL AND THE REST

With the passing of the Abdullah generation of politicians and the dislocations of the radical interlude of mid-1950s politics, the late 1950s and early 1960s saw the emergence of a new generation of politicians. Born in Jordan and from established families, these men had received considerably more formal education than their predecessors. In terms of background and aspiration, these were men with greater regional awareness and a modern outlook, rather than the traditional, introspective figures that had typified the profile of local elite figures in the past. However, owing to the tribally fragmented nature of the country, these politicians were implausible as truly national figures, which, of course, reduced the risk of their prominence for the king. Like their predecessors, their access to positions of political power was dependent on the patronage of the monarch.

The nearest that Jordan came to producing a man of genuinely national stature, during this period or indeed at any time since, was the controversial figure of Wasfi al-Tall,[1] whom Israeli historian Uriel Dann has called independent Jordan's 'outstanding statesman'.[2] A volcanic and seemingly contradictory amalgam, Tall was an Arab nationalist and Jordanian nationalist, a fighter for Palestinian rights and a suppressor of Palestinian activists, a patriot but someone who acquired a reputation as a British agent, a former journalist and reformer but a man whose first political appointment was as a government censor, a man who served three times as prime minister but was never a team player, Wasfi al-Tall is a much-debated figure in Jordan; even today his political legacy is a focus of competition among those lesser men who would claim him as the patron saint of their political movements.

The son of the Jordanian poet, Arar, himself a paradox,[3] Wasfi al-Tall was born in 1919 of a prominent line within the Tall clan of northern Jordan. After a childhood in Irbid, he attended the prestigious American University in Beirut (AUB), that was emerging as a regional centre of radical Arab nationalist ideas. He joined the British army during the Second World War, though in Beirut he had demonstrated in favour of the short-lived, anti-British Rashid Ali government in Baghdad. Ironically, in view of his later vilification by much of the Palestinian national movement, Tall risked his life trying to prevent the creation of the state of Israel, joining the Arab League's ill-fated Arab Liberation Army, which fought in Palestine during the first Arab–Israeli war. Its failures engendered in him what would become an active contempt for the theory and practice of what passed for pan-Arab action for the remainder of his career.

Various government positions in the 1950s, notably responsibility for Jordanian public diplomacy under the patronage of Hazza al-Majali, for whom by 1960 he had emerged as a close adviser, saw Tall become increasingly an establishment man. It was also during this time that he developed a visceral hatred for Nasser,[4] a man whom he correctly believed would ultimately bring catastrophe upon the Arab world. It was characteristic of Tall's imprudent straight-talking that he was never shy in sharing his contemptuous views of the Egyptian leader. Tall would meet his end in Cairo at the hands of a Palestinian assassin in 1971, apparently one of the first casualties of the Black September movement, which would seek revenge for the suppression of the PLO in Jordan in 1970–71, in which he had played a major part.

Government politics of the period between 1960 and the approach to war in 1967 came to be defined by an intense personal and political competition between Tall, as the natural successor to Majali, and the other leading politician of the day, the more senior Bahjat Talhuni. Their competition for office was just the latest example of Jordan's binary struggle between the big men politicians who head the political elite of the moment that has come to typify domestic politics, Jordan-style. Tall versus Talhuni was reminiscent of Tawfiq Abu al-Huda versus Samir al-Rifai in a slightly earlier age, and would be replicated in Zaid al-Rifai versus Mudar Badran in the 1980s. Such was the competition between the two that Tall and Talhuni came to represent everything that was the diametrical opposite in the other. Tall was a northerner; Talhuni was from the southern town of Maan. Tall was energetic, loud and, on occasions, coarse; Talhuni was quiet and careful. Tall was direct, stubborn and bullying; Talhuni was a more devious political operator, who would cement a political dynasty by marrying his daughter to Zaid, the son of Samir al-Rifai. Talhuni was corrupt and self-serving;[5] Tall was selfless to the point of foolhardiness.

With foreign affairs still an important signifier in the choice of premier, this diametrical opposition was also replicated in foreign policy. For King Hussein, Tall and Talhuni came to embody a diplomatic division of labour: while Talhuni became increasingly associated with good relations with Nasser, and, by extension, closer ties with the Arab world in general, Tall came to be identified with good relations with Baghdad, where he served as the first Jordanian ambassador after the restoration in 1960, and then in Riyadh. For Asher Susser, Tall's biographer, it was Wasfi's straight-talking that made him of immeasurably greater value to King Hussein than his peers:

Tall was one of the few, the very few, who would go a long way to impress his views on Husayn, at the risk of displeasing him. But Husayn also liked and appreciated Tall's sincerity. The King found in him a true partner with whom he could share the onus of government and also maintain a correct working relationship, based on mutual esteem and trust.[6]

Tall was first appointed as prime minister in January 1962 in succession to Talhuni, whose main task had been to provide stability after the assassination of Majali. King Hussein gave Tall a reformist brief.[7] Accordingly, he formed a cabinet that was drawn from among the new generation of younger, university educated government servants. By doing so, the king was coming to learn one of the key, though less politically partisan, lessons of the mid-1950s, namely to promote a circulation of elites. Through this device, younger members of the country's political elite could at last begin to entertain the realistic ambition that they would go on to enjoy high office, as ministers or senior public officials. Through such means a new generation began to develop a tangible self-interest in the survival of the regime. The device also worked in respect of bright members of the Palestinian elite, who could now see no prospect of benefit from radical opposition to the regime.[8] In reinvigorating its cabinet government, Jordan avoided the governmental and bureaucratic stasis that, until the mid-1990s, had come to typify Saudi Arabia. The attractions of the new government were not lost on the young.[9] This, combined with professional expertise rather than ideological zealotry, made for a more efficient and effective administration of the country.

Wasfi al-Tall responded to this brief with characteristic excess. He chose a government none of whose members had previously served as ministers and only one of whom had been an MP. Its members generally enjoyed a reputation for efficiency, and his closest ministerial partner, Khalil al-Salim, would go on to become the kingdom's first central bank governor. He also promoted promising, well-educated men within the ranks of the administration, of whom the best-known would come to be Sharif Abdul Hamid Sharaf, who would briefly star as a reformist premier in his own right in 1980.[10] Tell's motto for the cabinet was 'New Frontier'.[11] As the British ambassador wrote in a dispatch after the appointment of the first Tall administration, 'The air is full of hope.'[12]

Tall took seriously his commission from the throne to undertake administrative reform. For example, some 700 members of the bureaucracy, including a number of judges, were retired, fired or transferred in an anti-corruption and efficiency promotion drive, regardless of their tribal background. In order to bolster standards in the civil service, the Tall government set minimum educational levels for recruitment. This was implemented to great and visible effect with the holding of a public examination for a separate foreign service,[13] recruitment having previously been part of the civil service as a whole. The insistence that all Jordanian ambassadors be university graduates raised the quality of the country's envoys to a comparable level to those of the more advanced countries of the region. The office hours for civil servants were lengthened from 36 to 42 hours a week in return for a rise in pay. Meetings of the cabinet were increased from twice to three times a week.

As well as promoting efficiency, the new message from Amman was that anyone could get on in the Jordanian state, regardless of their ethno-geographic background. To emphasise this message, Tall put together a government 'with good West Bankers in it', half of its number being Palestinian, and dedicated to giving them 'a larger share in the Government'. He also made the dramatic gesture of giving a Palestinian, Kamal Dajani, the interior ministry portfolio,[14] the sign of a willingness to allow political co-option rather than mere coercion as the main instrument of stability.

Tall's government was also notable for its attempt to ease the kingdom back in the direction of a more inclusive institutional politics, in view of the easier regional atmosphere. This principally took the form of a new general election in November, which was one of the freest in Jordanian history, though one where political parties remained banned. This relative freedom contrasted with the national election of 1961 that, under the shadow of the threat from the UAR, had been blatantly rigged. Though some opposition

figures boycotted the November 1962 poll, as a function of the residue of
regional politics, on the whole the population of Jordan warmed to the
elections, with a turnout of up to 70% in some constituencies.

The outcome was a parliament that was awkward, though not anti-
regime. Including four members of his cabinet, the parliament was both
well educated and free-spirited. This appeared to suit Tall very well, in
that both executive and legislature seemed to be in reformist harmony.
He perceived the lower house as a partner for his government, and spoke
extravagantly at the outset of it making 'a real contribution'. He expressed
an interest in establishing a number of committees that might advise and
assist the cabinet on policy and proposed that the assembly should sit in
continuous session from November to May.[15] He proceeded to submit a
government programme to parliament that included the enfranchisement
of women, the expansion of government services and the distribution of
state lands to rural farmers.

However, Tall failed to capitalise on this favourable alignment. His
haughty character prevented him from lobbying the new members of parliament as they debated his programme, since he disliked the idea of being
beholden to them. Though he received the confidence of the new assembly, the casting of 18 dissenting votes, most of them from the West Bank
(including all five MPs for Jerusalem), brought the prime minister back
down to earth. This affront brought out the vindictive, authoritarian side
of Tall's character. He responded by sacking the governor of Jerusalem,
the urbane and capable Anwar Nuseibeh, replacing him with an East Bank
tough. Rather than ameliorating the West Bank–East Bank tensions, as had
been his original intention, Tall had ended up exacerbating them. It would
mark the beginning of his alienation from the Palestinians as a whole. With
Tall's petulance exacerbating rather than ameliorating an East Bank–West
Bank divide that the election had brought to the surface, the days of the
government were probably already numbered. Its demise was hastened by
renewed turmoil in Iraq and Syria that saw the resurgence of regional threats
and a need to appease Cairo.

Though the cabinet was only to survive until March 1963, and its end
was ignominious, the youth-oriented and meritocratic symbolism of it had
been clearly demonstrated. It was to be the kingdom's first technocratic
government, and hence the template for future non-crisis administrations.
For King Hussein, the stability and self-confidence of Tall's technocrats
were a reassuringly long way from the turbulent truculence of Nabulsi and
his associates. Dann has labelled it as being 'another milestone in the history
of modern Jordan . . . in some respects it was the birth of modern Jordan'.[16]

It is a sad reality but a distortion no less, that since his death Jordan has come to remember Wasfi al-Tall primarily for the brutal scourging of the Palestinians of his later years rather than as the government reformer of his early years.

THE DRIVE FOR ECONOMIC DEVELOPMENT

Apart from its technocratic and youthful symbolism, the most important aspect of Tall's first cabinet was the emphasis that it placed on integrated economic development as an important aspect of state-building. This was not the first time that the economy had been important in the stewardship of the kingdom. Under the auspices of the British, considerable efforts had been invested in development especially with the establishment of the Jordan Development Board in 1952. Later in the 1950s, the cause of economic development had been given a radical ideological bent through the emergence of such dynamic, reform-minded officials as Hamad al-Farhan. Increasingly important during the decade was aid received from the US under the Point Four programme. The process of systematic planning was initiated in 1957, with the establishment of the Reconstruction Council.[17] As Paul Kingston has concluded, this all made for a 'highly fragmented development effort'.[18]

Under Tall the economy was to emerge again as being of particular importance as a way of delivering prosperity, a prosperity that was viewed as a device through which to bind together the people of Jordan and act as a disincentive to political opposition. The broad approach of the Tall governments – of integrated indicative planning, of infrastructural development and of the building of public sector capacity – would characterise Jordan's approach to the oversight of the economy until the onset of the age of economic liberalisation at the end of the 1980s.

The centre-piece of the government's economic strategy was the unveiling of a five-year programme for economic development.[19] This was drafted by the Jordan Development Board, under the leadership of Kamal al-Sha'ir,[20] and was slated to run from 1962 to 1967.[21] This was the first time that the kingdom had attempted a balanced and integrated approach to economic development, with all the important aspects of the economy covered and allocative decisions taken on a holistic basis.[22] It was expected to deliver great things. The admittedly somewhat ambitious slogan of the second Tall government was 'self-sufficiency in 1970'.[23]

The plan had three main objectives. Its top priority was the expansion of the country's gross domestic output, bearing in mind that the average productivity of labour in all sectors in Jordan had hitherto been very low. The most disappointing results had been experienced in the agriculture sector, which occupied roughly half the workforce, but contributed between 20% and 30% of national income, depending on the level of the rainfall-affected harvest in any given year. In addressing this issue, the aim was to raise the standard of living in the kingdom, which, though higher than some less-developed countries, was generally considered to be inadequate.

Its second major objective was a reduction in the rate of unemployment, which was estimated to afflict about one-third of the workforce, or some 120,000 people. Such a high level of joblessness was in turn a major reinforcer of poverty. Its third goal was a considerable improvement in the country's balance of trade, bearing in mind that one-third of the total value of goods used in Jordan consisted of imports. Furthermore, the reliance on imports also helped to accentuate the rent-based dependence of the country, as an estimated 75% of imports were paid for by assistance from abroad.

The $356 million programme sought to tackle such problems first and foremost through the provision of investment in agriculture, which was to be the recipient of almost one-third of the total programme allocation. The focus of attention for such investment was the Jordan Valley, which Rami Khouri has described as 'the cornerstone of the overall development of Jordan'.[24] The main aim of this focus was to boost productivity through the construction of an ambitious irrigation system, the East Ghor Canal. As well as increasing the area of land under cultivation, it was also hoped to break the pattern of subsistence farming that threatened the viability of agricultural activity. Such ventures as this helped to foster the reputation that Wasfi al-Tall was especially well disposed towards the small, rural farmers of the East Bank. He certainly seemed to believe in trying to keep the rural population on the land, and was willing to devote resources accordingly. However, this appeared to be as much about stemming the security threat from the urban mob, made up in part of disaffected recent migrants from the countryside, as about a romantic mission to preserve the rural way of life.

Other sectoral recipients under the plan were to include: industry, embracing power generation, the extraction of phosphates and potash and the establishment of an industrial area around Zarqa; construction, that is the building of schools, hospitals, housing and government buildings; transportation, notably the expansion of Aqaba port, the provision of new roads and the extension of the railway to Aqaba; communications, especially radio; and tourism. Though there were some concerns expressed about the absorptive capacity of the country in the face of such new investments, the presence of such a large refugee population was regarded as likely to have a continuing deflationary effect. Even the most optimistic of estimates envisaged the creation of only 90,000 new jobs during the programme's span.

Though the programme enshrined the provision of an integrated range of investment, it was not an attempt to introduce a system of centralised, state planning. Nearly 40% of the plan's investment capital was expected to come from the private sector. The industrial sector investments in particular were aimed at mobilising private sector capital. The economic philosophy prevailing in Jordan was very much one of a mixed economy.

The forging ahead with a more effective and integrated approach to economic management necessitated the development of appropriate institutions. The most significant was the creation of a central bank, which opened for business in 1964. Though discussion about the need for such an institution had pre-dated the first Tall government, the bank was brought into existence in order to regulate financial activity in Jordan at this time.

There were, however, limits to the reformist successes of the Tall government. In 1962, Tall turned his attention to the army, which had been functioning semi-autonomously since it emerged as the crucial institution of power in 1957–58. Tall was concerned at the central position that it enjoyed within the state. In part, this concern was driven by the reality that the military ate up almost 50% of the national budget. However, the concern was not exclusively economic. Tall believed that the fact that the military was sucking resources out of the civilian economy could, ironically, contribute to an increased indirect political threat resulting from poverty and economic marginalisation. More directly, he was also concerned at the increasing manifestations of a national security state in Jordan, both in terms of the dependence of the regime on the army, and its own lack of accountability that had led to stories of violent abuse.

Initially, the signs were not auspicious, the 1959 Rifai government having been brought down by its efforts to reorganise the military. In the end, however, Tall was partially successful. Early measures, such as dispensing with the detachments of armed guards for senior figures, helped to reduce the profile of the army. Cost-of-living allowances were paid to military personnel as a sweetener. He won over King Hussein to the idea of streamlining the army in order to make it more efficient. He even managed to mobilise the army for civilian duties, such as afforestation, and dam and road construction. He was less successful in reducing the magnitude of the resources of the country taken by the military, which, with its entrenched social base in the rural political economy of the East Bank, was to continue as a powerful vested interest at the centre of the state.

CONFLICTS ACROSS THE REGION

The ground-breaking concentration of the Tall government on bringing in technocratic expertise and in giving priority to economic and administrative issues offered a glimpse of a new politics in Jordan. Rather than being able to build upon such a foundation, the waves of instability that were about to wash across the region proved to be too distracting for a state like Jordan that was small, relatively weak and whose borders were highly porous. Consequently, Tall's second government, between 1965 and 1967, was almost completely taken up with regional dynamics and their ever-increasing implications for Jordanian–Palestinian relations at home.

This was not, however, what the prospect had appeared to be in 1961. The collapse of the UAR was a sudden, dramatic and unexpected reversal of fortunes for President Nasser, which had seemed to be inexorably on the rise since 1955. For Jordan, which had so often been the butt of Cairo's propaganda and its attempts at promoting political discord, the end of the radical unity scheme was a boon in itself. Moreover, the eruption of recrimination and bad blood between Cairo and Damascus meant that Jordanian fears of being surrounded by radical, revisionist states were greatly eased.

If the aftermath of the collapse of the UAR gave Jordan a respite in which a reforming iconoclast like Wasfi al-Tall could be appointed to the premiership, the re-eruption of regional turmoil became manifest in September 1962 with the outbreak of the Yemeni civil war.[25] War in Yemen would prove to be a regional vortex for the next five years, comparable to the Lebanese civil war that would afflict the region between the mid-1970s and the late 1980s. Yemen would become a microcosm of the broader regional ideological struggle between conservatives and radicals, though from a Jordanian perspective, as again with Lebanon, better an arena elsewhere than at home. In the Yemeni case the conservative, religiously oriented Imamate regime was overthrown by radical republicans. Nasser backed the latter as a progressive force for change; Saudi Arabia came to the defence of the former in order to hold the line. The Arab world was polarised as never before.

There were only two choices on offer. For King Hussein and his prime minister, Wasfi al-Tall, the choice was not a dilemma. The resonance between Jordan in 1957–58 and Yemen in 1962 was too great. That Jordan adopted a pro-royalist and anti-Nasserite line was perhaps never in doubt. That it did so in an assertive way was a reflection of the leadership's assumptions about continuing stability at home. A boycott of parliamentary elections by some opposition figures was as bad as any direct protest was to get, although there was the embarrassment of the defection of the Jordanian

air force commander to Cairo; a more subtle cost was borne in terms of receding support for the Tall government, his reforms included. Though the
kingdom was too small and distant to make a decisive contribution to the
conflict in Yemen, its symbolic demonstrations, which Tall must have rel-
ished, antagonised Cairo disproportionately. These included the dispatch
of a small number of military advisers, the delivery of 12,000 somewhat
old-fashioned rifles, and a vitriolic propaganda campaign at which Tall,
given his earlier experiences in government, excelled.

For Hussein and Tall, the Yemeni war was not just about resisting radical
change and decrying Nasser. It was also about consolidating a conservative
bloc that would be strong enough to ensure that there would be no more
Yemens in the future. There was also the added prospect of aid from the
Gulf, the five-year programme, in spite of its determined protestations of
future self-sufficiency, being predicated on infusions from outside. The
clinching of several security and economic cooperation accords with Saudi
Arabia in the second half of 1962, which included the establishment of a
Joint Defence Council, appeared to deliver on just such an agenda.

The abandon with which Tall egged on the king's cavalier line on Yemen
was brought to an abrupt halt in February and March 1963, when coups
d'etat on the seventh of both months in Iraq and Syria respectively profoundly transformed the regional context. In Baghdad the quirky leader
of the Free Officers, Abdul Karim Qasim, who had metamorphosed from
an assumed Arab nationalist into an Iraq-first leader, was overthrown and
killed by more orthodox Arab nationalist officers. In Syria, the overthrow
of the secessionists from the UAR led to renewed interest in relations with
Cairo. Suddenly, Jordan was again surrounded on three sides and faced
with the prospect of the unity of its three most implacable neighbourhood
foes, a platform that was announced on 17 April 1963.

Though King Hussein tried to assuage the growing pressure by replacing
Tall, it would have been surprising if such a dramatic change in regional
fortunes had not made an impact on domestic politics. Though Samir al-
Rifai formed what would end up being his sixth and final administration,
and immediately sought to ameliorate relations with Cairo, it was a case
of too little too late for the veteran politician. Rioting reminiscent of 1957
broke out across the West Bank and in the northern city of Irbid. For
Rifai it was pay-back time. He received a mauling in the national assembly
for his track record of corruption, nepotism and authoritarianism as he
sought a confidence vote. His subsequent failure marked the first time that
parliament in Jordan had proved to be sufficiently vigorous and united to
bring down a government.

In spite of the inauspicious regional circumstances, domestically 1963 was not 1957. The army remained united in combating the rioters. King Hussein called the opposition's bluff by replacing Rifai with a Hashemite, his benign uncle, Sharif Hussein, who served as an interim prime minister. The king felt sufficiently confident of his position to turn down US-hinted offers of military support. New elections in July 1963 were exploited to ensure a more malleable lower house. It would be more than 25 years before Jordan would again see the election of such an independent parliament.

If adroit moves by the king alleviated pressures internally, the external environment remained problematic. Faced with the active enmity of Egypt, Iraq and Syria, and with relations with Saudi Arabia still crystallising, King Hussein began to explore relations with the only other serious player in the picture, Israel. It was, for instance, from September 1963 that King Hussein held the first of a series of clandestine meetings with senior Israeli figures. On this occasion the meeting was held in London with the head of prime minister Levi Eshkol's office, Dr Yaacov Herzog. For the pragmatic Hussein, such meetings evolved into get-to-know-you sessions, although he made the mistake of thinking that a dialogue with officials represented a dialogue with Israel as a whole; the king would still have to learn a painful lesson about the centrality of the defence establishment in security-related decision-making in the Israeli state. Though the initiation of such a dialogue would not save the king from the disaster of 1967, it would come to provide a sound basis on which relations could be stabilised in the 1970s and 1980s and a full peace treaty could be forged in the 1990s.

In the end, external pressure was alleviated by fast-moving developments within Jordan's neighbours. The consolidation of Ba'thist rule in Syria quickly resulted in new frictions with Baghdad and Cairo. In Iraq, nine months of political jockeying ended with the confirmation of the leadership of Abdul Salam al-Arif, a man whose admiration for Nasser was more a reflection of his desire to emulate the Egyptian leader's control of state power than a wish to be his regional subordinate. With President Nasser disconcerted by the emerging competitive power centres of Baghdad and Damascus, and Ba'thism now established as an ideological rival to his version of Arab nationalism, Jordan began to be viewed in a new light, as a state of geopolitical significance. With Wasfi al-Tall's influence at its low point, and with the likes of Rifai and Talhuni once again having the malleable king's ear, a shift towards rapprochement with Egypt was not difficult to understand.

THE AWAKENING OF PALESTINIAN NATIONALISM

It was out of the flux and instability of 1963 that the Middle East began to lurch towards a war that finally came in June 1967. The primary drivers of conflict were the emerging competition between Egypt and Syria, and the diplomatic and rhetorical devices sought by Nasser to maintain the edge in regional leadership. This emerging competition among radicals resulted in the resurrection of the Arab–Israeli struggle, which since 1956 had been relegated to a secondary importance in comparison with the radical–conservative division within the Arab world. For Jordan, it was a case of out of the frying pan and into the fire. King Hussein may have been relieved and perhaps rather flattered to be invited to play a central role in an Arab world where the old divisions had been somewhat attenuated. But he should have been more alert to the consequences. The looming confrontation with Israel, with the Palestinians at the centre, could hardly but have direct implications for the kingdom.

Nasser's concerns at the events of 1963 led him to a strategic change as far as regional Arab politics was concerned. He largely abandoned his propaganda campaign against Jordan, with the implication that its regime remained weak and defensive. He also set aside the language of unity, which had hitherto governed the way in which the radical states dealt with one another. Instead, he initiated a period of Arab summitry, with its assumption of mutual respect, and sought to involve all in its activities, radical and conservative alike.

King Hussein embraced the Egyptian turnaround with relish, being the first head of state to accept Nasser's conference invitation. It was an opportunity that fitted and bolstered the foreign policy template to which he was committed after the fall of the Tall government. Such an approach offered the short-term benefits of reduced pressure from Egypt and other radical Arab states, through a reduction in the bile broadcast from Cairo and other capitals. Most importantly, it presented a chance for the management of Nasser and Egypt, through coordination and the undertaking of collaborative activities. So pleased and relieved was Hussein at the short-term implications of the new departure that he was disinclined to think through the consequences of the concessions that he would shortly be obliged to make.

Hussein's embrace of the new regional departure may also owe something to the fact that he always seemed a little in awe of Nasser. Hence the chance for cooperation at last, after so many years of opposition and vilification, to be blessed by the benediction of Nasser, simply proved to be irresistible.

This psychological asymmetry is understandable if one bears in mind that Nasser was still the hero of the Arab world, widely admired across the region, ends to which the younger Hussein still dearly aspired. Hussein would display a similar, but less easily explicable awe-struck incredulity in his dealing with Saddam Hussein of Iraq in the 1980s. Whatever the role of such personal-cum-psychological aspects, as Lawrence Tal has written, Hussein's acceptance of the two most important substantive by-products of this Nasser-led summitry would be monumental errors.

Three Arab summits were held during this time, in January and September 1964, in Cairo and Alexandria respectively, and in September 1965 in Casablanca. The main outcome of the first of these was of profound significance for Jordan. First, it was decided to create a Palestinian liberation movement, the Palestine Liberation Organisation (PLO). Second, it was decided to establish a unified Arab command, with Egypt ominously given responsibility for it. Though it was the latter that provided the context in which King Hussein would sign away responsibility for the military conduct of war to the Egyptians in 1967, it was the formation of the PLO that was to be the more momentous development for Jordan.

There can be no doubt that Cairo's Palestinian initiative was a product of narrow state interest. And it would be the case that for the first three years of its existence the PLO would remain largely under Egyptian patronage. Like the All-Palestine government before it in the 1940s, the PLO was intended to be an instrument of Egyptian foreign policy, with the Palestinian issue made to serve the interests of Egypt and her leader and to create leverage with the other Arab states. If King Hussein believed that the basing of the PLO in Jordan would give him control of the institution, his patchy management of the West Bank component of his own national assembly hardly gave grounds for optimism. As in the 1940s, it was Jordan that would be disproportionately affected by its creation, for three reasons.

First, the establishment of the PLO helped to crystallise a dominant Palestinian identity in an area where competing supra-national identities of Arabness and Islam, and more parochial identities of clan, village and region, had been hitherto much more important. Second, the emergence of a new organisation self-consciously dedicated to the pursuit of Palestinian rights against Israel was to have an unsettling effect upon the Palestinian population of the West Bank of Jordan, in particular, that had shown itself to be at very least ambivalent towards its membership of the state of Jordan, and the all-embracing Jordanian identity that that state had sought to propagate. More particularly, it helped to trigger the emergence of a distinct and self-conscious Palestinian nationalism and, by way of reaction, to regenerate the nascent Transjordanian nationalism of the late 1920s and early 1930s, which had been predicated on the resentment of foreign influences. In that way, support for the creation of the PLO helped to negate the will for a national unity that had been a central strategy of the Hashemites since 1950. Third, Jordan's physical acceptance of the PLO, as was agreed at the Arab summit, opened the gates of the state to the Trojan horse of Palestinian radical nationalism, the effects of which would become alarmingly clear after the 1967 war.

Once the summit had taken place, the logic of the king's dangerous flirtation with Palestinian nationalism began to be seen. A Palestine conference was convened in Jerusalem at which Ahmad al-Shuqairi was elected to be the PLO's first chairman, thereby edging out the aging Hajj Amin al-Husseini, whose career had peaked some three decades earlier. The PLO agreed to respect the territorial integrity of all Arab states, with Shuqairi proving adept at soft-soaping the king with assurances that Jordan and the West Bank were included in this pledge not to interfere in their domestic affairs. But this commitment stood somewhat uneasily with the PLO's assumption of its own flag and anthem, and the agreement that it should open its own offices both at the UN and in states of the region and of the Communist bloc. Indeed, from the outset Shuqairi worked hard to bolster his own position as a regional political player, amassing significant funds from the Gulf and packing the new organisation with his supporters.

The second Arab summit consolidated the decisions of the first. The PLO would be allowed to train military forces in Gaza and Jordan. It would also be allowed to levy its own taxes, even on Palestinians working for the Jordanian state. Jordan's bandwaggoning of Egypt also continued in other areas, notably in a wider diplomacy, with diplomatic relations being established with Eastern bloc countries like Bulgaria, Czechoslovakia and Poland. Aspects of domestic policy also reflected Hussein's new-found friendship. Some of the dissidents of the mid-1950s were pardoned and allowed to return home, notably Ali Abu Nuwwar. There is no doubt that such measures were immensely popular, especially on the West Bank. As was the case immediately after his expulsion of Glubb, Hussein basked in the short-term popularity that such measures brought, oblivious to or disregarding of the longer-term implications.

With misgivings multiplying within Jordan's small and closely knit policymaking circles, Hussein was persuaded to slow down the pace of this pro-Nasser strategy. In February 1965, Talhuni was replaced as premier by his great rival Wasfi al-Tall. But in spite of this return to prudence it proved to be difficult to extricate Jordan from its new predicament. In particular, momentum was building rapidly behind the emergence of an independent Palestinian national movement. Ominously, Fatah, which was destined to become the mainstay of an independent PLO, also set up around this time, announced its arrival with its first, albeit ineffectual, guerrilla operation in January 1965. With Tall refusing to countenance the opening of a PLO office in Amman or the levying of a 5% tax on state employees of Palestinian origin, relations quickly soured. It was no surprise when Egyptian propaganda began to charge Jordan with the dangerous accusation of undermining the PLO. The third of the three Arab summits simply saw such differences come out into the open.

With Cairo-brokered mediation failing to deliver a sustainable compromise, Jordanian–PLO relations came to a head, not for the last time, over the issue of rights of representation. Insisting on the monopoly right to represent the Palestinians, the king ordered the Jordanian security machine into action in June 1966. The PLO's offices were closed and its activists arrested. The organisation would not become active again in the kingdom until after the 1967 war.

THE 1967 WAR

The breakdown in relations between Jordan and the PLO, and Amman's subsequent gravitation towards Saudi Arabia's emerging Islamic alliance strategy, proved costly in terms of Egyptian–Jordanian relations. By mid-1966 they had deteriorated to such a degree as to parallel the wretched level of relations when Wasfi al-Tall was last in power in early 1963. This bad blood would continue through the year and into 1967. As late as February in that year, for example, the Jordanians recalled their ambassador to Cairo in protest at Nasser's highly personalised invective against Hussein in a speech delivered on the 22nd of that month. Yet, just a few days later, Tall would be obliged to resign, marking a renewed willingness in Amman for rapprochement. On 21 May, King Hussein would send an envoy to Cairo expressing support for Nasser in what had become a precipitous decline towards war. On 30 May, King Hussein would fly to Cairo and in person conclude a Joint Defence Agreement with Egypt. On 5 June, Jordanian forces under their Egyptian commander would attack Israeli positions. By 8 June, Israel had occupied the whole of the West Bank. By 10 June, the war was over and Egypt and Jordan, together with Syria, were beaten and Jordan's military was in tatters.[26]

Many among both commentators and protagonists have sought to explain Jordan's policy zig-zag in 1967, and ultimately its decision to join in on the Arab side in the fateful war. There is no consensus and never is likely to be on Hussein's motives and calculations. Favoured explanations include: Hussein's fear of a popular uprising if Jordan left Egypt to fight Israel alone with Syria; a range of flawed perceptions on Hussein's part, from Israel's willingness to go to war to an over-estimation of the relative military strength of the Arab side to a presumption that total defeat was out of the question; an assumption that the superpowers would intervene diplomatically to head off, quickly curtail or reverse the consequences of a conflict, à la 1956. The main book on the 1967 war from the Jordanian side, by Samir Mutawi, states that the 'major mistake was to rely on the help and leadership of other Arab nations'.[27] The thrust of this and other explanations, what has become the conventional wisdom, as Lawrence Tal has shown,[28] suggest the inevitability of war and hence that King Hussein had no choice but to take part in the war on the Arab side. At very least, such explanations tend in part to absolve the king of much of the responsibility for the defeat, either because of the unwarlike communications emanating from the Eshkol government in Tel Aviv, or because he was duped by the claims of prowess on the part of the Egyptian military.

But to these factors listed above, none of which are unimportant, need to be added two additional elements that are invariably given less prominence if they are mentioned at all. First, the mercurial nature of Hussein's personality, especially at a time of crisis, operating in a highly individualised and uninstitutionalised domestic decision-making context. At very least, the lurches in Jordanian policy at this time exacerbated a sense of uncertainty and instability in the region. Second, Hussein's genuine fear of the expansionist threat from the state of Israel, which led him to exaggerate the direct Israeli military threat to Jordan. Adding both of these factors to an overall consideration of events suggests that King Hussein has to take a greater degree of personal responsibility for his disastrous decisions than has previously been the case. It also shows how easily perceptions of the enemy can be formed, and, once made, how difficult it can be to change them. For the 1967 war as a whole, Richard Parker's argument that the conflict was a culmination of multiple miscalculations on all sides is the most persuasive.[29]

For Hussein's Jordan, the lead-up to the 1967 war begins on 13 November 1966 with the Israeli attack on the West Bank village of Samu, to the south of Hebron. It was a devastating attack, involving a brigade-strength force with air support, the biggest Israeli military operation since Suez, and killed between 15 and 21 Jordanian soldiers, and even more civilians.[30] The attack came in the context of a series of Israeli retaliatory raids on the West

Bank commencing in early 1965 in response to cross-border operations by Fatah, now based in Syria, which the Jordanian army, though it tried,[31] was powerless to halt in their entirety. It differed, however, from previous Israeli operations, which had been proportionate and largely directed against non-human targets.

The Samu attack also had a negative effect upon the cohesion of Jordan. It exposed the relative weakness of its army, which explains the absence of any form of retaliation. It fed Palestinian frustration at the Jordanian state's inability to protect them, or provide them with the means to protect themselves. Riots followed in the West Bank towns and there was further loss of life in the ensuing clashes, as the army was called upon to maintain order. Rioters called for the arming of the people, the abdication of the king and his replacement with a PLO government. As Clinton Bailey has written: 'The need to wield the Arab Legion against the Palestinians wiped away six years of effort to win legitimacy in the eyes of these very people.'[32]

However, as Uriel Dann has argued, the greatest impact of the Samu operation was on Hussein himself.[33] Taking place on his birthday, Samu was interpreted by the king as a highly personalised message that Israel sought his destruction. The covert dialogue that King Hussein had helped establish in 1963, and which had conspicuously omitted the military, seemed to count for nought. As Laura James has concluded, the Samu attack was a crucial event in helping to shape King Hussein's image of the enemy.[34] It also entrenched the leadership's conviction, based on the recollections of 1948–49 and the seizure of the Sinai in 1956, that Israel was a fundamentally expansionist state. In short, it convinced many among the Jordanian elite that sooner or later Israel would try to conquer the West Bank in the name of consolidating its security.[35] The hardening of such views would not only underlie Jordanian decision-making in the run-up to the June war, such convictions would result in subsequent assurances from the Israeli government, aimed at the avoidance of conflict, being treated with the utmost suspicion.

In addition to its impact on the psyche of the king, the Samu attack also eventually propelled Jordan into a closer relationship with Nasser's Egypt. This was based on the assumption that only Egypt was large and strong enough to provide the deterrent to further Israeli attacks. The price of the mobilisation of that deterrent was closer political relations with Cairo. It took a little while to effect the domestic political realignment necessary for Jordan to pursue such a strategy. But, once Tall had been sacked,[36] and the pendulum of elite politics had swung towards the much larger pro-Egypt lobby in the kingdom, there was no one left to temper the king's strategic mood swing that now pitched the kingdom into its pursuit of relations with Nasser. By the time such a policy was in place, after managed parliamentary elections in April 1967, Egypt had already embarked upon a foolhardy strategy of provoking Israel, the effects of which would end in war.

The chief reason for Nasser's increasing willingness to take risks was the growing chorus of criticism from different parts of the Arab world towards the conservative nature of Egyptian policy towards Israel. At the forefront of such irresponsible propaganda was Syria, which, ruled by a radical variant of the Ba'th since 1966, had belittled Nasser for spinelessness towards the Jewish state. Ironically, however, Jordan also contributed to this state of affairs. Through the final phase of its propaganda retaliation against Egypt, Amman had criticised the Egyptian leader for cowering behind the United Nations Emergency Force (UNEF) that was established in the Sinai as a result of the resolution of the 1956 war. Coming from a small and relatively weak state, such accusations hit home.

From mid-May events took place at an inexorable pace. On 14 May, Nasser was moved to action by what would prove to be false reports that Israel was massing forces on the Syrian border; on 18 May, Egypt announced the termination of the presence of the UNEF from the Sinai, replacing the UN force with its own troops; on 22 May, Nasser announced that the Straits of Tiran, the access route to the southern port of Eilat, would be closed to Israeli shipping. Because Jordan was not one of the two central protagonists, it was powerless to affect the main course of events. All that Amman could do was to react to the actions of Egypt and Israel. It did so in a way that was determined by the logic of its rapprochement with Egypt; in so doing, it did not dispel the impression that war was inevitable. Thus King Hussein reacted to Egypt's decision to expel the UNEF by declaring support for the Arab side, ending the kingdom's propaganda campaign against Nasser, and sending the army chief of staff, General Amer Khammash, to Cairo as his envoy with the message that Jordan was willing to coordinate operational plans.[37]

The die was cast when, on 30 May, King Hussein flew to Cairo to conclude a joint defence agreement with Egypt, which fuelled Israel's growing concern at being surrounded. Under the terms of the humiliating deal that followed, the king agreed to withdraw his troops from the Syrian border, release political prisoners and allow Shuqairi to return to Jordan, which he did as a passenger in the king's plane. Most importantly, Hussein agreed to hand over command of the Jordanian armed forces to an Egyptian general, Abdul Mun'im al-Riyad, who arrived on 1 June, accompanied by a small staff, to take up the command ridiculously close to the commencement of hostilities. Riyad began working on a new strategy that would give the Jordanian military an offensive option, but it was not complete by the time hostilities commenced.

In spite of the recklessness of the move, Hussein was jubilant at the conclusion of the agreement. In commenting on the events of late May and early June, the Jordanian politician Zaid al-Rifai has reflected on 'a mass euphoria about the possibility of war', and it seems as if King Hussein too was engulfed by the mood.[38] The tumultuous reception he received on his arrival home appealed to his vanity and his deep desire to be liked. The agreement lay firmly within the context of the united Arab command strategy forged at the Arab summit in early 1964. The supposition was that Jordan was no longer isolated, as it had been during the raid on Samu, and to be treated just as Israel liked.

That June 1967 was to become King Hussein's conflict as well as Nasser's can be seen by the events of 5 June, following reports of the Israeli attack on Egypt that began the war. In a final attempt to avert war with Jordan, Israel let it be known that it would not initiate hostilities. With the lessons of Samu still firmly in mind, King Hussein brushed aside the offer. Though Riyad had operational command, King Hussein was still the supreme commander of the Jordanian armed forces. He apparently spent the first 24 hours of the conflict at army headquarters. He was present on the morning of 5 June when the Egyptian leadership claimed that it had destroyed 75% of Israel's air force during the first hours of conflict. In fact, it was the Egyptian air force that had been destroyed, in one devastating action that would seal the outcome of the war. Though many of Jordan's sceptical commanders, suspecting lies, urged a delay in order to receive independent confirmation of the success, King Hussein brushed aside such advice and Riyad was allowed to commit the Jordanian military to the fight. In doing so, he immediately abandoned Jordan's traditional strategy of selected defence,[39] based on the reality of its limited armed forces, in favour of a total defence approach. With the kingdom's military spread hopelessly thin, and the Egyptians creating widespread confusion through the issuing of unfamiliar and contradictory orders, its defeat was easier and quicker to execute.

MANAGING THE AFTERMATH

For Jordan it was a bit like 1948 again. Some 300,000 Palestinian refugees came flooding into the East Bank, causing initial problems of humanitarian relief and longer-term problems of loyalty and identity. In losing the West Bank, the Jordanian economy had lost some 40% of GDP, about half of its

Fig. 11. Palestinian refugees crossing the River Jordan to the East Bank during the 1967 war (JEM, 1.1505.1)

industrial capacity, and 25% of the country's arable land. The West Bank had generated over 60% of the kingdom's fruit and vegetable output, and also accounted for more than one-third of its grain production and its livestock. Gone too were most of the Christian holy sites, the West Bank having been responsible for 90% of a tourism sector that had begun to take off in the mid-1960s.

King Hussein emerged from the June war chastened but not crushed. He drew three main lessons from the conflict. First, that Israel was militarily too strong, and likely to remain so, to be defeated on the battlefield by her Arab neighbours working in unison, let alone working separately. The logic of this position was that he should seek to resume his dialogue with the Israelis with a view to stabilising their existing relationship. This led to the second lesson, which was that only diplomacy was likely to be successful both in regaining the West Bank and in stabilising the Middle East as a whole. Third, that as a relatively weak state Jordan was powerless to determine the trend for the region, and would therefore have to channel its efforts into trying to bring about the necessary circumstances to prevent war and to expedite diplomacy.

In this regard things seemed to progress auspiciously in the immediate aftermath of the June war. The Arab states instinctively fell back on the default option of an Arab summit to try to determine the way forward. That gathering met in Khartoum in late August/early September. The summit is best remembered for the 'three no's' sound-bite: no to peace, no to negotiation and no to recognition of the state of Israel. And indeed Israeli reaction did not get beyond the negative rhetoric as far as the summit's outcome was concerned. Substantively, however, Khartoum proved to be a positive development from King Hussein's perspective, because of the moderating impact of the war on Nasser that it revealed. The Egyptian leader had decided on the need for close inter-Arab cooperation, regardless of the complexion of the regimes in power. Most importantly, he agreed with the basic position of the king that peaceful means should be used in order to achieve the withdrawal of the Israeli army from territory occupied in the 1967 war. It was no coincidence that regional radicals like Syria and Algeria refused to attend in Khartoum.

This new spirit of moderation at Khartoum was followed soon after by a major breakthrough at the international level. The adoption of UN Resolution 242, which was passed by the Security Council on 22 November 1967, has formed the basis for an Arab-Israeli peace ever since. It laid down the basic principles of the inadmissibility of the acquisition of territory by force and the right of all states to exist within secure and recognised boundaries, and called for Israel's withdrawal from territories occupied in the recent conflict. Both Egypt and Jordan supported the adoption of the resolution, which enshrined the basis of a peace agreement in the exchange of occupied land for peace.

In spite of such positive developments at the regional and international levels, it was the relationship between the state of Jordan and the PLO that was soon to come to dominate the fortunes of the kingdom. The occupation of the remainder of historic Palestine had both a consciousness-raising and radicalising effect on the Palestinians. As Michael Hudson wrote at the time, there was a 'resurrection of a Palestinian political identity on a more modern basis than was the case before 1948'.[40] Increasingly, Palestinians expressed this new sense of political community by joining the various organisations that existed under the umbrella of the Palestinian national movement. Moreover, the devastating nature of the defeat of the Egyptian, Jordanian and Syrian armies in 1967 had convinced these activists that only through the efforts of their own organisations could they hope to realise their national political aspirations. Increasingly these activists gravitated to Jordan, as the Arab state with the longest boundary with Israel and the newly occupied territories.

At first, Jordan did relatively little to discourage them. Many in the country, as across the Arab world, sympathised with their plight. At first, even the Jordanian army and the Palestinian guerrillas to some extent viewed one another as comrades in arms. In any case, the Jordanian army had been so degraded as a result of war that it was demoralised and hardly in any position to do anything about such a development. For the three months immediately after the June defeat, the top priority of the Jordanian state was to rebuild its military capability. Jordanian intelligence, both military and general, made the monitoring of the activities of the various Palestinian organisations a top priority. From the outset, the Jordanian military remained confident that it could handle the issue of the Palestinian resistance, if needs be.[41]

Initially, Jordan and the PLO worked together in certain areas, though even at best never quite transcending the mutual suspicion that came to pervade the relationship. The battle of Karamah, on 21 March 1968, was as good as it got. On that occasion, Israeli forces attacked a Fatah stronghold in the Jordan Valley, which was where the majority of the guerrillas were concentrated. Jordanian troops joined with Palestinian fighters in stymieing the operation, bringing their artillery to bear on the attacking forces, which were forced to withdraw. It was a notable success thrown into relief by the relative absence of military successes against Israel. It was in victory, however, that the two sides began to diverge in view. Transjordanians resented the way Palestinians openly celebrated Karamah as their own success; the show of support for the PLO in Amman in particular that these celebrations represented indicated how potentially combustible the demography of the capital had become. Increasingly, the views of both sides were characterised by mutual disdain: for Palestinians the Transjordanians were *al-hufa*, the barefoot ones, implying that they were ignorant backwoodsmen; for the Transjordanians, the Palestinians were cowards, who had run like rabbits in 1967.[42]

The battle of Karamah led to a surge in recruitment for the various groups, with Fatah enrolment rising from 2,000 to some 15,000 three months after the battle. While most of these new recruits were Palestinian, some Transjordanians, mostly of a radical ideological persuasion, also joined up. Indeed, one of the main leftist groupings, the Democratic Front for the Liberation of Palestine (DFLP), which had split from the PFLP, was led by a Transjordanian Christian, Nayef Hawatmah, from Salt. The ranks of the guerrilla organisations were also swelled by an agreement between Jordan and the PLO that allowed Palestinians with Jordanian nationality to carry out their compulsory military service with the *fedayeen*, the ones who sacrifice themselves, as they liked to call themselves. With the Palestinian groups using the funding that they received from different Arab countries to pay their operatives a wage, there was an important pull factor for recruitment at a time when the Jordanian economy was suffering from the direct impact of the war.

As 1968 progressed, further points of tension began to open up between the PLO and the Jordanian authorities. Increased shelling of Palestinian strongholds in the Jordan Valley resulted in many of the new Palestinian recruits being based out of range of the Israeli gunners. This contributed to a more visible Palestinian militia presence in Amman, which was in any case a predominantly Palestinian city. New refugee camps established just outside the capital, like Wahdat and Jabal Hussein, seemed to become no-go areas for the police. Emboldened by the presence of such radical groups, some of the banned Jordanian political movements began to meet ever more openly. Sulaiman Nabulsi, the National Socialist prime minister ejected from power in 1957, made a notable reappearance as the head of a left-wing coalition that backed the guerrillas.

Peace diplomacy further exacerbated the rising tensions between the Palestinian guerrillas and the Jordanian authorities. When King Hussein went to Washington in March 1969 to meet the recently installed president, Richard Nixon, he proposed a six-point plan for peace with Israel, based on SCR 242, apparently undertaking to curb the guerrillas once an agreement was struck. But a hardening reluctance on the part of Israel to contemplate a withdrawal from the Occupied Territories helped such lingering tensions to come to a head.

The first major clash between the guerrillas and the Jordanian national security state came in November 1968, and involved a small group called al-Nasr. Whether or not, as the Palestinian side claimed, its leader was a Jordanian stooge, the purposeful way in which the Jordanian army struck back served as a warning to the guerrillas. Armed confrontations like this punctuated the period of the late 1960s, as did countless direct negotiations aimed at stabilising the situation. These continued after February 1969, when a leading member of Fatah, Yasser Arafat, succeeded in unseating

Shuqairi, and took over the leadership of the PLO. Arafat was committed to the undertakings made by the PLO not to precipitate regime change in the existing Arab states. However, he was largely unable or unwilling to control some of the smaller and more radical members of the PLO, notably the PFLP, who found that the shortest route to profile and resources was to breach such accords. In spite of these strenuous attempts, many of them sincere, none of them succeeded more than fleetingly. As Kamal Salibi has concluded about this period: 'Plainly, a sovereign revolution and a sovereign state could not continue living under the same roof.'[43]

BLOODY CONFLICT WITHIN

It was probably only a matter of time before a real and sustained confrontation took place. Under pressure from some of the hawks within his circle, King Hussein would make moves that seemed designed to face down the guerrillas. In July 1969, he appointed his uncle and hardliner Sharif Nasser bin Jamil as head of the army. The following February he attempted to introduce some steel into Talhuni's largely conciliatory cabinet with the appointment of the former *Mukhabarat* chief, Muhammad Rasul al-Kailani, as interior minister. Kailani was faithful to his brief, banning the carrying and firing of weapons within Jordanian towns, and insisting on the registration of all vehicles, even those used by the *fedayeen*. The PFLP's response to this initiative was to besiege the police station in one of the hills on which the capital is built, Jabal Ashrafiyah. In the face of this and other challenges, the king retreated and Kailani lost his job.

There are two views of King Hussein's actions at this time, though neither is without substance. The first is that Hussein was keen, desperate almost, to prevent a full-blooded confrontation, even to the extent of trying to appease the guerrillas, such as by his decision in May 1970 to declare the American ambassador in Amman *persona non grata*. Even if a confrontation proved successful, and the presence of hostile regimes in Syria and Iraq were a complicating factor, he would have known that it was unlikely that the country would escape without some death and destruction. More seriously still, a civil war would make it more difficult for the regime to claim that it represented Palestinian interests; Palestinian–Transjordanian relations within the kingdom would become markedly less harmonious, as the army–*fedayeen* tension was increasingly generalised to characterise the two communities.

The second view of Hussein's actions during this time is, as Salibi suggests, that the king probably knew that the Jordan–PLO relationship would end in conflict. He was merely giving the guerrillas as many opportunities to discredit themselves as possible before moving to a final confrontation. If this was indeed a conscious strategy, it was an effective one. Large sections of Palestinian opinion in Jordan became alienated from the guerrillas. This included the wealthy, who were affected by the arbitrary expropriations, notably of motor vehicles, by these groups. Foremost among those affected by such behaviour were shopkeepers and merchants, who were angered by their petty extortion, and the general atmosphere of fluctuating stability. It also included those of a conservative or religious outlook, who bridled at the immature displays of crude leftist ideology.

By June 1970 a confrontation at last seemed to be in the offing. In addition to a number of attacks on symbols of the state and its allies, King Hussein's entourage was fired upon at a roadblock. Though the lives of the king and his senior advisers were clearly no longer assured, claims that this was a deliberate assassination attempt rather than the product of a localised firefight are unproven. Characteristic of the fluctuating chaos of the times, July and much of August were then relatively quiet as both sides pulled back from the brink. All of that changed in early September, with the trigger coming from the regional diplomatic level.

In June, the US Secretary of State, William Rogers, had unveiled a new diplomatic initiative to bring peace between the Arabs and Israel, to be based on SCR 242. Egypt accepted the Rogers Plan, which in turn gave Jordan the cover to add its approval. The PLO did not accept the plan, because of its recognition of the state of Israel and because it confirmed the loss of a significant part of Palestine. Moreover, the various guerrilla groups, that were fast metamorphosing from revolutionary organisations into self-interested bureaucracies, profoundly objected. The response of the radical groups was a resumption of armed attacks on Jordanian military and civilian targets, which included an ambush of Hussein's convoy on 1 September. The king's response was to raise army salaries in mid-August and reinforce his troops in the capital.

Most spectacularly of all, the PFLP hijacked four international airliners with 425 passengers and crew on 6 September, flying three of them to a desert airstrip at Dawson's Field in Jordan. Though Arafat's Fatah-dominated PLO were uncomfortable with the direction of events, they appreciated their popularity among Palestinian and wider Arab public opinion. They therefore endorsed the hijackings. All three aircraft were subsequently blown up in the full sight of the world's media, and, while most of the passengers were released, 54 were kept hostage for a further two weeks. The whole event was a symbolic demonstration of defiance on the part of the PFLP. For Jordan and King Hussein it was a humiliating demonstration of weakness, and of the lawlessness into which the kingdom had sunk.

Now at last was the time for action. The alternative, in the belief of one of Hussein's biographers, James Lunt, could only have been abdication.[44] Just to ensure that there was no way back, Palestinian guerrillas took over the northern city of Irbid on 15 September, declaring it liberated and installing a 'people's government'. King Hussein responded by declaring military rule and setting up a military government; the Jordanian civil war, or Black September as the Palestinians were to come to call it, had begun. Once given the orders to move, a day later, the bedouin-dominated army units launched attacks on the Wahdat and Hussein camps near Amman, where the *fedayeen* had their main bases. They expected to win easily and quickly. In fact, fighting lasted longer and was more intense than had been predicted. According to the PLO, the death toll from the first 11 days of fighting reached 3,400. In one important way the Jordanian side had got it right: there was only limited support within the country for the guerrillas.

In spite of multiple appeals for help from outside, only Syria tried to respond to the PLO's growing plight. Damascus sent an armoured formation including 200 tanks across the border. However, Syria was not the only regional actor with a core interest in the outcome of the struggle. At the US's request, Israel had already reinforced its positions on the Syrian border and was prepared to cancel out the Syrian intervention. With Israel effectively giving the Jordanian regime defensive depth, the air force was sent into action, support that was conspicuously lacking on the Syrian side, as the operation became prey to domestic regime machinations in Damascus. Deterred by the Jordanian action and the Israeli show of support, the guerrillas were abandoned to their fate. Israel had learnt the lesson of where its interests really lay; Samu had been left behind.

In perhaps his last political act before his death from a heart attack, President Nasser arranged a cease-fire between Jordan and the PLO on 27 September. In a determined demonstration of single-mindedness, King Hussein had shrugged off Arab pressure to agree to an end of hostilities until he was sure he had the upper hand. In spite of the accord, the king was not finished. Significant numbers of fighters remained in different parts of the country. Hussein replaced a brief experiment in a benign cabinet led by a Palestinian notable in favour of a government of staunch Transjordanians led by Wasfi al-Tall, whose brief was for law and order, and sovereignty.

With Transjordanian nationalism surging in response to the strategic defeat of the guerrillas, for the next ten months the army and the cabinet together set about the task of systematically weeding out the PLO military

presence in the country. The Jordanian army was fortified by supplies air-
lifted by the US. By March 1971, the guerrillas had been driven out of Irbid.
A month later they had vacated Amman in the face of the determination
of the government. The final action came in July around Jerash and in the
Ajlun hills, where some 5,000 guerrillas, the last concentrations, remained,
choosing pointlessly to fight on rather than negotiate their departure. After
their conclusive defeat, the guerrillas fled or surrendered to the Jordanian
authorities, the latter being given safe passage to Syria. By 15 July, there was
only one state left in Jordan. Eventually, the *fedayeen* and the organisations
to which they belonged decamped to Lebanon, where the whole Jordanian
experience of civil war was to be repeated in a longer and more bloody
form.

CHAPTER 7

Illusions of Progress

The loss of the West Bank and the civil war with the PLO was not the end of the Palestinian issue in Jordanian history. Related issues, such as the nature of the representation of the Palestinian population in the East Bank, and who would speak for the Palestinians in peace-oriented diplomacy, had still to be decided. King Hussein would battle hard over this subject, both with the PLO within the regional Arab framework, and later with the Americans, as their emerging peace diplomacy eventually led to the Egyptian–Israeli peace process. In the meantime, the regional oil boom helped to ameliorate some of these tensions at home, through increased prosperity and predominantly Palestinian labour migration to the Gulf.

As the 1970s came to an end, Jordanian preoccupations moved eastwards. The Iranian revolution was seen as a destabilising development that had cost the region another of its conservative monarchies, and a man, the Shah, who was a friend of the king's. With the Arab leadership role now vacated by an Egypt ostracised for its peace with Israel, Saddam's Iraq mounted an attempt to fill the vacuum. Jordan soon found itself bandwaggoning Iraq, partly due to a growing economic dependence on Iraqi markets, partly because of the close relationship between the two leaders. However, a reversal in fortunes for Baghdad in the eight-year war with Iran, coinciding with the Israeli invasion of Lebanon, saw Jordan suddenly bounded by intensified threats on two sides. The loss of its guerrilla platform in Lebanon obliged the PLO to face up more fully to the realities of its position. But new diplomatic opportunities delivered little in spite of much perspiration.

Though the late 1970s and early 1980s were years of promise, by the late 1980s Jordan's fortunes were once again marked by uncertainty. The regional oil recession had ratchetted up the domestic pressures in the kingdom. The first Palestinian *intifada* had obliged the king to sever some of the sinews that still connected his state with the West Bank. Iraq's war with Iran was over, but prospects for the reconstruction of Iraq were limited. And lurking over the horizon were the triple disasters of debt default, riots and the Gulf crisis.

TWO PEOPLES, ONE STATE

The expulsion of the PLO may have ended the immediate, direct military threat to the kingdom from Palestinian nationalism, but more subtle realities, like demography, immigration and economic domination, offered the possibility of the increased Palestinianisation of Jordan. The emergence of the naked struggle for power between the Palestinian *fedayeen* and the Jordanian state had, moreover, brought such lingering tensions out into the open by the early 1970s. This would deepen as Transjordanians aped their fellow Palestinian inhabitants in the discovery of a separate and distinct national self-identity. With the PLO gone, the long-term prospects of inter-communal harmony depended on how the relationship between Palestinians, Transjordanians and those with confused, uncertain and ambiguous identities in the middle,[1] collectively the population of the state of Jordan, would be remade.

It would be misleading to suggest that, in spite of this growth of distinct national Palestinian and Transjordanian consciousnesses among many of the people, there was a simple binary divide between the two, especially over fundamental policy issues. Rather there were important divisions within each grouping. The division within the Palestinian people of Jordan, which had become evident during the civil war, was now deepened. On the one hand there were the Palestinian Jordanians, those who, though they continued to be conscious of their geographical origins, and were angry at the loss of Palestine, were committed by dint of the practicalities of life and career to the state of Jordan. The dominant profile of this tendency was Palestinians who had arrived in the East Bank in the aftermath of 1948, and whose children and grandchildren were now settled. They became increasingly preoccupied with the political and public policymaking arena of Jordan as the one that had the greatest effect upon their lives and fortunes.

On the other hand, there were the Palestinian nationalists, those whose ideological consciousness and commitment to the Palestinian cause eclipsed temporary chance geographical residence. In particular, this group included self-consciously Palestinian political activists.[2] More generally, it encompassed those who had arrived in the East Bank after the 1967 war, many of whom had been doubly displaced having also been initially uprooted to the West Bank in 1948. They tended to see their stay in Jordan as unwelcome and impermanent. They saw the PLO as their main political representatives.

In the aftermath of the civil war, they became largely disconnected from the politics of the kingdom, eschewing elections both as candidates and voters.

Meanwhile, Transjordanians divided between what Nawaf Tell has called 'Jordanian nationalists' and 'Pan-Jordanians'.[3] The former category comprised those who, once the stigma of defeat and loss in 1967 had dissipated, were increasingly relieved to see the back of the West Bank. They argued that its presence within the state of Jordan prior to 1967 had hindered the consolidation of a more territorially and subjectively Jordanian state. They believed that the PLO should speak on behalf of all Palestinians in the West Bank, as well as those living in exile, and that eventually the PLO should preside over liberated Palestine; Jordanian passport holders in the East Bank who identified themselves as primarily Palestinian should return to a PLO-controlled entity when conditions allowed. Indeed, as the period 1968–71 had demonstrated, Jordanian nationalists believed that the PLO and Palestinian nationalism as a whole were too potent a force for Jordan to combat without cost. Leading figures in this school were Sulaiman Arar, Said al-Tall, the younger brother of Wasfi, and Abdul Rauf al-Rawabdah, all of whom would hold high office over the next two decades, and Hamad al-Farhan (whose personal political journey from a leftist, Arab nationalist position in the mid-1950s was a long but by no means unusual one). The extreme fringe of this approach shaded into a visceral hostility towards the Palestinians as a whole and would later, in a reference to the main political party of the Israeli right, be disparagingly referred to as 'the Transjordanian Likud'.

By contrast, the Pan-Jordanians were 1950 Abdullahites. They believed in the unity of the two banks as the territorial basis of the Jordanian state, but with the centre of gravity of such a state remaining in Amman. They therefore regarded the PLO as a competitor, one to which no concession on representation or governance should willingly be made. This grouping tended disproportionately to consist of those Jordanians of clearly Palestinian origin, whose forebears had arrived in Jordan voluntarily, often before 1948, and had long made their careers in the East Bank, but for whom Jordanian nationalism as such would have been untenable. Their number included Zaid al-Rifai, a childhood friend of Hussein's and arguably the most consummate politician in the kingdom during the final three decades of the twentieth century, and Taher al-Masri, by the 1980s the most representative spokesman of the Palestinians in Jordan.

The emergence of these two distinct categories, Jordanian nationalist and Pan-Jordanian, also had implications for political relations between

Jordanian society and the Hashemites. As a Hashemite, with a broader Arab mission, and as a man with a personal desire to regain the West Bank that he had been so responsible for losing, King Hussein was an instinctive Pan-Jordanian. His long-standing adviser on foreign policy matters in the 1970s and 1980s, Adnan Abu Odeh, was of Palestinian origin, and a leading Pan-Jordanian. If there was a natural political affinity between King Hussein and the Pan-Jordanians, there was ambivalence in the relationship between the monarch and the Jordanian nationalist trend. Whenever the fortunes of the peace process revived, and the king was drawn into negotiations with a view to restoring Jordanian authority to all or part of the West Bank, Jordanian nationalists became noticeably uneasy. Under such circumstances Hussein was seen by some as no longer fully representing their interests. 'Whose king is he?' was an exclamation of exasperation periodically emanating from the leading political salons of a nationalist disposition in Amman on such occasions.

The tensions between Jordanian nationalists and Pan-Jordanians over peace process policy was particularly acute during the early to mid-1970s and in the mid-1980s, when successive Israeli Labour leaders displayed a strong preference for the so-called 'Jordanian option'. This had been Labour's preferred approach to matters of peacemaking since 1967, and became more tangible after 1972 with the Allon Plan, a security blueprint for the restoration of a truncated West Bank to the kingdom. According to the Jordanian option the Israeli government would be willing to deal with King Hussein as a favoured peace partner, not least as a device through which to exclude the PLO. The Israelis expected the king to speak on behalf of and ultimately resume some form of responsibility for the Palestinians in the Occupied Territories. However, as the Allon Plan demonstrated, the Israelis had no interest in let alone conception of the domestic and regional constraints on the king. For them, the Jordanian option meant King Hussein taking what was offered to him; he was expected to be grateful.

THE ROAD TO RABAT

King Hussein's main missions in the immediate aftermath of the civil war were to seek rehabilitation in the Arab world, stabilise relations with Fatah, as the only part of the Palestinian resistance with which Amman felt it could do business, and maintain Jordan's position at the forefront of peacemaking. Increasingly, however, the joint pursuit of these objectives proved to be incompatible. Many Arab leaders, governed increasingly by the logic of states, were not intrinsically hostile towards Hussein and Jordan in the aftermath of the civil war; presented with the sort of violent and radical challenge that had emerged in the kingdom by 1971 many of them would no doubt have acted in the same way. However, Arab public opinion was instinctively sympathetic towards the Palestinians because of their experiences of dispossession and dispersal, and Arab governments had to conciliate such views. This explains the sanctions that were introduced against Jordan in the context of the civil war, such as the closure by its Arab neighbours of their mutual borders and the cessation of financial aid. Stories circulating about the bloodthirsty conduct of some bedouin troops during the fighting, no doubt embellished and exaggerated, had intensified this sympathy at Jordan's expense.

The king's adopted route to the repair of broader relations across the region, and to ameliorate the rawness of inter-communal relations inside his kingdom, was to formulate a new vision, based on which Jordan and the Palestinian territories would be rejoined. Though never realised, it would be a plan the ideas incorporated in which would resurface from time to time. His United Arab Kingdom (UAK) scheme, which was unveiled on 15 March 1972, offered the prospect of a renewed unity between the East Bank and the West Bank 'and any other Palestinian territories'.[4] Under this blueprint, however, the political relationship was to be looser and more balanced than that which had prevailed between 1950 and 1967. More importantly, it was to overturn the ideological thrust of the earlier period whereby any separate Palestinian consciousness had been discouraged, and Palestinians and Transjordanians alike were expected to conform with what Laurie Brand has called 'a hybrid Jordanian identity'.[5] From 1972, however, the king indicated that he was prepared to recognise a distinct Palestinian consciousness and incorporate it into a wider political entity.

Under the terms of the plan, the Hashemite kingdom was to be renamed the United Arab Kingdom. The new state was to comprise two autonomous provinces, the East Bank and the West Bank, each with its own parliament and administration, and with Amman and Jerusalem as their respective centres of government. All Palestinian representation, even for those resident on the East Bank, would be channelled through institutions in the West Bank, a sure sign of the influence of the emerging Jordanian nationalist current on the plan's formulation. At a federal level, there would be a joint parliament with equal representation from the two component parts, a central supreme court and a joint army; Amman would remain the state capital. A federal government would enjoy powers over a restricted set of functional areas, to include foreign and defence policy.

The UAK idea was billed as a radical attempt to redesign the Jordanian state, taking into account the newly emerging Palestinian identity. In truth, it would only have been radical if it had been tabled six years before, when it is claimed that King Hussein had the genesis of the idea. Rather, it was a serious, if inadequate, attempt to catch up with the new realities of political identity on the ground. However, it did not address other key developments, such as the existence of an independent PLO or of Israeli occupation. In its conception of new state structures created within an old superstructure of an exclusively Hashemite monarchy it was decidedly conservative. It was little wonder that the plan was widely condemned by the PLO and other Arab states, notably Sadat's Egypt (which cut diplomatic relations), as a device through which to deprive the Palestinian people of self-determination and statehood.

With the UAK failing to attract wider supporters, it became increasingly difficult for the king to escape the regional consequences of the civil war. What became known as a 'battle of representation' entered its crucial phase in 1973. In November of that year, at an Arab summit in Algiers,[6] King Hussein had to resort to desperate, diplomatic measures to fend off collective Arab pressure for the recognition of the PLO as the political embodiment of the Palestinian people. Instead of attending himself or sending his prime minister, the king sent the chief of the royal court, Bahjat Talhuni, to the summit. Though the king's principal adviser, Talhuni lacked executive power, his presence thereby neutering the summit as a policymaking forum.

During the intervening 11 months until the next Arab summit, King Hussein and his prime minister, Zaid al-Rifai, manoeuvred feverishly in order to try to head off the intensifying pressure. Rapprochement with Syria, in order to break up the Cairo–Damascus–Riyadh axis that now dominated the Arab world, yielded fruit but not soon enough. An attempt to persuade Israel to withdraw from Jericho, as a symbol of a peace process that could deliver under Jordanian leadership, was always a long shot. In the end even the fabled skills of the American secretary of state Henry Kissinger could not avert the outcome, and all that could be accomplished was damage limitation. King Hussein managed to persuade Sadat to qualify the notion of PLO representation of the Palestinians to exclude those resident on the East Bank. Until the felicitous moment when Israel might eventually withdraw from the West Bank, Jordanians of Palestinian origin would not be forced to decide which was their overriding identity.

With this caveat, however, King Hussein was obliged to submit to the will of the Arab leaders, as expressed at the seventh Arab summit in Rabat in

October 1974. In effect this meant bowing to the inevitable in terms of the PLO eclipsing Jordan's position as the epitome of the political will of the Palestinians. Formally at least, Jordan accepted the primacy of the PLO as the dominant actor on behalf of the Palestinians, the Rabat summit having recognised the PLO as 'the sole legitimate representative of the Palestinian people'. Rabat also acknowledged the right of the PLO to establish an 'independent national authority' over any available Palestinian territory. With Israel and the PLO a long way from recognising the reality of one another's existence, Rabat effectively reduced the prospects for meaningful negotiations on the future of the West Bank for a decade to come.

King Hussein did not leave Rabat without reward. He had paid the price charged for Jordan's rehabilitation, and was duly included in the summit's $1,369,000 annual military aid allocation for the 'confrontation' states. Moreover, ironically, in view of the rebuff over representation, he gained an implicit recognition of Jordanian sovereignty in the West Bank, as Rabat avoided any reference to the status of the territory. President Sadat had even appealed to Jordan to continue its administrative and financial role in the West Bank, which it did, for fear of what Israel would do if faced with a political vacuum there.[7] In spite of such developments, however, there was no doubt as to whose summit it was. Rabat proved to be a triumph for Arafat and the PLO. For Hussein and the Pan-Jordanians, with their ambitions to reunite the two banks, and their increasingly zero-sum calculations, it was a defeat from which they would never quite recover.

If Rabat had been a victory for the PLO regionally, the outcome was much less clear-cut domestically. King Hussein's arrival home was met with celebrations by many East Bank tribesmen, and Jordanian nationalists as-sumed that they would now be able to shape Jordan according to the logic of Rabat. And it is true that following Rabat the number of Palestinians in the cabinets of Jordan was greatly reduced. Even so, after a moment's vacillation, King Hussein's Hashemite Pan-Jordanian inclinations got the better of him and he averted a 1950–1960s-style swing of the policy pen-dulum. Instead, Hussein kept Rifai as premier, a position he would hold until 1976. The king also recalled parliament in order to pass constitutional amendments that would allow him to put the national assembly, with its elected East and West Bank components, on ice. Hussein was biding his time. While the king was willing to bend with the wind of Rabat, he was not willing to give up a potentially important institutional asset which would allow him to dust down the claim to a legitimate right to speak on behalf of those Palestinians on the West Bank at some as-yet undetermined future time. As Asher Susser has concluded, 'Formally, Jordan accepted the Rabat resolutions, but in practice Hussein sought to undermine them.'[8]

THE OCTOBER WAR

Jordanian relations with the wider Arab world remained generally poor between the civil war and the eve of the next set-piece Arab–Israeli war, in autumn 1973, when, with war in mind, Cairo and Damascus moved to re-establish diplomatic relations with Amman. Not that Egypt seriously expected Jordan to take part in a new war with Israel. Firstly, in spite of the enduring warmth that Americans and Israelis have for both men, personal relations between Hussein and Sadat were never cordial; indeed Hussein subsequently made the withering observation that he found Nasser easier to deal with than Sadat.[9] Secondly, while the Jordanian army had been extensively re-equipped under the M-60 Program negotiated with President Nixon, it was not ready for war. Thirdly, Sadat suspected Hussein of being prepared to do a secret deal with the Israelis in order to have the West Bank restored to his control, regardless of the fortunes of the rest of the Arabs. And the biggest favour that Hussein could store up with the Israeli establishment would be to warn them about an imminent attack.

Cairo was right to be suspicious of Hussein, who was holding secret talks on a frequent basis with senior Israelis, including prime minister Golda Meir, and senior ministers Abba Eban and Moshe Dayan, at the time. There were, moreover, routine contacts between the intelligence services of the two countries, as Jordan continued to fear a security threat from Syria, remembering the intervention of 1970. Accusations have been made that the king informed the Israelis of an imminent attack following a three-way summit with Asad and Sadat on 10 September. King Hussein denies that he knew about the plan, though he did meet with Meir on 25 September, at which meeting he impressed upon her in general terms the gravity of the regional situation. In spite of this denial, it appears that the Jordanians used other channels to inform the Israelis of the plan. To the presumed relief of Egypt, the Israelis did not take the warning sufficiently seriously.[10]

What is clear is that King Hussein did not know the precise date for the attack, which came as a surprise to him. President Sadat phoned him soon after the beginning of the Egyptian–Syrian assault. Sadat asked him not to intervene. After the trauma of 1967, the king did not need any further encouragement, especially given the low opinion of the Egyptian military among its Jordanian counterpart. Besides, the Jordanian army was not deployed ready for an offensive across the River Jordan, while its air force was modest alongside Israel's. But as the initial successes of the Egyptian and Syrian armies became clear, and as the conflict became more protracted, so the pressures began to build upon King Hussein to join the fight. As its initial military advantage began to unravel, so Sadat became keener to elicit Jordanian participation.

In such a state of uncertainty, the king instinctively played for time. In an echo of 1967, he sent General Amer Khammash to Cairo, not as chief of staff with a mission to throw Jordan's capabilities behind the Egyptian war effort as before, but this time as a personal envoy and messenger. In the correspondence that Khammash carried, Hussein prevaricated, stating that it would be unwise for Jordan to intervene without adequate air cover. The king's discomfort increased with the news that the PLO had offered to send forces to fight in the Negev and would seek passage through Jordanian territory, an offer to make all but the most vigorous Palestinian nationalist in the East Bank shudder. As time went on, and arguments began to rage about Jordanian participation, it increasingly became clear that something had to be done to assuage the build-up of pressure, especially as the battlefield position of Syria began to decline precipitously. The compromise for Jordan therefore became to render assistance to the Syrians, thereby playing an active role in the conflict, yet avoiding any direct fighting with the Israelis.

On 12 October, Jordan sent a tank brigade to assist the Syrians in their engagement with the Israelis on the Golan Heights. An armoured division that was subsequently dispatched did not arrive until ten days later, only a few hours before President Asad accepted a cease-fire. The Jordanian military presence was therefore largely symbolic, although 27 of its soldiers were killed in the fighting. Of the 75 or so Jordanian tanks that actually saw action, 15 were destroyed. At no time did the Israelis seriously contemplate widening the conflict, either to attack Jordanian territory directly or to use it as a conduit through which to outflank the Syrians. During the 1973 conflict the Jordan Valley was, as Arthur Day has observed, 'almost bizarrely oblivious' to the bitter war being fought to the north and the south.

OIL WEALTH WITHOUT OIL

In the early 1970s, the Jordanian economy was mixed and modest, made up of a small number of public-sector ventures and family-dominated companies that were small in size and lacking in ambition. The early 1960s had offered a vision of growth and development. However, the ambitious plans laid down by the first Tall government of 1962–63 had been severely hampered in their implementation. A combination of administrative discontinuity, the dislocations of the aftermath of war and the domestic turmoil between 1967 and 1971 had retarded their implementation. In spite of these discontinuities, the paradigm of development had not been discarded. As it began to recover from the political turmoil of the preceding half-decade, the kingdom launched its 1973–75 three-year development plan, with the aim of revitalising the economy and re-establishing a coordinated approach to economic development.

In spite of Wasfi al-Tall's earnest desire to maximise Jordanian sovereignty through the achievement of self-sufficiency, Jordan remained structurally a rentier state. Throughout its existence it had been dependent on externally derived injections of cash in order to build the many institutions of the state and more generally to sustain the country's level of economic activity. Jordan had been able to attract this external rent, first from the British, and then the Americans and its Arab neighbours, by emphasising its strategic importance for its patrons. For Britain, Jordan's utility was as a buffer state against Wahhabi and French expansionism; for the US, Jordan emerged as a bulwark against Communism; for the principal Arab states, Jordan was important, both as a barrage against Israel and to avoid the kingdom becoming a client of any one of their number.

If the generation and maintenance of external strategic rents had been key to the establishment and consolidation of the Jordanian state, the role of externally generated funds would be crucial in the decade-long surge in economic development and prosperity that would characterise Jordan in the mid- to late 1970s and early 1980s. Key to these external monies was the main Arab oil-producing countries and the massive expansion in their revenue streams after the steep rises in the oil prices between 1973 and 1975. The big increase in incomes meant that such oil producers as Saudi Arabia, Kuwait and Iraq now had enhanced funds to distribute as grants and aid, and were willing to do so tied to a set of implicit or explicit political conditionalities.[11] By the early 1970s, as Laurie Brand has concluded, Saudi assistance had become 'the cornerstone of Jordanian budget security',[12] a trend that was set to continue. With this secondary distribution of Arab oil revenues, Jordan effectively began to acquire some of the economic attributes of an oil economy, without itself producing any oil at all.

The Jordanian economy also benefited indirectly from the regional oil boom, with significant inflows of foreign exchange accruing direct into private hands. The oil boom had also created a big demand for skilled labour within the oil-producing countries, especially the hitherto less-developed countries in the Arab Gulf. Palestinians holding Jordanian passports were well placed to meet this increased labour demand: because of their relatively

Table 7.1 *Foreign Grants and Government Revenues,*
1967–1982

Year	Foreign Grants (JDmn)	Grants/Total Govt Rev (%)	Grants/Dev Exp (%)
1967	40.4	57.6	172.0
1968	40.2	56.6	172.3
1969	38.4	45.4	165.6
1970	35.4	48.7	163.4
1971	35.4	38.8	157.7
1972	44.5	44.2	143.5
1973	45.6	40.0	111.5
1974	58.8	39.5	136.7
1975	100.6	47.3	127.1
1976	66.2	32.0	86.5
1977	122.2	36.2	85.9
1978	81.7	23.6	55.0
1979	210.3	44.9	108.2
1980	209.3	39.9	92.2
1981	206.3	33.4	80.7
1982	199.6	30.5	79.6

Source: Central Bank of Jordan, *Yearly Statistical Series (1964–1989)*
Special Issue, October 1989, p. 44.

high levels of education; because networks of Palestinians had existed in the Gulf states since the 1950s, thereby facilitating the process of labour migration; because Palestinians were more likely to welcome the so-called 'exit option', the alternatives being either a life lived under Israeli occupation or in the uneasy political environment of the East Bank. By the end of the 1970s, an estimated one-third of the Jordanian workforce was working outside the kingdom.

The relative peace experienced through the Middle East between 1973 and 1980, combined with the generation of surplus incomes, led to an unprecedented rise in confidence and spending. The impact of this juxtaposition on the Jordanian economy was rapid and profound. Positive consequences included high rates of growth, real GNP growth ranging between 7% and 11% each year during this period, and the swift disappearance of unemployment, a destabilising blight in the country since the late 1940s. Nevertheless, it also included a number of negative effects: an inflationary spiral, as the economy proved insufficient to absorb all of the new funds; a widening visible trade gap, in view of the country's modest production base; growing balance of payments current account deficits; unchecked population growth, as the myth took hold that Jordan's most valuable natural resource was its people; and rural to urban migration, especially to Amman, which, as it swallowed up adjacent settlements, was fast taking on the appearance of a city-state.

The increase in capital accruing to the public sector during this period stimulated an extraordinary expansion in the size and profile of the state. The impact of this expansion was comparable to two earlier periods in Jordan's economic history: the initial phase of state-building where there had been no state previously in the 1920s; and the building-up of Amman as a national power centre in the country in the 1950s. Three consequences in particular emerged as a result of the inpouring of these new funds, all of them with clear political ramifications.

First, the state itself expanded, acquiring new functions, increasing levels of spending and employing more people. Consequently, in a reflection of trends taking place elsewhere in the region, people in Jordan became more dependent on the state, especially for the provision of employment and services. For instance, between 1970 and 1985 the number of civil servants grew by getting on for 200%, from 27,000 to 74,000. Tariq Tell notes that by the early 1980s civilian employment in Jordan's urban areas had come to rival the army as a source of employment for Transjordanians.[13] Taking place in a context of the Jordanianisation of the country in the wake of the civil war and the 1974 Rabat summit, it was those who were Transjordanian in origin who benefited disproportionately from such a trend. If Palestinians in Jordan were increasingly coming to dominate the private sector economy, Transjordanians had tightened their grip on the public sector.

Second, the state increased its levels of intervention in the functioning of the economy. The best example of this new interventionism in action was the establishment of the Ministry of Supply in 1974. This was a placatory move by the Rifai government taken in the wake of an outbreak of army unrest at Zarqa, triggered by the high price of staples like bread and rice. In order to stem the disaffection and to mollify poorer, urban communities in general, the ministry was created in order to regulate prices. In order to ensure stability in the market the treasury had to be prepared to subsidise prices, which it did on a range of different products, from staple foodstuffs to fuel oil to the utilities. This supply strategy also stretched the responsibilities of the ministry vertically. It became responsible for the issuing of tenders for the supply of large consignments of basic commodities. Because only the large merchants in Jordan had the capacity to procure basic goods in the volumes required, this practice led to the development of a cosy, insider relationship between the larger trade-oriented businessmen and the relevant branches of the state.

Third, the state showed a particular preference for investment in large, capital-intensive schemes. This was done with the development of the country's infrastructure and the exploitation of its limited natural resources in mind. There was certainly a need for the former, especially in such growth areas as electricity generation and transmission and the creation of a modern road network, while the expansion of Aqaba port was to be important in servicing the Iraqi as well as the Jordanian economy. Investment in the latter saw the development of the kingdom's extensive phosphates deposits, making it the world's fourth-largest exporter, as well as potash resources in the Dead Sea.

There was also much profligacy here. A good example was the Queen Alia International Airport, the proportions of which were far greater than the level of traffic could justify. The potential of the Jordan Phosphates Mines Company was dragged down by chronic over-manning. Arguably the worst of all excesses was the national carrier, with a large debt of some $ 850 million (or the equivalent of 11% of GDP) being built up on the reckless acquisition of aircraft, and due scrutiny being warned off by an active royal patronage that reflected the king's personal weakness for flying. Such prestige projects undoubtedly enhanced the status of a small country. The subsequent revelation of debt and the reappearance of unemployment as a major social-cum-economic problem meant that the kingdom paid a big price for such a transient reputation. Jordan would probably have been better served by being more circumspect in its investment decisions, and targeting them towards smaller, more viable labour-oriented activities, rather than such capital-intensive outlets.

Expansion was not exclusive to the state. The inflow of funds from the kingdom's expatriate workers, together with rising levels of activity in the economy as a whole, from surging imports to increased banking activity, created new opportunities for the private sector inside Jordan. However, the impact of such activities was very patchy sectorally. Expatriate remittances tended to be used either to build villas and apartments, with retirement or rental income in mind, or to finance consumer spending on the part of those family members who remained in Jordan. This helped to push up the price of real estate, to stimulate construction and to boost the services sector,[14] from the provision of professional services to wholesaling and retailing. However, it did relatively little to drive forward the expansion of the productive sectors.

In spite of this unprecedented period of economic growth and the active involvement of the private sector, a risk-oriented, entrepreneurial stratum failed to emerge in Jordan. Indeed, actually quite the opposite occurred, as wealth creation was largely disconnected from risk-taking. Consequently, the big merchants, who had come to the country from Syria and Palestine in the early years of the state, or who were acquired from Palestine with the incorporation of the West Bank, and who had a grip on such lucrative areas as automobile distribution agencies and the import of consumer goods, now became very rich indeed. The old-established banks grew much bigger and declared rising profit levels, but with hardly having to develop their range of services at all. Industrial investment, with its long lead time on returns, and the vulnerability of fixed capital to nationalisation or physical attack, acted as a running disincentive to manufacturing investment.

If industrial growth was modest, not so the area of private services. A growing stratum of professional people, where in the past the country had struggled to produce university graduates of any sort, came to the fore as the bedrock of an emerging middle class. These people were trained as engineers, medical doctors and lawyers, and increasingly acquired a level of prosperity through private practice that had not been conceivable before.

THE TEMPTATION OF CAMP DAVID

If the Rabat summit proved to be a low point for King Hussein and the Pan-Jordanians, it did not take long for their fortunes to revive. The key to this improvement was relations with Syria, which had begun to repair in 1974. By 1975, Lebanon teetered on the edge of civil war as Jordan had done some five years before. Now, as then, the destabilising presence of the PLO, and the excesses of its radical fringe, had upset Lebanon's delicate power balances. With fighting erupting a year later, a leftist alliance with the PLO to the fore looked set to defeat a Maronite-dominated political right. Only the Syrian military intervention of June 1976, and its containment of the leftists, prevented an early and decisive outcome to the civil war.

With the PLO suddenly on the defensive and the beginning of an implacable enmity between Arafat and Asad, Pan-Jordanian interests were rapidly converging with Syria's. Rifai, who was to base his later political career on an ability to foster close relations with Syria, oversaw the rapprochement. A political unity project was declared as an expression of the sudden closeness of the relationship. Alarmed at the drift of developments, the PLO now assumed the role of the *demandeur*. Arafat and Hussein met briefly at the 1976 Cairo Arab summit, the first serious contact between the two sides since the end of the civil war, finally bringing to an end Jordan's semi-pariah status within the Arab world. With the PLO absorbed by the violent complexities of domestic Lebanese politics, King Hussein was increasingly free to try to retrieve the setback at Rabat.

The Cairo summit acknowledged Jordan's special relationship with the Palestinian issue, opening the way for its more intensified activities on the West Bank. The Rifai government was replaced by an administration led by Mudar Badran, a former intelligence head, that was sympathetic to Jordanian nationalist opinion, and therefore better placed diplomatically to engage anew with the PLO. Moreover, the notion that the PLO would simply emerge as the government of a Palestinian state based on the West Bank began to blur. The agenda for talks with the PLO delegation that visited Amman in February 1977, and which sealed the resumption in relations, was based upon King Hussein's UAK plan. In 1977 the PNC, often referred to as the PLO's de facto parliament-in-exile, passed a resolution reversing the organisation's policy for the overthrow of the Hashemite regime in Jordan. At last, Jordanian–PLO relations looked set to be conducted within parameters based on compromise.

Tentative attempts by Jordan and the PLO to feel their way forward were disrupted by high drama at a wider level of peacemaking. The election of Jimmy Carter as US president in November 1976 reawakened hopes for Middle East peacemaking. In particular, it was hoped to reconvene the Geneva peace conference, which the US and USSR, in an era of détente, had jointly hosted to little avail in December 1973. Increasingly bad blood between Egypt and Syria disrupted the preparations for such a meeting, with Asad distrusting Sadat's intentions and Egypt playing the PLO card against Syria. This bickering was finally swept away by president Sadat's monumental political gesture in visiting Jerusalem and addressing the Israeli parliament, the Knesset, on 19 November 1977, a trip that Hussein was not informed about in advance. At a stroke the Geneva formula for complex formal multilateral interaction was rendered irrelevant, and a process of US-sponsored bilateral negotiations between Egypt and Israel eventually got underway. Though the passage towards peace was far from smooth, the process eventually delivered, with the Camp David accords being concluded in September 1978 and a bilateral peace treaty being signed on 26 March 1979.

For King Hussein, Sadat's gamble and the process it engendered offered a tremendous opportunity, but also very great risks. The jump-starting of serious bilateral peace talks with Israel was very much in line with the sort of strategy conceived by Hussein following the 1967 war. Israel's willingness to return the Sinai to Egypt, that is a willingness to trade large-scale and tangible land assets in return for peace as a product of political negotiations, clearly offered Hussein encouragement for the return of the West Bank. The serious intervention of the US raised the possibility of constructive mediation by a superpower friendly to both parties. On the debit side, King Hussein knew that there had been widespread criticism of Sadat from Arab publics and governments alike. That criticism included Iraq and Syria, the two most potentially truculent regional powers, which had the presumed ability to destabilise Jordan from within and to pressure it from without, especially in harness with the PLO.

King Hussein was also to be encouraged by aspects of the substantive nature of the Egyptian–Israeli peace process, and its willingness to range beyond issues of narrower bilateral concern. For example, in mid-1978, Sadat made proposals that called for the establishment of a Jordanian administration on the West Bank for a five-year period. The proposal elicited 'cautious support' for Sadat from the king.[15] Even the Camp David meeting in autumn 1978 was far from discouraging. Of the two accords signed on 17 September, the former was entitled 'A Framework for Peace in the Middle East', and dealt with the West Bank and Gaza Strip, prescribing 'the resolution of the Palestinian problem in all its aspects'. There was even a presumption that Jordan and 'the representatives of the Palestinian people' would join Egypt and Israel in the subsequent negotiations. Of course, the widening of the scope of the peace framework was also self-serving: it offered the Israelis the possibility of enticing a second Arab state into a separate peace; for Sadat it potentially provided some Arab cover by enabling him to argue that he had not abandoned the Palestinian cause.

In the face of such conflicting pressures, King Hussein determinedly tried to sit on the fence. Initially, he was joined by Saudi Arabia, while Morocco, Oman and Sudan actually supported the process. The king's initial public diplomacy was not inimical to the peacemaking. He praised Sadat as a man of courage. He refused to condemn the Israeli–Egyptian peace talks, (though later he would adjust his position to express annoyance at Jordan's inclusion in the Camp David accords 'without prior consultation').[16] Such caution soon imposed a cost on Jordanian relations with the Arab rejectionists, with, in the absence of Rifai, its hard-won friendship with Syria a particular casualty.

The king's procrastination continued until after the conclusion of the Camp David agreement. Eventually, in the face of growing pressures that included 'strong arm persuasion tactics' from the US,[17] and pro-Palestinian demonstrations on the streets of Amman, the king was obliged to choose. He chose not to join the process because the deal on offer, which appeared not to include Jerusalem, did not offer enough land in order to justify the risks of a peace. In short, the deal was just not good enough. With a decision finally made, it only remained to dress up Jordan's rejection in the self-righteous rhetoric of Arab solidarity and Palestinian self-determination.[18]

Jordan's refusal to join the Camp David process ushered in a period of frostiness in relations with the US, whose wishes the king had flouted. The disappointment in the White House was exacerbated by the president's refusal to believe that the king would do anything other than join the process.[19] In order to demonstrate his displeasure, and assert his non-aligned credentials, the king threatened to purchase arms from the Eastern bloc, and did buy French arms. In spite of this gesture of defiance, relations with the US were rescued by events. The shock of the overthrow of the Shah of Iran in January 1979 obliged the US to consolidate its relations with friendly leaders in the region. King Hussein had been concerned by the train of events in Iran, and had even attempted to intervene, visiting Tehran in November 1978 and reportedly conferring with Ayatollah Khomeini in his exile in France as a way of searching for common ground between the two men. The Soviet invasion of Afghanistan in December 1979 sealed the restoration of both the strategic and the ideological convergence. In June 1980, during King Hussein's visit to President Carter, both sides were properly reconciled, and on the Camp David process finally agreed to disagree.

HUSSEIN AND SADDAM: THE ODD COUPLE

Jordan's decision not to join the Egyptian–Israeli peace process closed down one strategic pathway. With the majority of the Arab world implacably hostile to Sadat and his unilateralism, Egypt was cast from the fold. Diplomatic relations were collectively severed. Cairo lost the prestige of playing host to the headquarters of the Arab League. At the same time, the revolution in Iran and the fall of the Shah had seen Jordan lose a second traditional counter-weight to its two large and intrusive neighbours, Iraq and Syria. Consequently, as Jordan moved away from an Egyptian orbit it found itself being drawn, almost inexorably, towards the alternate centre of regional gravity, Arab rejectionism. Increasingly that spirit of rejectionism was coming to be epitomised by the aspirational regional leadership of Ba'thist Iraq.

It was Iraq, with Saddam Hussein the effective leader, that hosted the November 1978 and 1979 Arab summits, which included Jordanian participation, and at which Egypt was vilified and ostracised. It was the 1978 summit that saw the unveiling of the Arab states' ten-year programme of aid to the front-line states. Jordan's share was earmarked as $1.25 billion per annum.[20] Assistance for the West Bank was to be distributed through a joint committee based in Amman, thereby boosting Jordanian control and hence patronage. With Iraq and Saudi Arabia the major donors, the kingdom's economic dependency on the main Arab oil producers was deepening. For a fleeting moment it looked as though Jordan might enjoy converging relations with Iraq, without incurring a cost in ties with Syria, as between autumn 1978 and summer 1979 Baghdad and Damascus enjoyed a fast, furious, yet ultimately unconvincing rapprochement. As fast as rapprochement had appeared, it collapsed in July 1979, with Saddam assuming the presidency of his country and accusing Syria of plotting its own version of regime change in Baghdad. Faced with such a dramatic *volte-face*, Jordan had to choose.

That Jordan fully turned its back on Syria and opted for closer relations with Iraq was probably never seriously in doubt. After all, the twin Baghdad summits had demonstrated that, of all the Arab states, Iraq's diplomatic weight was currently the strongest. The driving personal ambition of Saddam Hussein might have helped convince the king that it would remain so. Moreover, the explosion of oil-related wealth made Iraq, as the Arab state with the second-highest oil reserves in the world, significantly more attractive than Syria, where hydrocarbon prospects were more modest. Domestic identity politics in Jordan were also important in the decision. As Nawaf Tell has shown, the Pan-Jordanian–Jordanian nationalist cleavage at home continued to make an impact on foreign policy.[21] If Rifai and the Pan-Jordanians consistently advocated close relations with Syria during the 1970s, the Jordanian nationalists were always likely to gravitate towards the opposite pole of magnetism. In 1979, with their emphasis on Jordanian national interest, the attractions of Iraq for Jordanian nationalists, both economic and diplomatic, were clear.

The remarkable thing about Iraqi–Jordanian relations, however, is not that they were forged initially, but that they continued for so long. In 1988, Amatzia Baram, Israel's leading Iraq analyst, could state that: 'personal relations between [King] Hussein and [Saddam] Husayn were closer than those between any two other Arab leaders'.[22] Though the extremities of war and sanctions after 1990 would diminish the personal bond between the two leaders, the sinews that bound the two countries together were not all severed. Even in the late 1990s, it could be argued that Jordan's first and only foreign policy lobby remained firmly in place and that that was in favour of Iraq.[23]

At the centre of this relationship were three features. First, the development of complex economic interdependencies between the two countries, the like of which tends not to be a feature of inter-Arab relations owing to the absence of commercial complementarities. By the end of the 1980s around 160 Jordanian firms had strong relations with Iraq, with three-quarters of Jordan's manufacturing exports bound for Iraq.[24] Second, the corruption of much of the Jordanian intellectual and governing elite as a result of the gifts showered upon them by the Iraqi leader over a prolonged period of time. Most infamously perhaps, Saddam Hussein sailed into town for the November 1987 Arab summit in Amman with a fleet of Mercedes cars that he proceeded to distribute to chosen recipients. This less-than-salubrious connection was further underpinned by the profits on offer from a range of different sanctions-busting and other scams, which helped to enrich those with close connections to the political establishment.[25]

Third, a close personal bond between the odd couple of Arab politics, Saddam Hussein, the ruthless peasant president, and King Hussein, the Hashemite patrician. While one can only guess at the reasons for the king's embrace of the new ruler in Baghdad, money was certainly not the least of it. Since 1976 Saddam Hussein had begun to send large sums of money for use by King Hussein personally,[26] the king having a deserved reputation, like his grandfather, as a spendthrift. The king is reputed to have felt more at ease with this source of funding compared to the alternatives, partly because Saddam was more generous than the Kuwaitis and the Saudis and partly because of the easier manner in which the money was dispensed. Saddam also seems to have developed a keen sense for how best to manipulate the king, his gesture of renovating the graves of the Hashemites in Iraq having touched the emotions of Hussein.

King Hussein was certainly no check on the Iraqi leader's ambitions and the risk-taking he was prepared to pursue in order to realise them. The king was, for example, a vehement supporter of Saddam Hussein's military adventure against Iran in September 1980, the first of a number of strategic blunders during Saddam's presidency, and, with more than one million casualties, arguably the single most appallingly costly event in the history of the modern Middle East. In a symbolic gesture, Jordan even organised and sent a military contingent, the Yarmouk Brigade, in 1982 to fight alongside Iraq in the war. Hussein also vigorously protested against the Israeli strike on Iraq's nuclear reactor at Osirik in 1981. In a related emotional outburst against the US of Ronald Reagan that was typical of the man, the king expressed his sense of 'futility and disillusionment' that the attack had been allowed to take place.[27] In such protestations of support for Baghdad, money was generally ascribed as being the dominant motivator at this time; it was disparagingly repeated in the region that in the case of the Iran–Iraq war 'Hussein will fight to the last Iraqi dinar'.

Iraqi money was certainly helpful in the king's attempts to preserve dignity in the face of a humiliating dependence on the US over the supply of arms. Under pressure from the Zionist lobby, the US Congress had refused to sell the kingdom the weaponry that it required for a long-overdue updating of its defensive capabilities without highly restrictive preconditions. These included the stipulation that Hawk anti-aircraft missiles should be set in concrete, thereby robbing them of their mobility, and that they should not be deployed in the Jordan Valley, where they could threaten Israeli aircraft. In response, King Hussein decided to purchase $200 million worth of SAM-6 missiles from the USSR, the first time that Jordan had shopped for armaments outside the West. A deal that had been on the cards since 1974 became feasible because of Baghdad's willingness to pick up the bill.[28]

Jordan was also willing to indulge and even collude in Iraq's use of Muslim extremists in order to try to destabilise the Syrian regime, a challenge that would generate a nasty spiral of violence in Jordan's northern neighbour between 1979 and 1982. The authorities in Amman appeared to have forgotten their own experiences of externally backed violence in the mid-1950s. A major sign of the precipitate decline in relations between Jordan and Syria was the killing of a leading Syrian Islamist in Amman in summer 1980, and the mutual mobilisation on their common border later in the year. King Hussein would later issue a *mea culpa* in 1985 for Jordan's military training of Syrian Islamists as part of a subsequent rapprochement with Syria.

Money alone, however, does not explain why Jordan's close relationship with Iraq would continue, even after the long and debilitating Iran–Iraq war started to bleed the Iraqi exchequer. By the second half of 1982, Iran had taken the military initiative and the war was being fought on Iraqi soil. Iraq had ceased to fulfil its annual Arab aid obligation of $185.7 million to the kingdom. Iraq was also forced to abandon the guns *and* butter policy that had characterised the first two years of fighting, resulting in a downturn in imports both from Jordan and from suppliers using Jordan as a conduit for trade. This jeopardised much of Jordan's fragile manufacturing sector, as well as hitting those involved in transport and other related services, most of which had put all of their eggs in one basket, expanding their activities solely on the basis of the Iraqi market.

Rather than see many of its manufacturers collapse, just at a time when the regional recession was emerging, Jordan decided to bail out the sector, evidence already of the influence that such interests had on the public policymaking process in the kingdom. A revolving credit line of the order of $400 million was created at the Central Bank of Jordan in 1983 to enable businessmen to continue to trade with Iraq in spite of the decline in foreign currency payments. This credit line was perpetuated through a deal whereby Iraqi crude oil would be processed at Jordan's Zarqa refinery, in what had evolved into an elaborate counter-trade relationship. Thus, at a time when the Jordanian exchequer was beginning to approach the Eurodollar market for sizable sovereign loans at commercial rates, it was also effectively subsidising the Iraqi economy, and rescuing its private business sector from its own profligacy.

There were some benefits to Jordan of the continuing relationship. Notable among these was the use of Aqaba as a terminal for Iraqi crude and fuel oil exported by tanker truck. By 1986 imports of Iraqi oil had risen to cover around 30% of the kingdom's needs, a figure rising to more than 80% by 1990,[29] thereby diversifying Jordan's dependence away from an exclusive reliance on Saudi supplies. However, the construction of a much-discussed oil pipeline to Aqaba did not materialise owing to persistent fears of security threats from Israel.

In part, Jordan maintained its initial loyalty to Iraq because of fears of the spread of the Iranian revolution and the possibility that the defeat of Iraq would result in an Islamist domino effect that would also threaten Jordan. In part, the maintenance of the relationship, especially beyond the span of the Iran–Iraq war, can be explained by the expectations of what the future would bring. For an economy like Jordan's, lapsing increasingly into stagnation, there were two possible *deus ex machina*: regional economic integration emanating from a successful outcome to the peace process; the post-war reconstruction of oil-rich Iraq. In July 1988, Iran finally agreed to an end to hostilities. Amman tried to galvanise the post-war situation by being the leading light behind the establishment in 1989 of the Arab Cooperation Council (ACC), a new sub-regional organisation grouping Jordan and Iraq with Egypt and Yemen. But the ACC was widely ridiculed in the region as a club of debtors. Meanwhile, an end to war with Iran brought little by way of an economic respite, as the political damage that war had inflicted on the Iraqi economy was too great. Instead of reconstruction, Jordan got a second strategic blunder by its neighbour: the invasion of Kuwait.

LIMITED DOMESTIC REFORM

The 1967 war, the standoff with the Palestinian guerrillas and then the civil war meant that for some years domestic politics had been retarded in the kingdom. This situation was further prolonged by the period between 1971 and 1974, when the formal relationship between Jordan and its former West Bank territory was effectively up in the air. The Rabat decision in favour of the PLO and King Hussein's unwillingness simply to consolidate politics on the East Bank meant that the Jordanian parliament, elected in 1967, was indefinitely dissolved. This, in turn, extended the period without a functioning legislature well beyond 1974, leaving successive governments as both law-giving and executive bodies. Though the absence of parliament may have made relatively little difference in terms of the quality of law-making or even the scrutiny of the executive, its absence as a safety valve and as a general arena of debate was certainly felt.

This political disability was difficult to sustain. Since the late 1920s Jordanians had become used to the existence of some sort of legislative institution in order to widen the base if not of decision-making then at least of consultation. Such legislative institutions had evolved incrementally into larger and more representative bodies. The onset of mass politics in the 1950s further increased the need for an inclusive body. At the same time, the younger generation of social elites was eager and ambitious to play a role in the politics of the country. By the 1970s the spread of mass education and the establishment for more than a decade of a higher educational sector further extended the pool of those who harboured personal ambitions of high position. Ironically, cabinet government was becoming less suited as a vehicle to assuage the ambitions of the growing ranks of the aspirant political elite. As domestic politics became more stable, governments could expect greater longevity, with the 15–18 ministerial portfolios consequently refilled less frequently. In the face of this institutional void, local politicians began to get increasingly restless and fractious.

For King Hussein, whose commitment to representative democracy had been much diminished by his experiences of the 1950s, the solution was to go for a half-measure. In April 1978, on the advice of his premier, Mudar Badran, and the increasingly influential Sharif Abdul Hamid Sharaf, now serving as the king's chief adviser, he announced the formation of a National Consultative Council (NCC). The 60-person council was to be an appointed body of leading figures. It was announced that the role of the NCC would be as a forum for debate and as a source of advice on major issues of the day. In order to give it standing among the elite and the wider public, leading political figures of the day, predominantly from the East Bank, were appointed to it. Through such a mechanism the king had finessed the situation, creating an institution representative of the new Jordan, while keeping the 1967 parliament up his sleeve as a device through which to resurrect his claims on the West Bank at a more opportune moment.

In spite of its appointed nature, the NCC was far from being acquiescent to the political centre, although criticism of the king and the royal family tended to remain off limits, not least because the ultimate political fortunes of all its members lay in the gift of the monarch. The new council included members of the opposition, such as Abdullah Rimawi, who had been the firebrand Ba'thist in the Nabulsi government of more than two decades before. There was also an attempt to give it a representative quality, functionally as well as geographically and ideologically, with some heads of professional associations and businessmen also being appointed. At a stroke, the king had provided a much-needed safety valve while also increasing his own instruments of patronage, as ambitious young politicians began to manoeuvre with its membership in mind. The NCC would fill the void in Jordan until its dissolution in January 1984. The king would return to the use of such a rainbow consultation device in drafting the National Charter, the basis for a new deal with the people of Jordan, in a very different political context in the early 1990s.

With Sharaf having developed the NCC idea while chief of the royal court, the traditional training ground for future prime ministers, his elevation to the premiership was only a matter of time. It came soon enough in December 1979, at the age of 40. Hussein's appointment of Sharaf was comparable to his elevation of Wasfi al-Tall, the promotion of a capable man with a royal mandate to reform. Though there were some parallels in their respective lives, and they were both can-do politicians, the comparison was otherwise limited: Tall was a rough and ready man of the people; Sharaf was a cultured intellectual.

Sharaf's family had left the Hijaz as part of the entourage of the Amirs Abdullah and Faisal as they had sought their fortune in the early 1920s. His father had briefly become embroiled in controversy, being appointed as regent of Iraq in 1941 during the Rashid Ali challenge to British power. After an uncertain life as political refugees, the young Sharaf and his family came to Amman in 1945. Like Wasfi al-Tall, a brief period of student radicalism at the AUB had been succeeded by a series of government appointments, especially in the fields of the arts, communications and diplomacy. As minister of information and culture in the Tall cabinet of the mid-1960s, he left his mark by founding a string of cultural institutions, such as the kingdom's national gallery and theatre, and establishing the first television channel.

Sharaf took office with a laundry list of areas that he wished to change. He was committed to making the NCC succeed as a vigorous platform for ideas, and wanted to extend the principle of participation to local government, with the development of regional self-government. He was associated himself with the idea of greater freedom for the press, and his wife, Laila, would later materialise as a liberal and reforming information minister in the Obeidat government of 1984. He was also an early supporter of women's rights and of environmental conservation in the country. It was also known that he viewed with distaste the conspicuous consumption so favoured by much of Jordan's glitzy political class. He made the curtailment of corruption an early priority, establishing a specialist court to deal with allegations of the bribery of officials, while a dedicated bureau was established for complaints against civil servants. Little else can be said of his policies, as he died just short of his forty-first birthday of a massive heart attack, before he had had the chance to introduce and embed them.

Deprived of its reformist leader to oversee their implementation, many of Sharaf's ideas, such as the new regional councils, were allowed to wither on the vine. It was not until January 1984 that King Hussein ventured to appoint another new and younger figure as prime minister in a context of change. Ahmad Obeidat was very different to Sharaf, especially in his views on political freedoms, and like his mentor, Badran, having a background in intelligence. An aloof and forceful person, Obeidat was nevertheless committed to stamping out corruption and was determined to be his own man. The fact that Hussein had made him premier without first giving him a stint in the royal court was a sloppy mistake, as it became progressively clear that the two men could not easily work together. The king sacked Obeidat a year after taking office, the experience being such that it deterred the king, who was becoming increasingly set in his ways, from bringing in new blood at the pinnacle of government.

The notable development of this period was King Hussein's decision to dispense with the NCC and recall the 1967 lower house of parliament. This he did partly as an instrument of pressure on the PLO to support an enhanced role for Jordan in the peace process. In part his hand was forced, as the deaths of a number of parliamentarians now threatened the quoracy of the assembly. Once recalled, the lower house was rejuvenated, through a combination of by-elections in the East Bank on 12 March, and the election of new representatives for the West Bank constituencies from among surviving parliamentarians. The latter was a dispiriting affair, with a series of Hashemite loyalists with little clout being co-opted into the assembly. The former was a much more vigorous experience, in spite of the ban on political parties and the continued existence of martial law, and it gave a pointer as to the new direction of the political winds within the East Bank.

Over 100 candidates stood for election for the eight seats available across the East Bank, with women voting for the first time at a national level, and a turnout of 50%. Candidates represented a wide range of views, drawn almost from across the ideological spectrum. The benchmark campaign took place in the Amman three constituency, which saw a three-way fight between Barjis Haddid, from the tribal incumbents, Faris Nabulsi, the leftist son of his father, the controversial prime minister, Sulaiman, and Laith Shbailat, a maverick Islamist, head of the engineers' syndicate and son of a former minister. Shbailat's electoral triumph in Amman three was accompanied by victories by two candidates from the Muslim Brotherhood slate. In the by-elections, Jordan's Islamists had established themselves as the ideological movement of the moment.

If the by-elections glimpsed the possibility of the transfer of the energy of NCC politics to parliament proper it was soon snuffed out. In spite of the vigour with which the newly elected MPs took up their seats, especially in opposing corruption and attacking the excesses of the national security state,[30] the noisy sessions did not go down well at the top. Obeidat's successor, Zaid al-Rifai, set about emasculating the lower house, which he did by manipulating its divisions and co-opting many of its members.[31] More generally, Rifai clamped down on freedom of expression in general. The short experiment in press freedom seen under the guidance of Laila Sharaf in 1984 was rapidly extinguished. It was a sad though not altogether unexpected irony that the cosmopolitan, Harvard-educated Rifai proved to be a much bigger enemy of personal freedom in Jordan, than either of his *mukhabarat* predecessor competitors, Badran and Obeidat.

In political wheeler-dealer terms Rifai may have been a big fish in the small political pond that was Jordan. In the end, however, he did his contemporary, the king, no favours. During the long period of Rifai's premiership incumbency between January 1985 and April 1989, the king virtually switched off from domestic politics, as he became more preoccupied than ever with the peace process, and enjoying the pleasures of life abroad. Rifai may have successfully wedged the lid on the political pot, but things were increasingly awry in the kingdom, especially with the growth in corruption

and the deterioration of the economy. The lid blew off in scenes of violent
mayhem in spring 1989.

The 1980s was a decade of Arab–Israeli peace plans, but ones that, though
strong on form, delivered little by way of outcome. Though the 1980s was
a frustrating decade, it was arguably a necessary one in terms of political
gestation for the peace process. During this time, Israel's strong preference
for the so-called Jordanian option continued. In reality, though, if Israel
was Pan-Jordanian it was never quite Pan-Jordanian enough. It controlled
the West Bank and could never summon the moral fibre necessary to take a
real chance on peace with King Hussein by restoring the whole of the land,
including east Jerusalem, to a Jordanian partner. Given this reality, Israel's
actual experience was fitfully and painfully to move towards the conclusion
that there was no alternative but to deal with the PLO.

For Yasser Arafat the decade was a painful process of learning that the best
way of eliciting recognition from Israel as a peace partner was to treat Jordan,
not as an out-and-out competitor, but as a bridge. During this time there
was not much activity in what has collectively and somewhat erroneously
become known as the peace process that King Hussein was not involved in.
Like a manic depressive, the king would engage in periods of intense and
exhausting activity when the moment appeared to be auspicious, only to
disengage in exasperated and often petulant anguish and depression when
the moment had appeared to pass.

Though the decade began with the Fahd Plan in August 1981, offering the
prospect of collective Arab recognition of Israel in the event of successful
negotiations, it was the June 1982 Israeli invasion of Lebanon that provides
the main backdrop for the peace process. It was the final attempt by an
Israeli government, using military means, to eradicate the PLO as an actor
in the region. While it was successful in that it exposed the emptiness of the
PLO as a military threat to Israel, its dispersal from Lebanon, as a result of
a US-brokered arrangement, left the organisation with no alternative to the
pursuit of a diplomatic strategy. For King Hussein and the Pan-Jordanians,
the squeezing of the PLO and the serious involvement of Washington in a
new phase of peacemaking was distinctly interesting.

In the immediate aftermath of the PLO's relocation from Beirut, the
US unveiled the Reagan Plan of September 1982. It was based on the twin
propositions that Israel should withdraw from the occupied territories but
that there should be no Palestinian state established in its stead, though it

did make mention of the 'legitimate rights' of the Palestinians. The issue of Jerusalem was fudged. A system of self-government in association with Jordan was to be introduced for the West Bank. It was in the distinct role envisaged for Jordan and the prior consultations conducted with Amman that made the Reagan Plan a departure from Camp David. Moreover, this Jordanian policy on the part of the US administration was backed up by an arms deal to include fighter aircraft and missiles. Unsurprisingly, the plan received support from the throne. In Israel, the right-wing Begin government was unhappy at the prospect of withdrawal and the lack of certainty about what would follow.

The broader Arab reaction, embodied in what came to be known as the Fez Plan, was not so positive. Embarrassed at their helplessness towards the Palestinians in Lebanon, an experience that had by now encompassed the massacres at the Sabra and Shatilla refugee camps, the Arab governments could not allow too much of a gap to open up between themselves and the PLO. Consequently, they fell back on the certainties of Rabat by emphasising the profile of the PLO as the exclusive representative of the Palestinian people, while ignoring any Jordanian role. Fez did, however, endorse the notion of direct talks with Israel, but under the multilateral auspices of a UN-brokered international conference. After Fez, the fate of the American initiative therefore rested on the ability of King Hussein to persuade Yasser Arafat to endorse a prominent role for Jordan.

King Hussein worked hard to pin down the notoriously elusive Arafat. Talks were held about the eventual nature of the relationship between the West Bank and Jordan, with discussions focusing on both a federal and confederal solution. A joint commission was established to explore Palestinian participation in future peace talks. But prospects for success began to recede as the US became sucked into the quagmire of Lebanese domestic politics, and failed to wring concessions out of Israel, notably on the issue of settlement construction in the Occupied Territories, even while increasing annual aid to the Jewish state. At the same time, the demands being made on the PLO for sweeping concessions on representation were too great, just nine years after the triumph at Rabat. A meeting of the PNC in Algiers in February formally rejected the Reagan Plan. For King Hussein the choice was stark: either accept the Algiers rejection of the plan and alienate the Reagan administration or go it alone like Sadat. Though his heart may have wanted to take a gamble, he played safe and effectively buried the Reagan Plan.

Exhausted and resentful, the king's disappointment came out in loose talk. To the delight of the Jordanian nationalists, who were worried at rising levels of Palestinian migration from the Occupied Territories, the king committed himself to 'confront the de facto annexation of the West Bank and Gaza Strip' which 'forces us to take all steps necessary to safeguard our national security in all its dimensions'. A series of measures was introduced to discourage Palestinians from leaving the West Bank that, with the 1988 Jordanian disengagement from the West Bank in mind, have been described as 'a mini disengagement'. By the end of the year, however, the king had regained his equilibrium and his appetite for the peace process. With a rebellion by radicals within Fatah having freed Arafat from some of the more hard-line pressures from within, Jordan and the PLO could resume diplomatic contact over how to proceed. The impetus for constructive engagement was strengthened in September 1984 when Jordan became the first Arab state that had previously severed diplomatic relations with Egypt to restore them. The king would now work for the reincorporation of Egypt into the wider Arab fold, its separate peace with Israel included. The message from the palace was clear: by making peace with Israel, Egypt had done the right thing, a course that the king wished to emulate.

Relations with the PLO steadily warmed through dialogue in 1984, so much so that in November the organisation chose Amman as the venue for the latest gathering of the PNC. At that meeting the PLO reaffirmed as its policy the convening of an international conference of all parties and the establishment of a process that would lead to the declaration of a Palestinian state. The king brushed aside the *pro formas* in making a pitch to the PNC for a Jordanian–PLO approach to the peace process, to be based on the principle of the exchange of land for peace, and expedited through a joint negotiation team. The success of the unfolding relationship can best be gauged by the Syrian reaction. So upset was Damascus that it commissioned a campaign of assassination against Jordanian diplomats, using the renegade Palestinian Abu Nidal as the instrument of violence.[32]

The fruit of the increasing interaction between Jordan and the PLO was harvested on 11 February 1985, with the conclusion of an agreement on peace process strategy, as William Quandt has put it, 'a new attempt to respond belatedly to the 1982 Reagan initiative'.[33] The two sides agreed to form a joint delegation to negotiate the return of all of the Occupied Territories at an international conference and then to establish a confederal state. The emergence of the confederation idea was especially important, as it moved on from the federal framework of the UAK. The confederation formula proved to be a convenience for both Arafat and King Hussein. For Arafat, confederation by definition included the notion of independent statehood, the basic component of confederation; for the king, confederation was a device through which he could legitimise his reentry into the politics of the West Bank. From the perspective of the wider peace process, crucially, the PLO had agreed to what it had baulked at in 1983: it was willing to accept an outcome that was less than full statehood; and it would no longer insist other than rhetorically on the sole right to represent the Palestinians. In return, the king had agreed to omit any reference to SCR 242, because of its failure to recognise the Palestinians as a people.

In order to operationalise the agreement it was decided that the first step would be for the US to meet a joint delegation of Jordanian- and PLO-endorsed non-PLO Palestinians. Much time was lost in agonising over who these individuals would be. With King Hussein resuming secret diplomacy with the Israelis, in the shape of the Labour leader of the national coalition government, Shimon Peres, it appeared as if a staged development of the process would be possible. In the end, the pre-negotiation cut and thrust was soon overtaken by violent events, especially the seizure in October of an Italian cruise-ship in the Mediterranean, the *Achille Lauro*, by radical members of the PLO. The murder of an elderly Jewish American passenger soiled the atmosphere, persuading the US that the PLO was not a worthy peace partner. It also convinced the king that the PLO would never be a credible actor unless it accepted SCR 242. With his frustrations with the PLO piling up, King Hussein ended political coordination with the organisation almost exactly one year after the agreement was struck, saying that it had missed a golden opportunity for peace.

There then followed a shabby and half-hearted manoeuvre by the Pan-Jordanians, which illustrated their increasing ineffectiveness towards the peace process. The king had ended his coordination with the PLO with a challenge to the Palestinians to decide who should represent them and what their future political course should be. Whether in an act of petulant revenge against the PLO or a genuine attempt to try to supplant it, the authorities attempted to organise a series of spontaneous demonstrations of adulation towards King Hussein on the part of various Palestinian communities. Palestinian tribal chiefs, refugee leaders and parliamentarians were obliged to traipse up to the royal palace in order to demonstrate loyalty to the throne. It is not clear whether this exercise in traditional politics was Hussein's idea or Rifai's way of pandering to the king's vanity. Whichever it was the lack-lustre way in which the popular demonstrations of loyalty were organised quickly undermined any impact that they might have had.

Further ineffectual attempts to tighten the Jordanian grip over the West Bank came later on in the same year. These included a tacit encouragement for the establishment of a dissident faction of the PLO under the former head of its military intelligence, Atallah Atallah. There also followed the subsequent announcement of a development plan for the West Bank to parallel the one being unveiled for the East Bank. The main problem with such an attempt at patronage creation was that the Jordanian state had no money. Amman failed miserably to attract donors either from the region or beyond, as the transparent nature of its intentions was clear for all to see. The entire strategy was soon exposed as being counter-productive, with traditional Hashemite supporters among the Palestinians being obliged to lower their profile.

In spite of the passage of time, the king's animus towards the PLO continued. It was evident when in April 1987 he concluded the London Agreement with Peres, who was now Israeli foreign minister as a result of a coalition government rotation. The two agreed to the convening of an international conference as a formal plenary, which would legitimise substantive negotiations taking place in a series of bilateral committees. The future of the territories would be negotiated by a joint Jordanian–Palestinian delegation, without the participation of the PLO, on the basis of SCR 242. In the end the agreement did not fly because Peres could not mobilise his Likud government partners for it and the US failed to take it up. The efforts invested in the London Agreement were not lost. Its procedures represented a maturation of the peace process, albeit one that clearly favoured Israel, and would form the basis of the Madrid process, which finally saw the opening of negotiations between Israel and her neighbours between 1991–93.

If King Hussein had been able to make the running on the peace process with regard to the future of the Palestinian territories since the aftermath of the Israeli invasion of Lebanon, he lost all ability to control the future with the outbreak of the first Palestinian *intifada* or uprising in December 1987. The spontaneous product of a car crash in Gaza, the uprising soon turned into a political mobilisation of the territories against Israeli occupation. Faced with a movement of energy, and a shift in the Palestinian centre of gravity from the diaspora to the territories, Arafat and the PLO had little choice but to endorse the process. With the local and PLO leaderships converging, and King Hussein perceived as hostile and, worse, enjoying a cosy relationship with the Israeli government, the balance of fortunes shifted decisively against the king and the Pan-Jordanians. More broadly, this deterioration was taking place against a backdrop of the Algiers Arab summit, at which the PLO's position had been strengthened, not least through the promise of new funds, even as Kuwait and Saudi Arabia, the kingdom's regular donors, refused to continue the ten-year Arab aid commitment made in Baghdad in 1978. The king once again fell into a mood of deep despondency.

This was the backdrop against which King Hussein decided on 31 July 1988 to sever 'legal and administrative ties' with the West Bank. This peculiar formulation was a gambler's throw of the dice, made from a position of weakness and intended to bring about a dramatic improvement in King Hussein's position *vis-à-vis* the West Bank. But the plan was poorly thought through and failed to realise its objectives. Indeed, it was a reflection of foreign policymaking in the kingdom at its worst: an impulsive decision-maker, with judgement especially flawed on Palestinian-related issues, and advised by only a handful of men, whose instincts were to second-guess or simply defer to such a long-serving monarch.

In practice, the disengagement involved a series of measures that were less than might have been expected: Jordan would cease to employ most of the 20,000 or more civil servants, barring religious officials and judges; the ministry of occupied territories affairs would be downgraded; the development plan, already moribund, was formally scrapped. The one measure of real importance was the diminution of the status of West Bankers, who would lose their citizenship rights and only be eligible for two-year passports instead of five. This was a defensive measure aimed at discouraging West Bankers from gravitating eastwards; it was informed by fear of transfer and the increasing Likud flirtation with the 'Jordan is Palestine' thesis.

It is important to understand exactly what the severing of ties meant. It was not a strategic decision by King Hussein to end all aspirations to win back the West Bank for Jordan. As a Hashemite, such a move would have gone against the ideological grain. Indeed, if that had been his goal then King Hussein would have managed events in a different way, asking, for example, that parliament end Jordan's notional sovereignty over the West Bank, or proceeding to amend the constitution as appropriate. The king did not make either of these moves, the severing of ties coming conveniently the day after he had dissolved parliament. This was not a mistake or an oversight, as Hussein had informed trusted foreign ambassadors some two weeks in advance of his intentions.

Furthermore, the move was not designed to hand responsibility for the territories over to the PLO; a sporting admission that the best man had won and that man was Arafat. It was much more tactically conceived than that, a product of the bad blood that still existed between Arafat and Hussein. The king made no attempt to smooth the transition. Rather his intention was to set a trap, to hand the PLO 'a poisoned chalice'.[34] The PLO was expected to fail to shoulder the burden as far as the West Bank was concerned, leaving the Palestinians with no alternative but to seek his leadership anew. The peevishness of Hussein's approach undermined the potential for exploiting the move to improve wider relations in the region and to improve the Jordanian reputation among Arab public opinion.

That King Hussein could have believed that such a possibility might exist and at such a time is evidence of the depths of the denial that he and the Pan-Jordanians now shared. In reality the game was up. The king had not meant to give the PLO the chance to establish proprietorial rights over the West Bank but this was in effect what would happen. Though the process would not be pretty, the PLO would go on to establish itself as the government of the West Bank. Though he had not intended to end his sovereignty over the West Bank, this was to be the consequence of his actions.

CHAPTER 8

Hussein's Choices

The last decade of King Hussein's life was among its most eventful, a reminder of the potential for turbulence, both at home and next door. It began with virtual economic collapse, including a plummeting dinar and debt default, leading to a decade-long stewardship of the Jordanian economy by the IMF. The conduct of structural adjustment triggered rioting, not from among Palestinians, but from within the heartlands of the East Bank. Suddenly, virtually out of the blue, the political base of the regime appeared to be fragile. Struggling to keep up, the king conceded liberal reform at home as a way of ameliorating economic austerity.

No sooner had Jordan returned to parliamentary pluralism than Iraq invaded Kuwait. Once again, the small state of Jordan was buffeted by regional political storms. Besieged by refugees, spurned by the US for its prejudiced efforts at mediation and vulnerable to a missile war over its territory, in the end the kingdom escaped lightly and with relief. The intuitive sympathy, both popular and regal, for Baghdad was quickly forgiven as the Arab–Israeli peace process once again moved ahead. Though the Madrid conference and the bilateral peace process that it spawned delivered little, it did provide a platform for an Israeli–Palestinian breakthrough in Oslo. Crucially, this secret, unilateral approach by Arafat freed Hussein of his obligations to the Palestinians. With the shadow of cancer lying across him, Hussein seized the day and drove forward to conclude a bilateral peace treaty with Israel in just over a year. The price of subsequent attempts at normalisation was paid for by the country's liberalisation process.

With the one big achievement of the second half of his reign now secure, the king had only to tend to the succession. In the end it was messy and public, a glitzy American-style soap opera with shades of Charles and Diana. Hussein got his way, as he so often did in Jordan during the later years of his life, with his brother dispossessed and his eldest son restored. And in the background stood the new crown prince, Hussein's favourite son, Hamzeh, 18 years old and bearing an uncanny, disconcerting, resemblance to his father when he succeeded back in 1953. With his work complete, Hussein could die, prematurely but in comparative peace.

WHILE JORDAN BURNS

The years 1988 and 1989 were disasters for Jordan as the country hit an economic wall largely of its own making, with raw political consequences. In 1988, the Jordanian currency, the dinar, hitherto regarded as a symbol of national prowess, was subject to two serious bouts of instability. This resulted in the loss of 23% of its value between April and October. At the beginning of the following year the kingdom had no choice but to default on its foreign debt,[1] the first time in its existence that it had ever done so. Once the truth was finally out the enormity of the situation became clear: Jordan's foreign debt was the largest in the world, measured on a per capita basis. As is the international norm in the case of debt default, this triggered a number of related measures, from the calling in of the IMF to the rescheduling of bilateral and commercial debt through the multilateral Paris and London Clubs of creditors. It was the ham-fisted way in which the resulting measures were introduced in April 1989 that precipitated the riots later that month. In the words of Adiba Mango, in her commentary on the Jordanian politics of this period, the kingdom was in the midst of a crisis that was 'shaking the regime to its core'.[2]

The origin of these calamities was the Rake's Progress that was government economic policy through much of the 1980s. The importance of the external economy to the rapid growth in public and private spending in the 1970s ought to have sensitised Amman to economic changes abroad. The waning of the post-Iranian revolutionary oil price spike, the onset of the Iran–Iraq war and conflict in Lebanon in 1982 all contributed to the end of the regional boom. The direct consequences for Jordan were becoming clear by 1983, by the end of which only some 45%, or some $550 million, of its Baghdad summit Arab aid, comprising those transfers from Kuwait and Saudi Arabia, was still being made.

The reaction of successive governments in Amman to this marked decline in the fortunes of the external economy was to ignore it. Budget austerity measures were largely eschewed in preference for real increases in current spending in every year between 1983 and 1988. This reflected successive governments' extreme reluctance to pass on the new straitened circumstances in the form of redundancies or pay cuts to the predominantly Transjordanian public sector. After all, these were Jordanian-dominated governments, and the public sector was its bedrock of support. A range of state subsidies built

Table 8.1 *Jordan's Deteriorating Government Budget (JD million)*

Year	Budget Deficit (excl. foreign loans)	Deficit (excl. loans) % of GDP
1979	85.1	12.7
1980	109.7	12.3
1981	106.4	10.2
1982	103.6	8.9
1983	76.6	6.2
1984	164.6	12.5
1985	201.5	14.5
1986	235.7	16.8
1987	159.1	11.0
1988	388.3	26.8

Source: Central Bank of Jordan, *Yearly Statistical Series (1964–1989)* and author's calculations.

up since the mid-1970s was also kept in place, as governments baulked at exacerbating the slide into recession. A nominal commitment to privatisation from 1985 was hardly translated into practical reform.[3] Rather than contracting, as economic realities dictated, the economy continued to expand, with government services the motor for growth.

Governments coped with the economic realities of the day through a combination of running down the country's foreign currency reserves,[4] and a resort to borrowing, the profile of which was moving from the soft money of bilateral and multilateral lending agencies to loans raised on the Eurodollar market at commercial rates. For example, Jordanian governments borrowed $225 million, $150 million and $215 million in 1983, 1984 and 1985 respectively; with the funds acquired being purely for budget support, there were no prospects of such monies generating new wealth to fund the repayments let alone further expansion. With an initial grace period built into each loan, governments were knowingly storing up trouble with the imminent prospect of bunched debt repayment obligations that would be enormously difficult for an economy the size of Jordan's to service. In the 1989 budget, just prior to the debt default, repayments of JD210 million were allocated for the servicing of the kingdom's internal and external debt, the equivalent of 20% of total expenditure. It was subsequently revealed that Jordan's debt repayment bill could be as high as $1.2 billion in 1989 and 1990.

Such dereliction did not succeed in protecting Jordanians from the creeping onset of economic erosion. Jordan began to pay for its largely unchecked approach to population growth through falling per capita incomes, and the re-emergence of acute structural unemployment. Increasingly problems of joblessness also affected the professions, with Jordan having produced a glut of such prestige occupations as medical doctors and engineers.[5] Jordanians coped with the incremental fall in living standards at this time through traditional practices of kin-based social solidarity. There were concerns at falling total levels of expatriate worker remittances. Increasingly, campaigns were introduced to weed out illegally employed foreign workers and reduce their overall profile in the labour market. Financial institutions began to fail, beginning with moneychangers,[6] and spreading to the commercial banking sector,[7] as the non-performing loans portfolios of banks began to come to light.

This fiscal irresponsibility of the mid-1980s can be explained in three ways. First, the kingdom had operated a rentier economy since the inception of the state, and it had survived tolerably well hitherto. This led to the perception that living beyond the means of the country was more of a routine, structural, economic reality than a new and dangerous development. It also explains the initial reluctance once the debt default had taken place, apparently on the part of the king and the premier included, to go to the IMF, even though the kingdom had no realistic alternative. Second, the conventional wisdom through the 1980s, both among the Arab oil producers and the hydrocarbons business more broadly, was that sooner or later oil prices would recover and the revenue trajectories of the late 1970s and early 1980s would be restored, thereby reflating the regional economy. In the face of such dogged expectation that something would turn up, and that something would be higher oil prices, even the oil price collapse of 1986 could be casually dismissed.

Third, there was widespread ignorance in the kingdom as to just how bad things were because of the opaque nature of the public finances and a general culture of secrecy. No better illustration of this exists than that which relates to the level of foreign indebtedness.[8] The activities of much of the public sector, such as the national carrier, which had significant volumes of debt, all government guaranteed, were kept off budget. In addition to being partially hidden, there was no clear way to aggregate debt in the kingdom. Furthermore, Jordan's military debt was notoriously untransparent. Justified on the grounds of national security, this opacity enabled the commission payments and skimming on military contracts that were taking place in Jordan, as across the rest of the Arab world, to be kept hidden. The one man who was well placed over time to know the magnitude of the worsening problem, the king, was totally uninterested in and hence unengaged in the subject.

In the division of labour that was policymaking in Jordan in the latter part of the 1980s, the king concentrated on foreign affairs, increasingly to the exclusion of all else. In the end, a small cabal presided over by the prime minister, Zaid al-Rifai, and including his brother-in-law, Maher Shukri, installed under his patronage as deputy governor at the Central Bank, attempted to prevent the inevitable. Their efforts included the clandestine sale of 350,000 oz of gold, one-third of the kingdom's gold reserves, in a vain attempt to buy time and stave off the collapse.[9]

Even when the game was clearly up in February 1989, King Hussein still refrained from sacking Rifai. There then followed the incongruous sight of the finance minister, Hanna Odeh, who had held the portfolio for the previous five years, now fronting the Jordanian team in discussions with the IMF. An agreement was quickly concluded, with the Fund and the World Bank doing what was expected of them in terms of extending a stand-by credit and a loan respectively in order to facilitate rescheduling. It was also agreed that the short-term aim of the agreement would be to cut the budget deficit. As part of this effort, the Rifai government implemented a series of steep price rises. Though it promised that staple goods would remain unaffected by the new strategy, the implementation of the austerity package was badly mismanaged.

It was in this context that riots broke out on 18 April. The disturbances began with taxi drivers in the southern city of Maan, who had been refused permission to raise their tariffs in response to the steep hike in petrol prices. The unrest quickly spread within Maan and then to other East Bank towns in the south, such as Karak, Shubak and Tafilah, the south being one of the most under-developed regions of the kingdom. A week later riots broke out in Salt, a matter of ten miles from the capital. The targets of the protesters were invariably symbols of the state, such as government offices, as Transjordanians demonstrated their feelings of anger and bitterness at the sudden and unexpected assault on their living standards. Amman, a predominantly Palestinian city, remained quiet during the turmoil. Palestinian areas in general were conspicuous by their restraint, encouraged by the PLO, which did not wish to see the central issue of the protesters clouded by the re-emergence of inter-communal tensions. At least eight people are known to have been killed in the unrest.

In addition to the price rises themselves, and the general decline in the standard of living that they represented, the outpouring of dissatisfaction was primarily aimed at the Rifai government. It was accused of having been both authoritarian and corrupt. Implicitly too, though not representing a direct challenge to the regime, the protesters were complaining about the conduct of the king, who was generally regarded as having become out of touch with popular sentiment. In the absence of any other institutional vehicle for protest, tribal and community leaders and the heads of professional associations led the way in articulating the demands of the protesters. These included: the resignation of the government; the revoking of the austerity measures; the punishment of corrupt officials; national elections; greater political freedoms, and a freer press. They were to get their way on everything but the reversal of the austerity measures and the prosecution of the corrupt.

Once the riots had broken out, King Hussein belatedly rediscovered some of his zip of old. He cancelled the remainder of a visit to the US, sacking Rifai upon his return to Amman. In his stead, Hussein appointed a distant cousin, Sharif Zaid bin Shaker, as the new premier, to oversee what was effectively to be a transitional government. The fact that Sharif Zaid had been, until the previous December, the kingdom's top military man indicated that the king would not allow law and order to be compromised. However, the king balanced this approach by giving his new prime minister a brief to reinvigorate the political life of the kingdom, as a *quid pro quo* for the price rises which remained in place. Hussein had finally caught up with the mood in the country. The assiduous way in which the king subsequently undertook visits to the various outlying parts of the East Bank was reminiscent of the young Hussein of the 1950s. Hussein's subsequent quiet removal of some of those accused of being the country's more egregiously corrupt officials, such as the head of the police and even the chairman and chief executive of his beloved national airline, showed that he had belatedly come to understand the depth of the crisis.

LIBERALISATION FOR AUSTERITY

The announcement of the restoration of participatory government in Jordan was a desperate attempt by a leadership that had become complacent over the past two decades, comfortable with the absence of real and effective mechanisms for scrutiny and accountability, to re-establish some sort of control over events. The king was widely regarded, in the words of one member of the opposition, as being 'all talk and tactics'.[10] In moving to a restoration of pluralist politics the king was responding not only to the demands of the rioters but also to the will of many on the

East Bank, who had been campaigning for the legalisation of Jordanian parties since the 1970s. Indeed, leading political figures, such as Sulaiman Arar (who would become the first parliamentary speaker after the election) and Jamal al-Sha'ir, had already tentatively pushed ahead with the creation of nascent political organisations, such as the Arab Constitutionalist Party (ACP) and the Unionist Democratic Association respectively, in the hope of prompting greater freedoms. Having regained control, the king would ultimately decide to halt progress towards greater political liberalisation in 1993 in favour of the strategic decision to conclude a peace treaty with Israel.

General elections were duly held on 8 November 1989.[11] They took place for a national assembly that was considerably revamped, with the number of seats being expanded from 60 to 80 and the dedicated West Bank component being removed. The decision to scrap parliament as a representative institution for the West Bank, something that had not been done either in the aftermath of Rabat in 1974 or the severing of administrative and legal ties in 1988, was a reflection of the depth of the crisis in the East Bank. The Hashemites had been pushed into a strategic retrenchment in the West Bank in order to ensure their survival in the East Bank. With Rifai in disgrace and the Transjordanians asserting themselves, it marked a crucial victory for Jordanian nationalism. The increase in the number of seats for East Bankers expanded the opportunities for advancement for members of the country's political elite, a fact illustrated by the willingness of 650 candidates to stand in the election.

The election, which was generally free and fair, was undoubtedly a success for the Islamists. Expected to receive 7–15 seats,[12] in fact as many as 34 of the successful candidates were regarded as being Islamists of varying hues. With the authorities relaxing the electoral provisions excluding candidates from banned parties running for election, the largest Islamist grouping, the Muslim Brotherhood, succeeded in the election of 20 of its 26-man slate. The willingness of the Islamists to play within the rules of a liberalising political process impressed many commentators, with the American Middle East specialist, Glenn Robinson, going so far as to describe them as 'capable democrats'.[13] A further ten deputies were elected from the ranks of the political opposition, comprising six nationalists and four leftists, a measure of the depth of the protest vote for those identified as not part of the political establishment, as economic issues and corruption dominated the electoral campaign. Of the remaining 36 deputies returned, some 22 were regarded as being tribal figures. Groupings of deputies then began to coalesce into broad, but ill-disciplined ideological factions within parliament.[14]

Soon after the election, the king changed governments again, appointing the experienced Mudar Badran, Rifai's great foe, as prime minister. Some expressed disappointment that the king had not chosen a younger, more liberal figure to govern the country at this time of accelerating openness. However, it soon became clear that the king had inverted this logic: it was because he realised the continuing need to pursue a strategy of openness and reform that he had appointed an older and more conservative figure, a man in whom he could have confidence to loosen up the political system but without making fundamental compromises on the security of the regime.

Those arrested during the rioting of the previous spring had already been released in an early amnesty. The government of Sharif Zaid followed this up by releasing a further 80 political prisoners. Badran built on this foundation in an effort to secure a vote of confidence from a potentially hostile lower house, a concern that also explains why he included ten deputies in his government. His early reforms reversed a range of repressive measures, including: ending the restrictions on travel abroad as a penalty for undesirable political activities at home;[15] rescinding the writing bans on some of the country's journalists; relaxing the hand of control on the Jordanian press;[16] allowing the restoration of the banned Jordan Writers' Association.

Such concessions alone did not prove to be sufficient to ensure a confidence vote, and Badran was subject to a bruising three-day debate, which included criticism of his past record in government, especially with respect to the management of the economy between 1980 and 1984. In order to succeed with the confidence vote, Badran was therefore obliged by this grilling to go much further than he originally seemed intent upon doing, and adopted much of the platform of the vocal opposition. The regime had still not regained control of the process. In doing so, Badran agreed to amend or revoke a number of draconian laws, to make the security apparatus more transparent and to ensure that an investigation into corruption was less restricted than initially envisaged.

Badran half-delivered on his promises. A further round of political prisoner releases, this time affecting those in prison before 1989 and serving long sentences, took place. The prime minister issued a directive ending the practice by which all those taking employment in the public sector had to be vetted by the secret police. He also issued instructions that former civil servants sacked for political activities should be reinstated. Such moves drew public applause, not least from the benchmark of international conscience, the human rights advocacy organisation, Amnesty International.

Elsewhere, the record was much less impressive, especially over the issue of corruption. Part of Badran's response to his mauling in parliament had been to move ahead in this area too. The public prosecutor was instructed to investigate nine cases of alleged corruption relating to a number of former officials, affecting such issues as the sale of the country's gold reserves, large import tenders, and the award of contracts for major public works. It is doubtful that the prosecutions would have taken place, as those initially pursued represented only the tip of the iceberg, corruption, it being generally agreed, being a phenomenon that, as the euphemism goes, reached right to the top. However, the government was saved from a difficult dilemma by the fortunate distraction of the Iraqi invasion of Kuwait, which resulted in the issue being kicked into touch. In mid-January 1991, shortly before the onset of hostilities in the northern Gulf, Badran announced that a number of the most controversial cases would be dropped. Due to the preoccupation of the Jordanian public with the Iraq crisis, the back-pedalling on corruption elicited little by way of protest. The explanation given was that there were no legal grounds for prosecution. Among the cases on which it was decided not to move forward was that of the gold sales. While other cases were referred to the courts, no successful prosecutions were to take place at all. Badran had succeeded in defusing what at one time promised to be a highly combustible issue.

The other notable political contribution of the Badran government was to start the process by which the challenge posed by the Muslim Brotherhood would be blunted. Immediately after his appointment as premier, Badran had opened negotiations with the organisation with a view to their joining his government. When talks became stalled, he opted to include three independent Islamist deputies instead. He resumed negotiations with the Brotherhood at the turn of the year, including five of their number (and two independent Islamists) in his reshuffled, 25-strong cabinet. It made good sense to widen the base of the government shortly before the onset of war in the Gulf. The price paid in terms of ministerial portfolios was modest, with the Brotherhood receiving only education and health of the significant spending ministries. Whether by chance or design, the former proved to be an astute move, in spite of general concerns that control of the ministry would be used to accelerate the recruitment of Islamist activists as teachers and administrators. The new minister, Abdullah Akayleh,[17] lost some of the wide-ranging respect that the Brotherhood enjoyed by introducing a rule preventing the fathers of schoolgirls from attending group sports activities, a move that drew far-reaching criticism as petty and dogmatic. The Muslim

Brotherhood enjoyed the fruits of limited power for less than six months, losing office considerably chastened with the fall of the Badran government the following June.

Running in parallel with the political liberalisation process in Jordan was an initiative for the adoption of a National Charter (*al-mithaq al-watani*). This initiative emanated from the palace, part of the king's urgent response to the violent unrest of April 1989. The original aim of the charter was to provide a political framework to regulate the transition towards a more liberal form of politics in the kingdom. Many feared that it would end up being a device through which the king would play for time, and hence hold back the cause of greater openness and participation. This appeared to be confirmed when a 60-strong drafting commission was established, taking until December 1991 to conclude its deliberations.

In reality, however, rather than obstructing the process, the charter emerged as being a document of significance. Arguably, its greatest importance was in the reassurance that it offered the king about the moves taking place in the direction of greater political liberalisation. The basic contract at the heart of the charter was that the king would allow the complete restoration of pluralist, democratic, participatory politics. In return, there would be a general *quid pro quo* from all of the people of the country that would do two things: first, acknowledge that Jordan was a legitimate territorial state; second, recognise that Jordan was a Hashemite monarchy, with King Hussein its legitimate head of state. The charter was, in short, an attempt to transcend the lingering ambivalences towards state and regime that were a hangover from the 1950s. It was also a reflection of the renewed insecurities felt by the throne.

There were two procedural ways in which King Hussein tried to ensure that the charter acquired widespread legitimacy in Jordan. The first was to appoint politicians from across the political spectrum to the drafting commission; in this way the king was employing a device that he had previously used very successfully in the establishment of the NCC. The appointment of Ahmad Obeidat, who enjoyed a reputation for probity and whose relationship with the king had often been far from smooth, as the head of the commission gave additional credibility to the exercise. The second was the way in which the charter was finally adopted: a 2,000-delegate popular conference, drawing its members from traditional and modern social formations, like tribes and professional associations, endorsed the charter by popular proclamation.

The process was not without its critics. While very few disagreed with the substance of the initiative, there were those who questioned the process. Some harked back to the 1952 Jordanian constitution, as providing a comprehensive normative bedrock for the political system. Unsurprisingly, perhaps, many of those connected with the national assembly were none too enamoured of the charter, because of the way in which parliament had effectively been sidelined in its drafting and adoption. Such complaints were far from being idle. The process used for the approval of the charter would be utilised again by the king in the autumn, to legitimise Jordan's participation in an international conference in Madrid, thereby skirting the potential hostility of an opposition-dominated national assembly, initiating at last a proper Arab–Israeli peace process. On 9 June 1991, the ad hoc national conference duly met and the charter was adopted.

There then followed a brief moment when liberalisation and democratisation were at their most intense in Jordan. The charter paved the way for the legalisation of political parties, a measure that finally reached the statute books in September 1992, and hence the competition among parties to become the dominant force in the elected lower house. Of course, such a measure still fell short of delivering a full democratic system. King Hussein was under no obligation to choose the leader of the largest party in parliament to form a government, while the upper house, an appointed chamber, formed an institutional check on its elected counterpart. Behind the scenes, no effective measures were introduced to promote the scrutiny or accountability of the intelligence service, the GID. Nevertheless, in relative terms, this was a big improvement on that which had existed before 1989, and positioned the kingdom as one of the leading liberalising states in the Arab world. There were some restrictions on the newly legalised parties, such as the banning of the creation of paramilitary wings. The most important restriction was that no party should be financed from or have links outside the country, and that its leadership should be Jordanian. In his residual caution, the king had not forgotten the traumas suffered at the hands of the transnational parties of the 1950s.

With the adoption of the long-awaited charter, some 20 political parties were formally registered with the interior ministry, as the law required, though some mergers took place as the system began to consolidate.[18] The Muslim Brotherhood (the mainstay of the newly created Islamic Action Front) was arguably the only mass party in the kingdom; parties of notables, such as the ACP, occupied the political centre; a clutch of small, fragmented parties were to be found on the left. Further measures then followed. The most symbolically significant measure was the lifting on 7 July of martial law, which had been in force since 1967, and which had been utilised in a range of ways, extending even to the prosecution of shopkeepers for breaking price controls.

THE IRAQ–KUWAIT CRISIS

In spite of the troubles at home, 1989 was an auspicious year for Jordanian foreign policy, especially as far as its central objectives were concerned. On the one hand, Jordan's tenacious diplomacy aimed at bringing about the reintegration of Egypt into the Arab fold was coming to fruition. At the Arab summit in Casablanca in May 1989, Cairo would be warmly welcomed back and the Arab League headquarters returned to its original home in Cairo. On the other hand, the Iran–Iraq war was now over and Jordan could look forward to developing its relationship with Iraq. Proof of the enduring nature of the Amman–Baghdad axis had come the previous August, with a public gift of captured weaponry. In return, Jordan reciprocated diplomatically, for instance, by rejecting accusations that Iraq had used chemical weapons against its own Kurdish population; such was the price of a small country bandwaggoning a state like Iraq.

King Hussein's Egypt and Iraq strategies appeared to meet in a happy convergence with the announcement in February 1989 of the creation of a new sub-regional organisation, the Arab Cooperation Council (ACC).[19] Combining Egypt, Iraq and Jordan with North Yemen (soon to be united with People's Democratic Republic of Yemen in the south), the grouping comprised demographic and military weight. The situation was altogether different when viewed from an economic perspective. It appeared that the ACC combined the indebted with the under-developed with the war-damaged.

For Jordan, the attractions of the ACC were at least threefold. First, it cemented closer economic relations with Iraq, in a way that would privilege the kingdom in the business of the reconstruction of its neighbour, whenever the foreign exchange might become plentiful enough for that to begin. Second, it implicitly galvanised Egypt and Iraq behind the defence of Jordan, at a time of great nervousness *vis-à-vis* Israel. The cause of this was the migration of some 800,000 predominantly Jewish citizens of the Soviet Union to Israel, and the fear that they would be settled in the West Bank, increasing fears of the displacement of Palestinians to Jordan. The king, utilising Rifai's good contacts in Damascus, was committed to bringing Syria into the new body in order to extend this strategy of deterrents. Third, it provided a means through which to manage the Palestinian issue, against a backdrop of heightened speculation that *finalité* for the Occupied Territories would involve the creation of a confederal relationship with Jordan; the ACC offered the prospect of the membership of a Palestinian entity in the future, thereby side-stepping what for Jordan was a most uncomfortable issue.

While the ACC seemed an attractive new departure for Jordan, the king did not seem to think through the potentially destabilising effects of the new organisation for the region. These ranged across Saudi fears of being surrounded, Syrian fears of heightened isolation, and Israeli fears of the recreation of an Arab confrontation front. The greatest testimony to the destabilising effects of the ACC, for the creation of which the king was so responsible, was that its active existence did not stretch beyond an 18-month period.

Most worryingly, given his famed close relationship with Saddam Hussein, it was the future of Iraqi foreign and security policy on which the king appeared to be the most unsighted. It was undoubtedly the strategic aspects of the ACC that proved most attractive to Iraq, impatient to reassert its position within the Arab world following a near-decade-long distraction to the east. Suddenly, though, rather than being a net contributor to Jordan's security *vis-à-vis* Israel, as was the expectation from Amman, Iraq's increased posturing was to have the opposite effect. Whether it was Iraqi Mirage jets flying along the Jordan Valley in summer 1989, the possible creation of a joint air squadron (even if only for training purposes owing to Jordan's penury) in February 1990, the Iraqi president's use of the Amman summit of the ACC in the same month to attack the US presence in the Gulf and its relations with Israel, and Saddam's threat 'to burn half of Israel' on 2 April 1990, they all served to ratchet up tension and increase the uncertainties between Jordan and Israel. With apparently little influence in Baghdad in spite of his excellent access, King Hussein was left with little by way of a role to play other than that of Saddam apologist, as he did, for example, over Iraq's execution of the British-based journalist Fazad Bazoft in March 1990. If Saddam was an unguided missile in 1989 and 1990, King Hussein failed to provide him with a guidance system.

In view of the asymmetric nature of the relationship between the two men it is unlikely that Hussein knew of Saddam's intention to invade Kuwait, which took place on 2 August 1990, in advance. King Hussein had visited both Iraq and Kuwait on the eve of the invasion, and did not return with a display of frantic action.[20] Indeed, one of Jordan's two leading Arabic dailies suggested that a peaceful settlement of the dispute was the most likely outcome.[21] This view of an essentially benign Jordanian role in the invasion was not shared by the Saudi establishment. It viewed the invasion as a crucial part of a wider ACC conspiracy to restore the Saudi regions of the Hijaz to the Hashemites and the Asir to Yemen. Jordanian–Saudi ties declined rapidly, as the clock of bilateral relations was turned back to before the 1950s, to a time when dynastic rivalry and open competition governed such links.

Once the invasion had taken place, King Hussein's instinctive reaction was to do two things: to declare that the issue was an intra-Arab one; and to try to mediate. The resort to a mediation-based approach to intra-Arab affairs had proved to be a useful device through which the king regularly punched above his country's diplomatic weight in the regional ring. It was also an adept way for the king to retain good relations with warring regimes that otherwise would insist that he declare his hand one way or another.[22] But, almost from the outset, as the US Middle East expert Ann Mosely Lesch has concluded, the king's 'unwillingness to distance himself from Saddam undercut his credentials as a mediator'.[23] For the veteran Israeli historian of Jordanian affairs, Uriel Dann, the situation was even more clear-cut: King Hussein 'stood out as a supporter of Saddam Husayn and an apologist for the invasion of Kuwait'.[24]

As long as Baghdad insisted on the fiction that its military intervention was aimed at aiding progressive forces in Kuwait and not at annexation, and hence was reversible, and as long as the Arab world had not formally entrenched what was fast emerging as a cavernous split, the king's insistence on a mediatory role and an Arab solution was just about tenable. By 8 August, and the formal Iraqi annexation of Kuwait, and 10 August, and the Arab summit in Cairo which endorsed the dispatch of a pan-Arab force to protect Saudi Arabia,[25] King Hussein's approach was dead in the water.

The prudent course of action for the king ought then to have been politically to keep his head down, domestically to have hidden behind the lengthening list of UN resolutions sanctioning Iraq, and, practically, to have concentrated on addressing the direct consequences of the crisis, notably the influx of more than half-a-million evacuees from Iraq and Kuwait. In reality, however, he could not resist picking at the wounds. Like Yasser Arafat, he seemed unable and unwilling to distance himself from his erstwhile partner. True, Jordan had opposed Iraq's annexation of Kuwait, and continued to recognise its amiri regime. But Amman had also been distinctly equivocal in refusing to condemn the original invasion, instead resorting to the longhand of reiterating its commitment to the

Arab League charter, which upholds the inadmissibility of the acquisition of territory through force. Indeed, by opting for such language, Jordan was also referencing SCR 242 and its focus on the Israeli occupation of Palestinian land, a linkage that Saddam was himself trying to establish in order to outmanoeuvre the US. Moreover, Jordan was also very late in implementing the UN embargo against Iraq, playing for time by seeking clarifications from the UN.[26] The subsequent strident emphasis placed by the king on the avoidance of war was similarly problematic, as by inference it would consolidate the gains made through force by Baghdad.

At the same time, the king's emotional rhetoric against the US, for its 'embargo on dialogue', and Israel, for the perpetration of a grand conspiracy, became increasingly impassioned and ill-advised. As Hussein took to the skies, it elicited a backlash from traditional friends. In Britain, Margaret Thatcher, whom Hussein admired, administered a tongue-lashing; in the US, President Bush snubbed him; Israel quietly but firmly reiterated that the arrival of Iraqi troops on Jordanian soil would be viewed as a *casus belli*. In the Arab world, King Hussein was left in a minority of the marginal that refused to join the international coalition, alongside such lightweights as Libya, the PLO and Yemen.

Virtually the only place where King Hussein's line went down well was at home, both among the Transjordanians, who had so profited from a decade and more's relationship with Iraq, and the Jordanian Palestinians, mesmerised by Saddam's apparent demonstration of strong leadership. Domestically at least, the king was sure-footed: approving the establishment of a popular militia, a gesture which saw 150,000 Jordanians undergo basic training prior to the onset of hostilities in the northern Gulf; allowing demonstrations to take place, whether organised by Islamists or leftists, as a safety valve for popular sentiment; quietly rebuilding bridges with the radical Palestinian groups like the PFLP and the DFLP, that had fought for his downfall two decades before. King by default he may have been after the riots of April 1989, by early 1991 Hussein was the subject of a desperate, almost intoxicated, adulation on the part of many of his subjects.

King Hussein maintained his mediatory stance until January 1991, when war became inevitable. Ineffectual from an Iraqi perspective, irritating in the extreme from the point of view of the international coalition, King Hussein was possibly the only man outside his kingdom who still viewed his stance as even-handed. On the brink of war, Hussein recovered some of his equilibrium, warning his neighbours, that is to say Iraq included, that Jordan would defend its territory and airspace against any possible incursion 'from any side'. Jordan duly condemned the coalition for its attack on Iraq on 16 January 1991. Rhetorically, King Hussein could not help himself in making increasingly impassioned criticisms of the US-led war effort. Practically, however, Jordan sat tight, and was gratified to be left unscathed by the ensuing hostilities.

Even after the war was over and Iraqi forces had been ejected from Kuwait, Jordan seemed reluctant to move on. Relations with Egypt, fully restored as *primus inter pares* in the Arab world, were needlessly antagonised by Jordan's official publication of a 'White Paper', seeking to justify its actions during the Iraq–Kuwait crisis.[27] An apparently equivocal attitude over the implementation of UN sanctions against Iraq only succeeded in riling the US, and provoking commercially costly searches of shipping bound for Aqaba port.

THE 'BREAK' WITH IRAQ

In spite of the 'almost dogmatic' way in which King Hussein leant in the direction of Iraq during the Gulf crisis, the invasion of Kuwait spoilt the close personal relationship between the two leaders. In time it appeared clear that Hussein felt let down by Saddam's invasion. King Hussein visited Baghdad during the early and middle weeks of the crisis, and was instrumental in helping to persuade the Iraqi leader to release his remaining foreign hostage 'guests'. From that point onwards, however, the visits ended. There was no falling out, but the distance between them grew.

This did not mean that Iraqi–Jordanian ties came to an end. On the contrary. Between 1991 and 1996, the period when the impact of sanctions was at its most intense, Jordan became Iraq's windpipe to the world. Those humanitarian goods not proscribed under the sanctions regime were imported via Aqaba. The land route to Amman was the only outlet to the outside world for Iraqi officials. Some 300,000 Iraqi citizens moved to Jordan to find work as anything from academics to prostitutes. The existence of such a community provided an excellent cover for intelligence and sanction-busting operations. The kingdom also benefited from the continuation of this relationship. The UN recognised Jordan's special need for Iraqi oil and exempted it from the ban on exports. The oil trade provided the motor for reciprocal exports from the Jordanian private sector. The continuation of this economic symbiosis, even at a low point in Iraq's economic fortunes, nurtured the Iraqi lobby in Jordan.

This relationship encountered one major upset, in 1995–96, following the defection to Jordan of Hussein Kamel Hasan al-Majid, Saddam Hussein's cousin and son-in-law, and arguably one of the most senior members of the Iraqi regime, following a dangerous falling out with the Iraqi president's

eldest son, Uday. Hussein Kamel attempted to reinvent himself as a puta-
tive leader of the Iraqi opposition and alternative president. King Hussein
initially welcomed Hussein Kamel and gave him political asylum. Moreover, the king appeared to support his ambitions, no doubt a means through
which to reawaken Hashemite ambitions in Iraq.[28] The king also somewhat
implausibly used the defection, and Hussein Kamel's 'revelations' about the
nature of power in Iraq, to scorn its past conduct and confirm the distance
that now existed between Amman and Baghdad. He also began speaking
in elliptical terms of a possible new era in Iraq in the future, established
relations with the wider Iraqi opposition movement, and appointed a new
prime minister, Abdul Karim al-Kabariti, who was known as being anti-
Iraqi. Though bilateral relations became noticeably rocky during this time
they never actually collapsed.

As quick as the potential for a new Iraq strategy emerged in Jordan, it
appeared to close down. The king's relationship with Hussein Kamel soon
waned, as the wider Iraqi opposition refused to endorse a man on whose
hands it believed there was still the stain of blood. With Hussein Kamel
now an embarrassment to the king, and apparently a virtual prisoner in
Amman, he was persuaded to return to Baghdad, only to meet his violent
death at the hands of regime henchmen in February 1996. Though only of
symbolic importance, his death seemed to suggest that the opportunity for
regime change in Baghdad had passed. Neither did King Hussein help his
own cause more directly. The unveiling of a new initiative in Amman for a
future federal Iraq was received with coolness by the Iraqi mainstream, who
perceived it as a recipe for fragmentation. Jordan did allow one leading Iraqi
opposition group, the Iraqi National Accord, to open an office in Amman,
but its activities there remained low key.

By April 1996, King Hussein had adopted a new, conciliatory approach
towards Iraq. The reason seemed to be Baghdad's acceptance of UN SCR
986, the so-called 'oil for food' resolution, which gave Iraq the right to
export significant levels of crude oil in return for importing 'humanitarian
goods', such as food and medicines. With a more realistic opportunity to
increase bilateral trade, and the possibility that Iraq might otherwise take
its new purchasing power elsewhere, the king quietly reversed his policy of
the previous eight months.

STRUCTURAL ADJUSTMENT

The centrality of economic factors in the continuing relationship with
Iraq is illustrative of the straitened circumstances that characterised Jordan

through the 1990s and the close relationship between foreign policy and foreign economic policy. In the period between 1988 and 1991, the value of the dinar declined by half and the standard of living of Jordanians fell by about one-third. Unemployment stood at over 30%. State salaries were frozen, and new public-sector recruitment curtailed. Though the kingdom's debt was subject to a rolling rescheduling, the magnitude of it exercised a psychological effect in deterring new investment in the economy. Though the 300,000 or so returnees from Kuwait stimulated the economy temporarily, with their new investment in real estate, retail and construction, the main impact of this fillip was concentrated in Amman, rather than the rural areas. By the mid-1990s, this effect had worked its way through the system and the Jordanian economy was once more in the doldrums.

Dominating the commanding heights of economic policy in Jordan through the 1990s was the IMF. Its first foray into the kingdom in 1989 was superseded by the direct economic consequences of the Gulf crisis. The relationship was resumed in October 1991, through a seven-year agreement, subsequently extended, that initiated what would be a long and painful process of structural readjustment, away from the spendthrift and macro-economic irresponsibility of the recent past. The headline objectives of the new agreement were typical of IMF programmes in general, seeking to: cut the budget deficit; decrease public expenditure; cut private consumption; increase the domestic revenue component of government income; reduce inflation; reduce the need for foreign and domestic borrowing; and build up foreign currency reserves. By doing so, the agreement aimed to deliver higher but sustainable growth, promote greater macro-economic stability, remove many of the distortions from the economy, and create an environment under which a range of services could be provided more cheaply and efficiently.

In spite of the disadvantageous position of the Jordanian economy, the impact of the IMF on practical policies in the kingdom was slower, more cautious and more limited than one might have imagined. In part, this was probably due to the political influence on the IFIs (International Financial Institutions) wielded behind the scenes, especially by the US, not least as a function of Jordan's cooperative participation in the emerging peace process. In part, it also reflected the emergence of a give and take relationship between the IFIs and successive Jordanian governments, whereby the latter would in the end conform to the basic conditionalities of the former, but in a style and at a pace that would not jeopardise domestic political stability. Consequently, limited privatisations did take place, but with the state continuing to enjoy a majority stake in such diverse areas as telecommunications and cement production, while movement on the sale of the national carrier remained painfully slow. Governmental supervisory structures were changed, especially in the provision of water and electricity, but again only slowly and only at the prompting of the World Bank. Revenue raising also met with cautious success, both in terms of one-off capital injections from asset sales, and through the introduction of a national sales tax. Delayed in its initial introduction, owing to the noisy opposition of special interests, notably the merchants, the sales tax became a case study of structural change in Jordan: introduced in 1994 at a 7% level, it rose by stealth amid little subsequent disputation to 10% in 1995 and 13% in 1999.

Careful, incremental change also typified reform in areas with a strong impact on social policy, mindful of the fact that perhaps as much as 40% of the kingdom's population now exist below the poverty line.[29] Thus, subsidies were phased out in areas like fuel, but kerosene and unleaded petrol were exempt, in order not to hit the least well off. The general subsidy on bread was also removed, but targeted assistance was maintained for the very poor. In case of the IMF and the World Bank trying to force the pace too quickly, events, notably in the form of renewed disturbances in the southern towns of the East Bank over the price of bread in August 1996, could be invoked to justify further delay. The plight of the poor was also partly assuaged by the introduction of the beginnings of a social safety net, notably through the establishment of: the Social Productivity Programme, which includes new public sector agencies like the National Aid Fund (NAF), Community Infrastructure Programme and the Small and Micro Enterprises Development Programme; and the Family Income Supplement (FIS). Though vulnerable to accusations of being little more than a band-aid, the NAF helps 22,000 of the kingdom's most destitute families each year, while the FIS is aimed at lifting families above the poverty line.

More than a decade later, Jordanian perseverance and IFI patience have won the structural adjustment programme praise from a range of leading world players. For the IMF too its performance in the kingdom has come to be regarded as a success story amid a much larger catalogue of obvious failures in the world, thereby deepening the caution in its approach for fear of harming this positive view. This perception of a broadly successful structural adjustment programme has served Jordan well in the post-Cold War era, where a flexible and liberal approach to economic policy is seen as the only one worth supporting. Amman has also been shrewd in its positive approach to international economic understandings, correctly perceiving that economic accords can be a useful instrument through which to underpin political relationships. In order more firmly to orient itself in the Western camp, Jordan concluded under the Barcelona process an Association Agreement with the EU, which came into force in January 1999. It successfully gained membership of the World Trade Organisation in December 1999. Jordan's collection of the membership cards of liberal respectability was completed when it concluded a free trade agreement with the US in 2000, joining Canada, Mexico and Israel as the only other states to enjoy such a privileged agreement with the Americans.

HUSSEIN'S GAMBLE ON PEACE

Shortly before the onset of hostilities in the northern Gulf, the US and the USSR declared that once war was over they would move purposefully to address the outstanding aspects of the Arab–Israeli conflict. In spite of widespread scepticism, the US was as good as its word. The product of such a strategy was the convening of an international peace conference in Madrid on 30 October 1991, at which all of the country protagonists were in attendance. The presence of the affable Jordanian foreign minister, Kamel Abu Jaber, at the head of a joint Jordanian–Palestinian delegation was an illustration both of the impact of the Gulf crisis and the swiftness with which King Hussein had been rehabilitated as a regional partner.

Ironically, it was the Israeli government that played a leading role in the rapid healing of wounds, fronted though it was by the hard-line prime minister Yitzhak Shamir. For Shamir, who had until recently seemed to gravitate towards the 'Jordan is Palestine' camp within his Likud party, was a recent convert to the strategic necessity for Israel of preserving Jordan as it was, that is to say, independent and Hashemite. With Israel's support and the impossibility of keeping out both Hussein and Arafat, the focus swung back to the peace process conundrum of the mid-1980s, namely how to accommodate Palestinian representation, but without dealing directly with Arafat and the PLO. The answer was also a legacy of the 1980s: the inclusion of Palestinian personalities endorsed by the PLO in a joint delegation.

The return to late 1980s-style peace diplomacy was completed by the convening of a peace summit in Madrid, a ceremonial plenary that legitimised a subsequent series of bilateral negotiations between Israel and its neighbours. Peace talks began by preserving the presentational fiction that Jordanians and Palestinians were part of one negotiating team. Over time, however, this cumbersome framework broke down, and Israelis and Palestinians increasingly came to talk directly. With the Oslo breakthrough in Israeli–PLO mutual recognition just months away, Jordan's representational and facilitational roles were both now over.

Once the Palestinian component had been taken out of Israeli–Jordanian peace talks, there was relatively little for the two countries to negotiate bilaterally. Water rights and the fate of an under-populated strip along the common border from the Dead Sea to the Red Sea, that is to say unconnected with the West Bank, were the two most pressing issues. Yet, Israeli–Jordanian talks were inhibited by this newly emerging Israeli–Palestinian track. King Hussein could not be seen to be moving swiftly ahead with his own peace talks, as that would be interpreted as breaking solidarity with the Palestinians. If in the new post-Cold War world the Syrians no longer had a veto over Jordanian peacemaking with Israel, as had been the case with the campaign of assassinations in the mid-1980s, a Palestinian veto nevertheless remained in place. With the Madrid process failing to deliver, the Israeli government, once again led by Labour, began to look for alternative channels of negotiation. Whereas in the 1980s, it would have been the Jordanian option, it was rather to the PLO that the indefatigable Israeli politician, Shimon Peres, now serving as foreign minister to Yitzhak Rabin as premier, now turned.

King Hussein's reaction to the Oslo deal between Israel and the PLO was one of surprise, outrage and resentment. Such emotions were not difficult to understand. Hussein had not known about the track two initiative underway through the good offices of the Norwegians, a bilateral device that was being utilised while he was insisting on the need for multilateral Arab coordination. He was angry because it momentarily appeared as if the PLO had stolen a march on Jordan, leaving Amman to negotiate its peace with Israel from a disadvantageous position. It seems probable that there was a fair bit of envy involved as well. After so many years of being courted by world leaders, it looked as if Hussein would have to come to terms with the fact that the state he presided over was small, weak and once again of only marginal significance.

It did not, however, require much reflection for King Hussein to conclude that Oslo could be turned to his own advantage. Most importantly, Arafat's secret and unilateral diplomacy had freed Jordan from any obligation to coordinate with the PLO or tie its peacemaking to the fortunes of the Palestinians. It had also prompted the king to move ahead with Jordan's bilateral peace diplomacy for fear of getting left behind. In this urge to move quickly the king's calculations were also affected by his own health and the impact that this had had on his relations with the Jordanian people. In 1992, after a number of incidents of minor ill-health, it was announced that the king had undergone a serious operation in the US for cancer of the left ureter. When the king returned to Jordan following the public revelations, he was greeted by a massive and spontaneous demonstration of support and affection, hundreds of thousands strong. This experience convinced the 57-year-old king of two things. First, that he had less time than he might otherwise have expected to deliver a stable peace with Israel, and hence, as he imagined, to secure Jordanian stability and survival in perpetuity. Second, that he enjoyed the popularity and confidence of his people, thereby giving considerable leeway for leadership in moving as swiftly as possible in such a direction. Oslo therefore gave the king the opportunity to seize the moment.

Just 22 hours after the signing of the Israeli–Palestinian Declaration of Principles, on 13 September 1993, Israel and Jordan signed an agenda for negotiation,[30] an accord that had long been concluded but which the Jordanians were hitherto reluctant publicly to endorse.[31] In keeping with such urgency, confidence-building measures were quickly put in place. These included: the establishment of a US–Israeli–Jordanian Trilateral Economic Committee to promote regional economic and developmental coopera-tion; King Hussein's public admission that he had met with every Israeli prime minister with the exception of Menachem Begin; and a meeting between Peres and Crown Prince Hasan, the highest-level public meeting between the two countries. If Jordan had soon caught up with the PLO as far as peacemaking with Israel was concerned, the king remained cautious about forging further ahead. It took the Israelis until the following spring to accept the residual caution on the king's side. When finally they did, the Jordanian track was placed on ice, in favour of Israel's other peace options, an attempt to reheat the Syrian track and then a new initiative with the Palestinians.

King Hussein's coyness persisted until May when he finally judged the timeliness of a conclusion to bilateral peacemaking. At a meeting with Pres-ident Asad in Damascus, the king appeared to have covered his political back. A flurry of high-level meetings between Israeli and Jordanian leaders then followed, leading to a series of symbolic breakthroughs in June and July, of which the most important was the ending of the state of hostili-ties between the two countries, a formal hangover from 1967. A summit between Hussein and Rabin, who had by now established a considerable rapport, led to the Washington Declaration, in which Israel, playing politics with the Jordanian–PLO relationship and conscious of the king's lingering Hashemite ambitions, acknowledged a role for the monarch in the adminis-tration of the Islamic sites in Jerusalem. The king was further enticed down the road of peacemaking by the economic inducements of $950 million worth of debt forgiveness by the US and new military aid to modernise the Jordanian armed forces. The occasion also allowed the king finally to bury the hatchet with a Congress that had inevitably been more sceptical about rapprochement with Jordan than the administration following the Iraq–Kuwait crisis.

With negotiations stalling over such issues as border demarcation and water resources, the final conclusion of a formal peace seemed uncertain. Uncertain that is until Rabin's surprise visit to Amman in early October, and the achievement of a compromise breakthrough as a result of direct dealing between the two chain-smoking leaders. With Israel agreeing to return 116 square miles of desert to Jordanian sovereignty, in return for 'private ownership rights' by neighbouring kibbutzim, the way was open to the signing of a formal peace treaty on 26 October on the mutual border in the Wadi Araba. Most importantly, Israel agreed to recognise Jordan's 'sovereignty, territorial integrity and political independence' (Art. 2, 1), accepted that 'involuntary movements of persons in such a way as to adversely prejudice the security' of Jordan 'should not be permitted' (Art. 2, 6), and to 'refrain from the use of force or weapons, conventional, non-conventional or of any other kind' (Art. 4, 3a). In finally neutralising the potential threat from Israel, both direct and demographic, Hussein had completed the goal that he had set himself after the 1967 war. One cannot but concur with the king, who described the agreement as his 'crowning achievement'.

DEMOCRATISATION ON THE BACKBURNER

The speedy movement in the direction of peacemaking with Israel was always going to be controversial at home, both among Palestinian nationalists and those ideologically ill-disposed towards peace with Israel.[32] During the main period of peacemaking, between September 1993 and October 1994, events such as Israel's expulsion of Palestinian activists to south Lebanon and the massacre of some 28 Palestinians by an Israeli settler in Hebron inevitably made the pursuit of such a process difficult to sustain. As the Israeli–Jordanian peace track became increasingly successful, so the temptation to curtail the kingdom's newly acquired liberal freedoms grew. However, the nature of the regime's threat perceptions and the limited nature of institutional reform indicated that even before September 1993 the potential for change was still limited.

As early as 1991, Jordan had to cope with an increasing terrorist threat, emanating from the end of the war against the Soviet occupation of Afghanistan. Jordanian 'Afghans', some 1,000 of whom had fought alongside the *mujahideen*, had begun to return to the country, and had gravitated towards extremist Islamist politics. In July, the Jordanian authorities arrested around 100 activists linked to the so-called Prophet Muhammad's Army, purported to be the military wing of the Muslim Brotherhood, a charge the organisation rejected. There would be other examples of state action against terror threats from the Islamist right through the decade.[33] Though most of these threats seem to have been real enough, the authorities were not above their abuse. The arrest, charge, conviction and immediate royal pardon of two MPs, one of whom, Laith Shbailat, had been a tireless campaigner against corruption,[34] simply drew attention to the continuing lack of accountability in the kingdom.

The detentions of those connected with the Prophet Muhammad's Army elicited a controversy in the kingdom about the residual methods used by the GID. The recently established Public Freedoms Committee of the National Assembly, dominated by opposition MPs, whose membership also included Shbailat, accused the intelligence service of continuing to use torture, which had been routine before 1989. While the GID denied that this was still part of its *modus operandi*, bad blood had come to typify the relationship between the Islamist-dominated opposition and the core of the national security state. A state security court was established to take on some of the functions hitherto dealt with by the now defunct martial law courts, but an automatic right of appeal was now built into its operation.

Growing concern about the size and influence of the Islamist mainstream, exacerbated by the emergence of a violent fringe, prompted the authorities to try to take preventive action sooner rather than later. Even in 1992, it was clear that the government was considering a revision of the electoral law. When it came, it did so in the form of a simple amendment to the existing law, promulgated by King Hussein on 4 August after the assembly had been dissolved in the run-up to the November 1993 general election. The amendment changed the electoral system from one where each voter would cast the number of votes corresponding to the deputies to be returned from the country's multi-member constituencies to a situation where each voter would cast only a single vote. The aim of what the government came to call a 'one man, one vote' system was to remove the ability of individuals to vote for tribal *and* ideological candidates, based on the assumption that in the event of a choice the system would favour the former. In a further reflection of his dwindling enthusiasm for democratic activity, King Hussein appointed his chief negotiator with Israel, Abdul Salam al-Majali, as prime minister with responsibility for overseeing the poll.

The amendment to the electoral law had its desired effect. In Jordan's first multi-party election since 1956, the IAF suffered a serious reversal of fortunes, with 16 of its number successfully elected out of the 36 candidates fielded. Among its casualties was Dr Abdul Latif Arabiyat, its former spokesman, and the speaker of the national assembly for most of the previous term. With only five independent Islamists also returned, the Islamist trend in the lower house was reduced from 34 to 21. Though the IAF remained the largest party in the national assembly by some distance, its nearest rivals winning five and four seats, the considerable political momentum gained in 1989 had been dissipated.[35] Though generally disappointed by the outcome, the IAF would not have been too dismayed to remain in opposition. With the election coming just two months after the conclusion of the Israeli–Jordanian agenda for peace, a much better showing for the Islamists would have risked a confrontation over the peace process with the Jordanian establishment, and there was wariness of such a development in view of recent bloody events in Algeria.[36]

In spite of their reversal of fortunes in November 1993, the IAF and its fellow travellers still presented a potent challenge within the main political arenas in Jordan. As if to underscore this point, the Islamists won control of two professional associations in early 1994, the Engineers Association and the Agricultural Engineers Association, the former in particular being a high-profile organisation. Increasingly, the king faced such developments with defiance, for example retaining the irascible Majali as prime minister, whereas convention would have expected a different premier to the one who had overseen elections. With Majali retaining the foreign affairs and defence portfolios he had held before, it was clear that a successful outcome to the peace process remained at the top of the royal agenda. Such issues also had an impact on external relations, with 33 Iranian diplomats leaving Amman in March following growing Jordanian concerns at the embassy's size and its contacts with local Islamists.

With the peace process, and more specifically the expected conclusion of a peace treaty with Israel, increasingly dominating the political agenda in late spring 1994, the opposition coalesced to register its opposition to such a direction. In May, eight Islamist and leftist political parties, including the IAF, the Communists and the Ba'thists, formed the 'Popular Arab and Jordanian Committee for Resisting Submission and Normalisation'. The list of anti-normalisers would grow, to include even a former prime minister of the stature of Ahmad Obeidat. With the opposition still cautious and the king hell-bent on having his peace treaty with Israel, such developments had little immediate impact. When the peace agreement was signed, there were protests in Amman, but they were muted. A demonstration by 5,000 opponents, predominantly Islamists, was followed by an official ban on public meetings. It seemed as if the majority of the people of Jordan were willing to wait and see what the treaty would bring. For the opposition, this marked the beginning of a process rather than the end. Jordan's ideological opposition would fight the normalisation process that followed the formal peace tooth and nail.

UPHILL STRUGGLE FOR NORMALISATION

The Israeli–Jordanian peace treaty was concluded at a time of expectation in the region. Peace negotiations were taking place between Israel and the PLO and Israel and Syria. Egypt, eager to be vindicated for its stance in the late 1970s, was encouraging the process. Shimon Peres had unveiled his vision of a 'new Middle East', with mutually beneficial cooperation and integration replacing the confrontation and conflict of the previous five decades. Jordan's business and governmental elites were similarly excited about such a prospect as it offered a route to salvation for the kingdom's economic problems. Regional peace would clear away the barriers to foreign direct investment. Jordan could emerge as the regional conduit that its cheap but educated workforce, relatively tolerant atmosphere and important geographical location would seem to justify.

Before the turn of the century such a view had already been exposed as wishful thinking. The Syrian track had failed over arguments about what constituted all of the Golan Heights. The Israeli–Palestinian track had never quite recovered from the assassination of prime minister Rabin in November 1995, becoming, at least until 2000, immersed in endless wrangling. Egypt, concerned at being marginalised by Peres' narrow focus on Israeli–Palestinian–Jordanian integration, became more of a hindrance than a help. Increasingly, King Hussein's peace with Israel took on the appearance of an isolated and risky gamble rather than the crest of a wave. Crucially, the expected economic resurgence, whether as a result of a Camp David-style US aid programme,[37] or a more forthcoming global private sector, failed to materialise. Instead, with the Palestinian returnees from Kuwait by now having spent their capital, the kingdom seemed to be sinking into recession.

If the popular view of the peace treaty with Israel evolved from quiet expectation or scepticism, depending on the audience, into widespread disillusionment and even hostility, it was not for the want of effort on the part of the palace. King Hussein, closely supported by his brother, Crown Prince

Hasan, was a tireless campaigner for the deepening of the relationship. The treaty was quickly ratified by the new Jordanian parliament, an ambassador was appointed and, with foresight, the palace cultivated the Israeli opposition leader Binyamin Netanyahu, who visited Amman 17 months before he won the Israeli general election in May 1996.[38] By the end of 1995, the Jordanian parliament had voted to remove three specifically anti-Israeli laws from the statute book. These laws, dating back as far as the 1950s, had banned Jordanians from having contacts or doing business with Israelis. A law banning land sales to Israelis was also rescinded, but then, in recognition of the controversial nature of the issue, readopted in a more acceptable way, with land sales to 'non-Jordanians' being proscribed other than with cabinet approval. In January 1996, the king paid a state visit to Israel.

Neither was Jordan shy in exploring ways in which the peace with Israel could be turned into economically advantageous outcomes. In April 1994, the two states signed a tourism agreement, to integrate their marketing of the Holy Land abroad. Israeli tourists flocked to Jordan's ancient sites, notably the deserted Nabatean city of Petra in the south. Even here, however, increased interaction proved far from happy. Businessmen in the Jordanian tourist sector complained that visiting Israelis came only on very short visits, spent little money, and conducted themselves in a rude and arrogant way. A preferential trade agreement between the two countries was concluded just before the first anniversary of the peace treaty.

In October 1995, Amman hosted a regional economic conference, the second of four that proved to be a vain attempt to stimulate the regional economy. The two states did achieve some limited activity in the area of joint-venture investment, especially after an agreement with the US on the establishment of Qualifying Industrial Zones (QIZ).[39] With Israeli companies interested in outsourcing manufacturing in the textile sector in particular, where Jordanian land and labour were proximate but cheaper, Irbid became a centre of such activity.[40] By 2000, a number of joint-venture companies had been established, employing around 6,000 people, and with good potential for expansion.

As the palace tried to push ahead with the normalisation of relations with Israel, a perceptional gap started to appear between the elite and the street. For example, when King Hussein went to Jerusalem to deliver one of the funeral orations for his slain peace partner, the anti-normalisers drew attention to the involvement of Rabin in violent operations against Arab targets. When Hussein condemned suicide-bomb attacks and attended an anti-terrorism summit at Sharm al-Sheikh, a fig leaf to help with the re-election of Shimon Peres, the opposition attacked Israel's selective definition of terror. When a Jordanian soldier, Ahmad Dakamsah went berserk in March 1997 on the border killing seven Israeli schoolgirls,[41] and the king visited each of the bereaved families individually, many Jordanians complained that he had rarely responded the same way upon the death of Arabs.

As the king became increasingly exasperated with the process of normalisation he began to lose patience with the opposition, and the remaining liberal freedoms provided by the system.[42] The king precipitated action towards the country's press, and its tabloid weeklies in particular. An amendment to the Press and Publications Law, furnishing the state with punitive measures, was passed in May 1997.[43] Such was the deterioration in relations that much of the Jordanian opposition decided to boycott the November 1997 parliamentary elections, thereby robbing them of much of their legitimacy.

Meanwhile, King Hussein himself was getting frustrated by the disappointing performance of successive Israeli governments towards the issue of peace. Peres, whom since the London Agreement of 1987 Hussein had never really trusted, tried shamefully and unsuccessfully to reinvent himself as a hard man just prior to the 1996 election, with a military adventure in southern Lebanon. Netanyahu, of whom Hussein unusually among Arab leaders had some hopes immediately after his election, quickly showed himself to be shallow and uninterested in the peace process. The failure of a top Netanyahu aide to mention that the Israeli government intended to open a controversial tunnel under the Muslim holy places in Jerusalem during a visit to Amman the day before increased the king's frustrations. The king's response was to put himself forward as a peace process troubleshooter, making good use of the trust that existed between the monarch and the Israeli people and his improving ties with the PLO. His intervention in January 1997 in support of the US mediator helped to resolve the stalled deal on Israel's redeployment in Hebron. He famously turned up at the Israeli-Palestinian negotiations in the US in October 1998, though seriously ill, which resulted in the Wye River Accords. By the end, the king was as popular in Israel as he was in Jordan, if not more so.

If the palace had resolutely tried its best to make the peace with Israel work, even it was shaken by the events of late September 1997. Looking for a short-term boost to his poll standings just before a public holiday, Prime minister Netanyahu sent a Mossad hit squad posing as Canadian tourists to Amman with the task of assassinating a leading figure in the political wing of the Palestinian Islamist grouping, Hamas, Khalid Mish'al. The whole affair rapidly turned from Ian Fleming to farce, as the agents succeeded in spraying poison in Mish'al's ear, but were apprehended by his bodyguards. King Hussein acted quickly, demanding that Israel supply the antidote, saving Mish'al, and insisting that the spiritual leader of Hamas in Gaza, Shaikh Ahmad Yassin, who was in Israeli custody, be released in return for the agents, a deal with which an embarrassed Israel complied. Through his quick thinking, the king had turned a potentially disastrous position for Jordan into a diplomatic success that helped re-establish his credibility with the opposition. After such a cavalier attitude towards peace with Jordan, relations between the palace and the Netanyahu government were conducted through the altogether more reliable conduit of Ariel Sharon, ironically a strong proponent of the 'Jordan is Palestine' thesis in the late 1980s, but since reconstructed.

A MESSY SUCCESSION

In July 1998, King Hussein returned to the US suffering from lymphatic cancer, treatment for which would see him remain out of the country for the next six months. During his absence his youngest brother,[44] Prince Hasan, who had been crown prince since 1965, acted as regent. As the gravity of Hussein's illness became clear – he nearly died under the knife in the autumn – it seemed as though the perfect succession was taking place, with Hasan as apprentice king. However, this was not how the king viewed it. By December there were clear signs that he wanted to change the succession. Upon his brief rally at the end, Hussein returned to Amman, sending a rambling public letter to Hasan disinheriting him. Instead, Hussein named his eldest son, Prince Abdullah, as the new crown prince. Once the cancer finally got him on 7 February 1999, the crown prince duly succeeded as King Abdullah II, with his younger half-brother, Prince Hamzeh, as the new heir apparent.

With 12 years between them, Hussein and Hasan had never been close. Temperamentally, they were very different: while Hussein was the four times married, dare-devil, bon viveur, Hasan was the quiet, stable, studious family man. Hussein had initially made Abdullah, his son by his second and British wife, Toni Gardiner, crown prince upon his birth in 1962, in accordance with the 1952 constitution. In view of the unstable times in the 1960s, the 'dark atmosphere', as Hussein would later refer to it, the king had changed the order of succession when Hasan reached the age of 18, Article 28 of the constitution being amended to allow the king's brother to succeed.[45]

Like Britain's Prince Charles, for Hasan the role of crown prince was a frustrating one. On occasion, such as during the approaching civil war

Fig. 12. King Hussein embraces Prince Abdullah the day after having restored him as
crown prince, Amman, 26 January 1999 (Popperfoto AMM04)

with the PLO, he was brought into the centre of decision-making by his
eldest brother. Most of the time, however, he was kept to the margins. It
did not help that Hasan was ill at ease in the crucial contexts of power in
Jordan, especially in army uniform or in attending set-piece tribal occasions.
Instead, Hasan played to his strengths. Domestically, he carved out a role

for himself as a thinker, establishing a clutch of innovative institutions from the Royal Scientific Society to the Arab Thought Forum. He developed an interest in the economy, overseeing the launch of Jordan's 1986–90 five-year plan, and patronising a range of businessmen's activities. He also emerged as a sponsor of the education sector. Internationally, Hasan became one of the youngest members of the club of the great and the good, establishing personal relations with a number of UN bodies, and being a tireless participant in inter-faith dialogue. When they worked together, such as over peace negotiations with Israel, Hasan and Hussein were the perfect foils for one another: Hasan the tireless man with an eye for detail and Hussein the gregarious big-picture man. In general, though, King Hussein was happy to see Hasan busying himself in marginal ways, as he did not want Hasan to build a solid power base for himself within Jordan.

In spite of his political marginalisation at home and a growing reputation for being dour and verbose, Hasan's position as heir seemed unassailable until the consequences of Hussein's rather messy private life began to become manifest. Having divorced his first and second wives, Hussein married a Palestinian, Alia Touqan, a match seemingly made in heaven, at a time when the king was manoeuvring vigorously in order to re-establish his authority over the West Bank. After Queen Alia's death in a helicopter crash in 1978, Hussein married for a fourth time, to a 26-year-old Arab-American, Lisa Halaby, who took the name Noor. As part of the succession settlement at the time of his final marriage, Hussein instructed Hasan in writing that he in turn should be succeeded by Prince Ali, the single son of his union with Alia.

The revelation of the king's cancer in 1992 once again drew attention to the issue of succession. By this time, Prince Ali, and his sister Princess Haya, adrift in the unforgiving atmosphere of the royal court, were regarded as going off the rails; Prince Abdullah and his younger brother Faisal were carving out promising careers in the military, the army and air force respectively; the sons of Prince Muhammad, notably Prince Talal, had come of age and was regarded seriously; Hussein now had four children by Noor, including two boys, the eldest of whom was Prince Hamzeh; while Hasan and his Pakistani-born wife,[46] Sarvath, also had four children, including one son, Prince Rashid. Ominously, at best King Hussein's attitude towards a Hasan succession appeared to be lukewarm.[47]

Yet, with the looming proximity of the issue after 1992, King Hussein seemed to answer the succession question in favour of Hasan. Significantly, Hussein brought Hasan into the centre of policymaking during the negotiation of the peace treaty with Israel. In April 1995, King Hussein referred to Hasan as 'my right arm', following one of his regular cancer check-ups. In the mid-1990s, the two men seemed closer than they had ever been. It was in this context that the king pronounced anew on the issue of the succession. While Crown Prince Hasan would succeed him, the decision on the subsequent succession would be for Hasan, with 'a great role' for a family council. Prince Ali was now out, and the future decidedly more open.

Yet, just as Hasan's fortunes seemed more secure, the king's equivocation re-emerged. King Hussein froze Hasan out of his attempts to calm the south following the August 1996 riots, and refused to sack his prime minister, Abdul Karim al-Kabariti, when his working relationship with Hasan broke down. Then came the first real sign that a Hasan succession might be in trouble, the eighteenth birthday of Prince Hamzeh in September 1997. During very public celebrations, the king sent an open letter to Hamzeh stating that he felt the prince was destined for 'great achievements', and pointing out that he himself had been 18 years of age when he had acceded to the throne. This less than subtle attempt to advance the fortunes of his favourite son seemed both to reveal Hussein's true wishes, and the growing influence behind the scenes of Queen Noor, Hamzeh's mother, especially with the recurrence of illness. Queen Noor would hardly leave the king's side during his coming hospitalisation. With long-standing tensions between Noor and Sarvath now exacerbated by the endgame of the succession, palace politics was increasingly to take on a Shakespearean atmosphere over the months ahead.

The first that Amman knew of Hussein's manoeuvre to change the succession came in January 1999, a month of high drama for the kingdom. The king returned home on the nineteenth of the month, looking awful, but supposedly in improving health. As it became clear that his rally was simply a prelude to relapse, King Hussein had to move quickly. On Monday 25 January, he declared that the succession would return to Prince Abdullah, in compliance with the original principle of primogeniture in the constitution. The one condition for such a change was that Prince Hamzeh become the new heir apparent upon Abdullah's succession; it seemed that Abdullah was the compromise candidate for a monarch who feared that rushing the succession to his favourite would be a step too far.[48] In order to justify his actions, and to ward off factionalism, he sent a long and rambling letter to Prince Hasan explaining his actions on the same day.[49]

With the king's sentiments now out in public, the hangers-on quickly distanced themselves from Hasan. Apart from some of his old technocratic colleagues he was left quite alone, and was certainly ill-placed to make a stand. Wisely, he chose a demeanour of quiet dignity as a mask for his deep sense of loss. With many foreign observers perennially doubting that Hasan had what it took to be a successful king, only the Israelis, with whom Hasan had struck up a close relationship since 1994, seemed to mourn his political demise. For the now-elevated Crown Prince Abdullah, the change in fortunes was breathtaking. Up to this point his best hopes had been to emulate Sharif Zaid bin Shaker, as the country's most senior soldier under a Hasan succession.

CHAPTER 9

Abdullah's First Steps

The death of King Hussein was always going to be a difficult time for Jordan and the Jordanians. In the later stages of his career commentators had thought aloud about the Franz Josef effect: a monarch who had reigned for so long that his passing was unimaginable and any replacement, by implication, implausible. In the event the analogy proved false. As with the succession in Syria little more than a year later, the leader has been replaced, the succession has stuck and life has continued more or less as before. There was undoubted shock and sadness at King Hussein's death, but he has certainly not proved to be irreplaceable.

There are three broad reasons why the succession has taken place so smoothly. First, the succession of King Abdullah II was widely viewed as being legitimate. It was legitimate because, in spite of the rather messy way in which the build-up to the succession had been handled, it was clearly perceived to be the will of the dying king. Though Hasan's supporters put it about that Hussein's faculties were already impaired when he changed his mind about the succession, making him susceptible to the manipulation of others, most Jordanians could understand that a father would want his own son, rather than his brother, to succeed. Equally importantly, the succession was legitimised by the original constitutional provision, which favoured primogeniture.

Second, for the practical purposes of the transfer of authority, the main power centres in the kingdom – especially those identified with the national security state – remained united. Of crucial importance here were the army and the intelligence service. The new King Abdullah's background in the army, where he had been the head of the special forces and held a senior rank, meant that the loyalty of the military was easier to secure. Abdullah was a real soldier, someone who instinctively led from the front and enjoyed jumping out of aeroplanes; his was not a manufactured soldiery. The loyalty of the *mukhabarat* was secure under the leadership of Samih Batikhi, who had lobbied hard with Hussein during his illness for Hasan's exclusion.[1] Batikhi's Syrian origin underlines the residual importance of the external elite, which had been so pivotal during the double succession of the early 1950s. Having worked hard to bring it about, Batikhi was a crucial figure during the first months of Abdullah's reign in stabilising the political transition of power.

At a social forces level, many of the broader constituencies within Jordanian society tended to favour the newly designated succession. For Transjordanian insiders in the bureaucracy and the coercive state, and those who depended on them for patronage, it was important to ensure a conti-nuity that would maintain the existing power structure. The wealthy and the well-to-do, embracing a range of groups from the merchants to the pro-fessional middle classes, needed the preservation of stability, thereby pro-tecting property, as well as the commercial environment in which economic transactions could continue to take place. For Palestinian nationalists, the dominant mood was one of cynical disinterest; this was not perceived to be their political succession. For those who potentially might have opposed the succession, from radicals on the Islamist right through to the more disaffected groups such as parts of the urban unemployed and the rural poor, there was no breakdown, however fleeting, that might have provided the opportunity to make trouble.

The smoothness of the process was also helped along by the nature of King Abdullah himself. Though contemporary foreign reportage tended to play up the inexperience of the new monarch, it was easy to forget that, at 37, he was actually at a reasonably good age to take over, and 20 years his father's senior at a similar stage. He may not have served an apprenticeship in statecraft, but he was well known to the next generation of Arab royals, especially in the Gulf, and had developed close relations with the Americans. Like his father, he looked and felt at home in an army uniform, a prince who was prepared to get his hands dirty. For many, with his army background, his unbookish nature and an earlier reputation as something of a playboy, he was recognisable as 'a chip off the old block'.[2] For those of a liberal disposition or Palestinian in origin, who worried that his army background might have made him into a narrow, intolerant Transjordanian nationalist, he had by marriage acquired a balanced political ticket. His consort, soon to become Queen Rania, was a middle-class Palestinian who had grown up in Kuwait, her family sharing the trauma of dislocation caused by the Iraqi invasion of 1990.

Having secured the succession, Abdullah started well as king. He quickly shored up his position by making changes in the upper echelons of the army, and sidelined both Prince Hasan and Queen Noor. The king and the new queen threw themselves into their work with tremendous energy, with Abdullah, in spite of his faltering Arabic, making frequent public appearances around the country to demonstrate that he was monarch for real. Abdullah showed himself to be especially determined in the area of foreign affairs, where he seemed intent upon improving relations with all. Though an 'all things to all men' foreign policy might have been untenable in the long run, a number of successful foreign visits, notably to the Gulf and the US, helped to alleviate outside pressures during the period of settling in. Mindful of the history of Syrian interference in Jordan, Abdullah made a special effort to establish warm personal relations with the Syrian successor-in-waiting, Bashar al-Asad. After the multiple difficulties in regional relations during his father's last decade, Abdullah had adroitly used his accession to begin a set of relationships anew.

Nowhere was King Abdullah's management of foreign relations more careful than in relation to Israel. Abdullah came to the throne knowing full well that Jordan had a 'peace of the palace, not of the people'. He therefore moved to dampen down the bilateral relationship in a way that King Hussein was most unwilling to do. Indeed, Abdullah paid his first public visit to Israel only some 14 months after his accession, in spite of the impatience of the political establishment to the west. Of course, this adjustment towards a more restrained public diplomacy made little difference either to the continuation of the bilateral peace treaty, to which the Jordanian establishment and much of the Transjordanian nationalist current were fully committed, or to the substance of the subterranean relationship, namely security cooperation. Here, the continuing close and mutually beneficial cooperation, towards Palestinian and Islamist radicalism alike, remains paramount for both parties.

Abdullah's success was more mixed in relation to the Palestinians. Careful attempts to play down continued claims over Jerusalem helped soften relations with the Palestinian Authority (PA). They also suggested that Abdullah might be a more pragmatic leader than his father, whose Hashemite hang-ups had given an intensity to policy towards the West Bank in general and Jerusalem in particular. Less successful was Abdullah's handling of the Hamas crisis in the kingdom, commencing in August 1999. Abdullah's expulsion of three members of the Hamas political leadership was designed as a foreign policy manoeuvre to win plaudits with the Americans, Israelis and the PA alike, which it did. However, it failed to take into account the domestic implications, especially in terms of Palestinian sensitivities, for which Hamas' resistance against Israel is viewed as heroic.

It suggested that the new king was more sure-footed in foreign affairs than in domestic politics.

As far as the peace process is concerned, Jordanian anxiety was discernible every which way, underlining that the ambiguities of the Hussein era had not disappeared with his demise. Thus, when a final peace between Israel and the PA looked feasible in 2000, Jordanians fretted at becoming ever more marginal and losing their external subsidy. When the second *intifada* or uprising broke out in September 2000, they fretted anew at the rising tide of regional instability. As Yasser Arafat and Ehud Barak came close but not quite close enough to brokering a final agreement at Taba in January 2001, Jordanians felt relieved at having divested themselves of responsibility for the peace process, even as they worried that they no longer had a negotiating role in issues of direct material interest, notably the fate of the Palestinian refugees.

On the domestic scene, Abdullah and Rania established an early reputation for compassion, through his unannounced visits to inspect conditions in state hospitals, and his secret forays into Amman at night in order to take the public mood; and her patronage of a range of liberal causes against ills such as domestic violence and honour crimes. This image of the caring royals was consolidated through such institutions as the Jordanian Hashemite Charity Organisation, which was vigorous in raising humanitarian funds for Palestinians under occupation, and through the king's leadership in the establishment of the Plan for Socio-Economic Transformation (PSET) at home. The PSET initiative aims to channel extra income from privatisations and foreign aid into new spending on education, health and job creation for the poor. This earnestness, though important in explaining the continuing popularity of Jordan's glamorous couple, has been somewhat tarnished by a fondness for appearing in the pages of *Hello* magazine and other glossies.

If most observers were prepared to give him the benefit of the doubt during his early months, there was one area of state in which King Abdullah clearly struggled. This was in the management of the country's political elite, a class who are in the main conceited, shallow and self-serving. This was where Abdullah's inexperience most showed through, and where his army background proved to be poor preparation for kingship. It also provided echoes of the early Hussein years. The root of Abdullah's difficulties seemed to lie in deciding exactly what he wanted in terms of government and advice. His first change of government in March 1999 resulted in the installation of a conservative administration under the new prime minister,

Abdul Rauf al-Rawabdah, nicknamed 'the bulldozer', a strange choice given
Abdullah's private protestations of liberal values. Rawabdah was expected
to coexist with the newly installed Chief of the Royal Court, the impatient
liberal, Abdul Karim al-Kabariti. This was either incoherent confusion or
a misguided attempt to replicate his 'all things to all men' foreign policy at
home. If it was the latter, it was naïve. Differing in views and temperament,
the relationship between the two men soon degenerated into a running exchange of petulant jibes, over such issues as women's rights, press freedoms
and economic liberalisation. These unseemly spats only came to an end
with the resignation of Kabariti. With concerns mounting that Abdullah
had made a serious error of judgement, Rawabdah went further and implemented a conservative agenda. His close association with a narrowly
East Bank approach to politics, together with persistent accusations of corruption, increased the awkwardness of this period. It was with a frustrated
sense of starting anew that Abdullah replaced Rawabdah after the minimum
decent period of 15 months in the post.

King Abdullah's second cabinet was more recognisably his own. His
new premier, Ali Abu Ragheb, with his private sector background and
neo-liberal inclinations, is a man better known to the king and someone
who shares his general outlook. Abu Ragheb was chosen because he enjoyed
good relations with the national assembly, was prepared to act as a motor
of liberal economic reform and favoured more equitable relations with the
kingdom's Palestinians. However, it is further evidence of King Abdullah's
lack of a sure touch that he has clung onto Abu Ragheb as premier for more
than three years, even when the felicitous conditions that accompanied his
appointment have long since passed.

Before the intentions of the new government could be put to the test,
the second Palestinian *intifada* broke out in the Palestinian territories. Just
three months into its term, the government was obliged to focus more on
managing the new realities rather than implementing a reformist agenda.
The new *intifada* gave a fillip to the anti-normalisation movement, and a
new organisation, the National Coalition for the Support of the *Intifada*,
supported by 16 parties and 14 professional associations, rose to prominence.
Mass demonstrations and other less ruly protests had to be firmly contained.
Though the intelligence agencies, the army and the police were comfortably
able to deal with such protests, the subtle balances on the inside of power
shifted away from a more liberal approach to governance.

Evidence of the emergence of a less liberal form of politics, in spite of
the nominal wishes of both king and premier, has become increasingly
clear as the *intifada* has dragged on. This trend in the direction of a more

authoritarian approach was boosted by the events of 11 September in 2001, as the king eagerly affirmed his relations with the US by demonstrating a staunch commitment to the 'war against terror'. Growing domestic unease following the election of Ariel Sharon as Israeli prime minister in February 2001 and the looming, slow-motion showdown between the US and Iraq also deepened these illiberalising tendencies, as the political centre has sought to maintain its hold. Sporadic violence against American and Israeli targets in the country has been used to justify such policies. Consequently, more than 120 emergency laws have been implemented since the start of the uprising in September 2000, further restricting press freedom and freedom of speech, and implementing a more restrictive penal code. Parliamentary elections, which were due in November 2001, have been repeatedly postponed.

To date, King Abdullah has offered two things to try to balance this uncompromising, security-first approach to policy realities: image-building and economic improvement. The former has crystallised in a political vision that has been called 'Jordan-first'. In spite of its Madison Avenue feel, the initiative represents something much older; it is the latest in a number of attempts to articulate a political community to correspond with the state in Jordan, a search that has been taking place since 1948. Abdullah's Jordan-first concept is an attempt to override all of the disparate divisions that cross-cut the kingdom and to offer an over-arching basis upon which people should cleave together. The slogan exemplifies loyalty to Jordan over loyalty to other causes, whether ethnic, religious, ideological or tribal: in short, to foster unity in diversity. The reactions of a sceptical and dissatisfied population indicate that the search for a common basis on which to forge a new idea of shared political community will have to continue for some time to come. It is difficult to imagine such deep divisions within Jordanian society being alleviated, at least as long as occupation and violent conflict characterise the experiences of life in the Palestinian areas across the Jordan River. Meanwhile, conflict and uncertainty elsewhere on Jordan's borders, notably Iraq, will hardly allow for a more settled and stable politics to emerge within the kingdom in the near term.

From the outset, King Abdullah has stated time and again that the economy is to be his top priority, in recognition of the hardships experienced in the kingdom over the previous decade. In so doing he is displaying an interest and concern that easily outstrip those of his father. He has made a particular point of trying to encourage a younger generation of small businessmen, especially in the knowledge economy. In keeping with the relaxed and unpompous demeanour of his persona as a modern royal, King

Abdullah has even made a tourism promotional film for the Discovery Channel.

In spite of such hard work, however, Abdullah has learnt the lesson of his father and his great-grandfather before him that the swiftest and most effective way of aiding an ailing economy in Jordan is to seek strategic rents from abroad. Consequently, by 2003, the US had re-emerged as Jordan's main economic backer in an experience resonant of the 1950s and the Eisenhower Doctrine. US aid to Jordan had been rising in the late 1990s in any case. Amman's growing usefulness to Washington increased as it provided the US with intelligence on al-Qaeda post-9/11. It further grew with the deployment of Jordanian medical and mine-clearance teams to Afghanistan by way of symbolic support for the new US-backed, post-Taleban regime.

The biggest test for Jordan and King Abdullah has, however, come with the US-led war against Iraq. With the US organising a further debt-rescheduling under the Paris Club in the summer of 2002 and virtually doubling aid to Jordan between fiscal years 2002 and 2003, it was always clear on which side the Jordanian bread was buttered. Jordan is now the fourth-largest recipient of US aid worldwide, after Israel, Egypt and Colombia. Though formally neutral in the war against Iraq, Jordanian low-key, 'deniable', yet extremely useful help to the American military in the eastern desert has cemented the client relationship anew. Eight decades after its founding, Jordan's position now is eerily reminiscent of its position in the early years of its existence: a favoured dependency of the regional superpower of the day.

Notes

I ON THE EDGE OF EMPIRE

1 For a detailed illustration of the importance of the leading shaikhs, such as Kulaib al-Shraidah, see Richard T. Antoun, *Arab Village: A Social Structural Study of a Transjordanian Peasant Community* (Indiana UP, Bloomington, 1972).

2 Raouf Abujaber, *Pioneers Over Jordan* (Tauris, London, 1989), p. 46.

3 Suleiman Mousa and Munib al-Madi begin their formidable history of Jordan in the twentieth century by reflecting on the Ottoman age. Though now somewhat dated, it remains the definitive work in Arabic on Jordanian history. See *Tarikh al-urdun fi al-qarn al-'ashrin, 1900–1959* (Maktabat al-Muhtasab, Amman, 1988).

4 For background to the *Tanzimat* reforms, see Justin McCarthy, *The Ottoman Turks* (Longman, London, 1997), and William L. Cleveland, *A History of the Modern Middle East* (Westview, Boulder, 1994).

5 For a succinct commentary on the undulating fortunes of Ottoman state authority in the territory of what is now Jordan, see Eugene L. Rogan, 'Bringing the State Back: The Limits of Ottoman Rule in Jordan, 1840–1910', in Eugene L. Rogan and Tariq Tell (eds.), *Village, Steppe and State: The Social Origins of Modern Jordan* (British Academic Press, London, 1994).

6 *Khuwa*, a tax with what Suleiman Mousa has called a sugar coating (see his 'Jordan: Towards the End of the Ottoman Empire 1841–1918', in Dr Adnan Hadidi (ed.), *Studies in the History and Archaeology of Jordan* (Department of Antiquities, Amman, 1982), p. 386, literally means 'brotherly' tax, and was extracted in the form of grain, cattle or money by the bedouin in return for protection.

7 Eugene L. Rogan, *Frontiers of the State in the Late Ottoman Empire* (CUP, Cambridge, 1999), p. 55.

8 Rogan, 'Bringing the State Back', p. 45.

9 Claude R. Conder, *Heth and Moab* (Alexander P. Watt, London, 1892), p. 158.

10 Raouf Abujaber, *Pioneers*, p. 90.

11 Lars Wahlin, 'As-Salt: A Trans-Jordanian Town Through Time', personally produced, undated monograph.

12 As perhaps befits its destiny, Transjordan was to have only a marginal influence on the course of the conflict during the First World War in comparison with Palestine.

13 Interview with Kurdi's son, Ali Seydu Kurdi, 15 October 1986.

14 For an authoritative summary of Transjordan under the Arab government see Yoav Alon, 'State, Tribe and Mandate in Transjordan, 1918–1946', unpublished D.Phil thesis, University of Oxford, 2000, pp. 45–63.

15 Writing about the new term of League of Nations mandates, St John Philby, who had served as chief British representative in Amman, wrote: 'Under the conditions of the modern world imperial expansion is no longer fashionable as the avowed aim of diplomacy and war, and we talk more politely of mandates and spheres of influence.' See his 'Trans-Jordan', in the *Journal of the Royal Central Asian Society*, Vol. XI, Part 4, 1924, p. 296.

16 Deedes to Tilley, 27 September 1920, FO371/5123.

17 Jarvis tells the story that Tafilah had its own *qa'im makam* (district officer), *qadi* (judge), *mufti* (religious leader), postmaster, telegraph master and minister of finance in spite of having no post office, telegraph or money in the exchequer. See C. S. Jarvis, *Arab Command* (Hutchinson, London, 1942), p. 66.

2 FOUNDING STATE AND REGIME

1 Samuel to FO, 29 November 1920, FO 371/5290. These men consisted of Utayba tribesmen, Hijazi ashraf and former Ottoman officers from Iraq.

2 For example, in one such letter sent to the shaikhs of Karak, the Adwan and the other Balqa tribes, King Hussein stated that he would soon be sending one of his sons northwards, and appealing to the tribes, in the name of 'your religion and country', to unite to deliver 'our country from the infidels'. Text included in Samuel to FO, 21 September 1920, FO371/5123.

3 Abdullah's arrival in Maan was viewed as being 'a nagging worry' for the British administration in Jerusalem, but, to illustrate that he had got the balance right, it concluded that his 'posture was hardly threatening'.

4 Abdullah's diwan became a magnet for many of the leading political figures in Jordan, notably Sa'id Khair, the mayor of Amman, Sa'id al-Mufti, the Circassian leader, Mithqal al-Fayiz of the Bani Sakhr and Hamad ibn Jazi and Awdah abu Tayih of the Huwaitat. This support was not, however, unanimous, with other leading Transjordanian tribal leaders, such as Rufaifan al-Majali and Sultan al-Adwan, staying away.

5 Uriel Dann, *Studies in the History of Transjordan* (Westview, Boulder, 1984), p. 38.

6 Raslan, from Homs in Syria, had been an official of Faisal's Damascus government, the *mutassaraf* based at Salt. He had initially opposed Abdullah's presence at Maan because of his efforts to render viable the local government at Salt.

7 Dann, *Studies in the History of Transjordan*, p. 40.

8 Hashim was allowed to stay on and serve in the administration once he had 'given an undertaking to sever his connection with the Istiqlal party'. Monthly situation report, December 1923, FO371/10106.

9 Kirkbride's supplementary report to Philby's, undated, FO371/9009.

10 Yoav Alon, 'State, Tribe and Mandate in Transjordan, 1918–1946', unpublished D.Phil. thesis, Oxford University, 2000, p. 140.

11 For more on Philby's life see Elizabeth Monroe, *Philby of Arabia* (Faber and Faber, London, 1973).

12 Some formal ambiguities did dribble on until 1927, it only being in that year, for example, that the functions of the high commissioner were separated out as far as Palestine and Transjordan were concerned, and in dealings with Amman he became known simply as the high commissioner for Transjordan.

13 Britain, with the consent of the League of Nations, took this decision in September 1922. Even so, Jewish representatives were arguing strongly as late as 1930 for the extension of Jewish land-settlement provisions in Palestine to be applied to Transjordan.

14 Mary Wilson, *King Abdullah, Britain and the Making of Jordan* (CUP, Cambridge, 1987), p. 74.

15 See the front pages of the respective reports, both issued by the Colonial Office as Colonial No. 5 1924 and Colonial No. 12 1925.

16 Cox is usually assigned only fleeting references in works on Jordan, and often of a disparaging kind. For example, Kamal Salibi, *The Modern History of Jordan* (Tauris, London, 1993), states that Cox 'appears to have conceived of his position as being essentially that of a colonial governor', p. 97; Ma'an Abu Nowar, *The History of the Hashemite Kingdom of Jordan, Vol. 1* (Ithaca, Oxford, 1989), describes Cox as 'a soldier with an attitude tinged with military discipline rather than political acumen', p. 126. Such dismissive views scarcely do justice to the state-building achievements made on his watch.

17 Monthly situation report, October 1923, FO371/8999.

18 Clayton to Samuel, 1 February 1924, FO371/10101 and monthly situation report, January and February 1924, FO371/10101.

19 Clayton to Thomas, 24 July 1924, FO371/ 10101.

20 Text of letter from Clayton to Abdullah, 14 August 1924, FO371/10102.

21 Samuel to FO, 4 January 1921, FO371/6371.

22 P. J. Vatikiotis, *Politics and the Military in Jordan* (Frank Cass, London, 1967), p. 62.

23 Jarvis puts the size of the levy at around 250, comprising various nationalities, but including Egyptians and Sudanese who had remained in Palestine after the First World War in the hope of gainful employment. See C. S. Jarvis, *Arab Command* (Hutchinson, London, 1942), p. 87.

24 For a breakdown of the composition of the 859-strong Arab Legion in 1928, see undated comments of HMG on the petition from some Karak notables to the League of Nations, 24 November 1928, FO371/13748.

25 Report of HMG for 1928 to the League of Nations, p. 112.

26 For an excellent discussion of the impact of missionaries on inter-confessional relations see Eugene L. Rogan, *Frontiers of the State in the Late Ottoman Empire* (CUP, Cambridge, 1999), pp. 122–159. Rogan concludes by stating that the missionaries had 'entered a tolerant land and by the time they had established themselves, they had transformed it into a land of sectarian divisions', p. 159.

27 There is a disagreement as to the composition from these three countries, with Vatikiotis stating that they were drawn from Syria and Lebanon. See Vatikiotis, *Politics and the Military in Jordan*, p. 71 and L. K. Lockhart, 'The Trans-Jordan Frontier Force', in *Journal of the Royal Artillery*, Vol. 56, April 1929, p. 80, claiming that they were 'mostly "fellahin" from the towns [sic] and villages of Palestine'.

28 This estimate is based on a letter by Lt-Col. C. H. Miller to *The Times*, 7 June 1939.

29 Report of HMG for 1936 to the League of Nations, p. 317.

30 Report of HMG for 1936 to the League of Nations, p. 316.

3 THE LONG ROAD TO INDEPENDENCE

1 For a wealth of descriptive material on how Amman has grown see *Amman, 'asimah al-Urdun* (Amman Municipality, Amman, 1985).

2 It was only published in the official *Gazette* No. 210 on 30 December 1928.

3 Report by HMG to Council of the League of Nations on 'Palestine and Trans-Jordan, 1928' (HMSO, London, 1929), p. 99.

4 For example, one local newspaper called it 'humiliating' and 'resembling rather those of a contract between a workman and his employer', *The Times*, 2 April 1928.

5 To quote Tariq Tell, 'The Social Origins of Hashemite Rule: Bedouin, Fallah and the State on the East Bank', unpublished D.Phil. thesis, University of Oxford, 2000, p. 157.

6 To quote Lord Cushenden in his reply to the final minutes of the third meeting of the 13th session of the Permanent Mandates Commission, India Office W8511/170/98, 1 September 1928.

7 Kamal Salibi, *The Modern History of Jordan* (IB Tauris, London, 1993), p. 114.

8 See G. W. Rendell, 'Policy of HMG regarding the Status of Transjordan', 13 May 1931, E2665/2665/31.

9 The Organic Law was published in the official *Gazette* No. 188, dated 19 April 1928.

10 For a list of the members of the first and subsequent parliaments see *Majlis al-amah al-Urduni, 1921–1984* (Ministry of Information, Amman, 1984).

11 These also included two from the northern and southern areas of the badia, invariably represented by senior figures of the Bani Sakhr and the Huwaitat respectively.

12 The elected members of the Council would be drawn from three multi-member constituencies: Ajlun (four members, including one Christian); Balqa (eight

members, including two Circassians and one Christian), and Karak & Ma'an (four members, including one Christian).

13 The paternalistic view of the British authorities had been to discourage the creation of a 'representative assembly', as the name would imply 'that the country had advanced further down the road to responsible government than is, or can be, the case in TransJordan'.

14 Most of the major tribal groupings were represented in the first executive committee of the TNC. These included: the Adwan from the Balqa group of tribes; al-Akrad and Awamlah from Salt; the Tarawnah and Majali from Karak; the al-Fayiz and Kharaishah lines of the Bani Sakhr; the ibn Jazi (though not the abu Tayyih) of the Huwaitat. See Tell, 'The Social Origins of Hashemite Rule', p. 193.

15 For example, by 1934 the Bani Hasan tribe in the Zarqa area was 'in a critical state of poverty', having lost most of its cattle and not having raised a successful crop in four years. See RAF monthly summary of intelligence, Palestine and Transjordan, February 1934, in E1794/1794/31, 1 March 1934.

16 For example, notables tried to block the appointment of a Chief Secretary in 1926 on the grounds that he should have been elected by a representative assembly. See *The Times*, 21 October 1926.

17 Published in the official *Gazette* No. 162, 1 August 1927.

18 In the 1934 election the amounts paid for secondary votes were as high as £P200. See RAF October intelligence report in E6944/1794/31, 1 November 1934.

19 For example, Hussein al-Tarawnah was imprisoned during the 1934 election, his sentence subsequently being cut to one month on appeal, RAF October intelligence report in E6944/1794/31, 1 November 1934.

20 Report by HMG 1933, p. 243.

21 For the results of the first election see E1359/318/65, Cox-Chanceller, 'Election Results for the Legislative Council', 20 February 1929.

22 Mary Wilson, *King Abdullah, Britain and the Making of Jordan* (Cambridge University Press, Cambridge, 1987), p. 96.

23 For a methodical account of land registration and the land tax that followed see Michael Fischbach, 'British Land Policy in Transjordan' in Eugene L. Rogan and Tariq Tell (eds.), *Village, Steppe and State: The Social Origins of Modern Jordan* (British Academic Press, London, 1994).

24 Report by HMG 1933, p. 248.

25 *The Times*, 4 April 1934.

26 John Bagot Glubb, 'The Economic Situation of the Transjordan Tribes', in *Journal of the Royal Central Asian Society*, Vol. 25 (1938), p. 455.

27 Riccardo Bocco and Tariq Tell, '*Pax Britannica* in the Steppe: British Policy and the Transjordan Bedouin', in Rogan and Tell (eds.), *Village, Steppe and State*, p. 108.

28 Hatem A. Al-Sarairah, 'A British Actor on the Bedouin Stage: Glubb's Career in Jordan, 1930–1956', unpublished Ph.D thesis, Indiana Univesity, 1989, p. 100.

29 Godfrey Lias, *Glubb's Legion* (Evans & Bros, London, 1956), p. 29.

30 John Bagot Glubb, *The Story of the Arab Legion* (Hodder and Stoughton, London, 1946), p. 93.
31 Major T. N. Bromage, 'Jordan', in *Journal of the Royal Central Asian Society* Vol. 49 (1962), p. 20.
32 RAF intelligence summary, February 1934, in E1794/1794/31, 1 March 1934.
33 India Office, Cox to High Commissioner, 18 June 1932.
34 According to Riccardo Bocco's estimates the population of Transjordan's urban centres in 1946 was: Salt 14,479; Maan 8,000; Ramtha 9,790; Irbid 6,693; Karak 6,698; Aqaba 2,900. While Amman had emerged as the main population centre by this time with 65,754, this number was still somewhat modest if one remembers that it had been the capital for two-and-a-half decades and had received an additional boost through the economic activities of the British military effort during the Second World War. See Bocco in Tell, 'The Social Origins of Hashemite Rule', p. 187.
35 For an informative discussion of the merchants in Transjordan see Abla M. Amawi, 'The Consolidation of the Merchant Class in Transjordan during the Second World War', in Rogan and Tell (eds.), *Village, Steppe and State*.
36 Kirkbride's August 1939 report in E6665/263/31.
37 A rare exception came in August 1939, when the amir 'accepted the Prime Minister's final proposals without demur'. See Kirkbride's August report in E6665/263/31.
38 Report by HMG 1938, p. 312.
39 Peter Gubser, *Politics and Change in Al-Karak, Jordan: A Study of a Small Arab Town and its District* (Oxford University Press, Oxford, 1973), pp. 102–103.
40 India Office 132/1, Plumer to Amery, 6 May 1927.
41 Cox's March report in E2688/89/31, 2 April 1936.
42 There is disagreement among scholars as to the extent to which Palestine was a priority for Abdullah. For Ron Pundik (*The Struggle for Sovereignty*) 'the events starting in 1936 were decisive in developing a real interest and concern for the Palestine issue', p. 30. Mary Wilson (*King Abdullah*) disagrees, stating that 'Palestine was never the sole or even the chief focus of Abdullah's ambitions, at least until 1947', p. 103.
43 Joseph Nevo, *King Abdallah and Palestine: A Territorial Ambition* (Macmillan, Basingstoke, 1996), p. 14.
44 Nevo, *King Abdallah and Palestine*, p. 13.
45 Report by HMG 1929, p. 143.
46 British thinking in encouraging this development had been both to give Abdullah a stake in the country and as an alternative source of funds. See comment by Mr Hall, CO, 24 December 1929, on letter from Harry Pirie-Gordon, correspondent of *The Times* to Sir John Shuckburgh, India Office, CO831/6/69489, 1929.
47 Abdullah signed a document with the Jewish Agency for the lease of 60,000 dunums in the Jordan Valley. See political report for January 1933 by Cox in India Office E1163/169/31, 3 February 1933.
48 Paragraph 3 of the Resolutions of the Trans-Jordan Congress, 7 June 1933, in FO371/16932.

49 Avi Shlaim, *The Politics of Partition: King Abdullah, the Zionists and Palestine* (Oxford University Press, Oxford, 1990), p. 50.

50 *Daily Telegraph*, 5 November 1937.

51 Wilson, *King Abdullah*, p. 112. Later on Wilson is equally withering, writing: 'If Faysal's death created an opening on the pan-Arab stage, Abdullah's dealings with the Jewish Agency underlined his unsuitability to fill it', p. 115.

52 Cox's April report in E3442/89/31, 2 May 1936.

53 Cox's November report in E263/263/31, 2 December 1938.

54 Kirkbride's May report in E4696/263/31.

55 Kirkbride's April report in E3790/263/31.

56 Kirkbride's March report in E3583/263/31.

57 Ron Pundik, *The Struggle for Sovereignty: Relations Between Great Britain and Jordan, 1946–1951* (Blackwell, Oxford, 1994), p. 33.

58 Abdullah had to travel through the area of the Karak government, to which Kirkbride was the British officer attached. Kirkbride relates the story that he had a choice either to try to stop Abdullah's advance, or 'to meet the Amir hat in hand and to say, "Sir, welcome to Transjordan!" '. He chose the latter. See Sir Alec Kirkbride, *A Crackle of Thorns: Experiences in the Middle East* (John Murray, London, 1956), p. 26.

59 Kirkbride's September report in E7205/263/31.

60 Kirkbride, *A Crackle of Thorns*, p. 131.

61 Kirkbride, *A Crackle of Thorns*, p. 131.

62 'A Report on the Role Played by the Arab Legion in Connection with the Recent Operations in Iraq', Glubb Papers, Iraq 1941–42 ALC/48, Middle East Private Papers Collection, St Antony's College, Oxford.

63 Lias, *Glubb's Legion*, pp. 127–130.

64 Interview with Yaqub Salti, officer in Desert Patrol, 1931–1947, 11 December 1985.

65 Vartan M. Amadouny, 'Infrastructural Development under the British Mandate', in Rogan and Tell (eds.), *Village, Steppe and State*, pp. 142–143.

66 Martin W. Wilmington, *The Middle East Supply Centre* (State University of New York, Albany, 1971).

67 Amawi 'The Consolidation of the Merchant Class in Transjordan', in Rogan and Tell (eds.), *Village, Steppe and State*, p. 175.

68 Interview with Adeeb Shibli, Amman, 21 August 1988.

69 Amadouny, 'Infrastructural Development under the British Mandate', in Rogan and Tell (eds.), *Village, Steppe and State*, p. 150.

70 Elizabeth Monroe, *Britain's Moment in the Middle East, 1914–1956* (Chatto & Windus, London, 1963), p. 156.

4 LOSS OF INNOCENCE

1 For a discussion of 1948 and the historiography of Transjordan see Eugene L. Rogan, 'Transjordan and 1948: The Persistence of an Official History', in Eugene L. Rogan and Avi Shlaim (eds.), *The War for Palestine: Rewriting the History of 1948* (Cambridge University Press, Cambridge, 2001).

2 Esmond Wright, 'Abdallah's Jordan: 1947–1951', in *Middle East Journal*, Vol. 5, No. 4 (Autumn 1951), p. 459.

3 Robert Satloff sums up this moment very nicely when he describes it as 'The Passing of an Era Already Past'. See Robert B. Satloff, *From Abdullah to Hussein: Jordan in Transition* (Oxford University Press, Oxford, 1994), p. 3.

4 Elizabeth Monroe, *Britain's Moment in the Middle East, 1914–1956* (Chatto & Windus, London, 1963), p. 160.

5 Mary C. Wilson, *King Abdullah, Britain and the Making of Jordan* (Cambridge University Press, Cambridge, 1987), p. 164.

6 Trevor Royle, *Glubb Pasha* (Little, Brown and Company, London, 1992), p. 355.

7 Wilson, *King Abdullah*, p. 166.

8 Uri Bar-Joseph, *The Best of Enemies: Israel and Transjordan in the War of 1948* (Cass, London, 1987), p. 50.

9 For example, in his memoirs King Abdullah associates the actions of his father during the First World War with those of the Prophet Muhammad: 'the army of the Prophet was revived, as is well known, by the awakener of his Arab people, the Commander of the Believers al-Husayn ibn Ali, may God be pleased with him'. See *My Memoirs Completed* (Longman, London, 1978), p. 75.

10 Rogan, 'Transjordan and 1948', in Rogan and Shlaim (eds.), *The War for Palestine*, p. 112.

11 P. J. Vatikiotis described the Arab Legion at this time as 'mainly a corps d'elite fighting force'. See his *Politics and the Military in Jordan: A Study of the Arab Legion, 1921–1967* (Cass, London, 1967), p. 7.

12 Wilson, *King Abdullah*, p. 174.

13 James Lunt, *Glubb Pasha: A Biography* (Harvill Press, London, 1984), p. 146.

14 John Bagot Glubb, *A Soldier with the Arabs* (Hodder and Stoughton, London, 1957), p. 157.

15 Simha Flapan, *The Birth of Israel: Myths and Realities* (Croom Helm, London, 1987), p. 100.

16 Avi Shlaim, *The Iron Wall: Israel and the Arab World* (Norton, New York, 2000), p. 38.

17 Uri Bar-Joseph, *The Best of Enemies: Israel and Transjordan in the War of 1948* (Cass, London, 1987).

18 Shlaim, *The Iron Wall*, p. 44.

19 Bar-Joseph, *The Best of Enemies*, p. 17.

20 Cited in Bar-Joseph, *The Best of Enemies*, p. 234.

21 Joseph Nevo, *King Abdallah and Palestine: A Territorial Ambition* (Macmillan, Basingstoke, 1996), p. 166.

22 Wilson, *King Abdullah*, p. 195.

23 Peter Mansfield, 'Jordan and Palestine', in Patrick Seale (ed.), *The Shaping of an Arab Statesman: Sharif Abd al-Hamid Sharaf and the Modern Arab World* (Quartet Books, London, 1983), p. 30.

24 Avi Plascow, *The Palestinian Refugees in Jordan, 1948–1957* (Cass, London, 1981), p. 26.

25 Satloff, in the most intensive and authoritative piece of scholarship on the double succession in Jordan, makes the point that in spite of the myriad of different theories we just do not know who ultimately was responsible for the assassination. See Satloff, *From Abdullah to Hussein*, p. 32.
26 Kamal Salibi, *The Modern History of Jordan* (Tauris, London, 1993), p. 166.
27 In fact, the law stated that the succession should pass through Abdullah's nearest male relative. However, it also provided for the exclusion of such a figure on the grounds of unsuitability through a royal proclamation.

5 THE ROARING FIFTIES

1 Charles Johnston, British ambassador to Jordan in the mid-1950s, describes his view of the outlook for Jordan as 'hopeless' when he arrived to take up his post in November 1956. See his *The Brink of Jordan* (Hamish Hamilton, London, 1972), p. 17. Even with hindsight, commentators have struggled to explain its continuation; Donald Maclean describing its survival as 'something of a freak' in *British Foreign Policy Since Suez* (Hodder & Stoughton, London, 1970), p. 189.
2 Robert B. Satloff, *From Abdullah to Hussein: Jordan in Transition* (Oxford University Press, Oxford, 1994), p. 43.
3 For example, even the main Communist party in Jordan regarded the constitution as a good document and was prepared to abide by the ground rules that it laid down. Interview with long-standing party leader eg, Yacoub Zayadin, Amman, 24 September 1989.
4 See, eg, Article 8 of *The Constitution of the Hashemite Kingdom of Jordan*, p. 7.
5 For example, for fear of Talal's temper and disfavour, it proved to be impossible to find two Jordanian doctors willing to confirm Talal's illness.
6 This is the title given to the fourth chapter of his book, *Jordan: A Political Study, 1948–1957* (Asia Publishing House, London, 1965), pp. 85–108.
7 Avi Plascow, *The Palestinian Refugees in Jordan, 1948–1957* (Cass, London, 1981), p. 60.
8 J. C. Eyre, 'Frontier Village of Arab Palestine' (MEDD Library Documents), May 1952, p. 2.
9 R. S. Porter, 'Economic Survey of Jordan' (MEDD Library Documents), September 1953, p. 26.
10 Fawzi A. Gharaibeh, *The Economies of the West Bank and Gaza Strip* (Westview, Boulder, 1985), p. 10.
11 Gharaibeh, *The Economies of the West Bank and Gaza Strip*, p. 15.
12 Annex II 'The Movement of Palestinian Funds to Jordan, 1948–1952', 5 November 1952, pp. 2, 4.
13 Porter, 'Economic Survey of Jordan', p. 21.
14 For example, see Mordechai Nisan, 'The Palestinian features of Jordan', in Daniel Elazar (ed.), *Judea, Samaria and Gaza: Views on the Present and the Future* (American Enterprise Institute, Washington DC, 1982), p. 115.
15 Plascow, *The Palestinian Refugees in Jordan*, p. 37.

16 Daniel Lerner, *The Passing of Traditional Society* (The Free Press, New York, 1958), p. 303.

17 Don Peretz, *The West Bank* (Westview, Boulder, 1984), p. 34.

18 Figures cited in Joel S. Migdal (ed.), *Palestinian Society and Politics* (Princeton University Press, New Jersey, 1980), p. 39.

19 Kamel Abu Jaber, *The Jordanians and the People of Jordan* (Royal Scientific Society, Amman, 1980), p. 98.

20 Uriel Dann, *King Hussein and the Challenge of Arab Radicalism: Jordan, 1955–1967* (Oxford University Press, Oxford, 1989), p. 169.

21 Hussein actually acceded to the throne on his 18th birthday according to the lunar calendar.

22 One contemporary source refers to 'the condescending "old gang" politicians in Amman', and of Hussein being 'pathetically ill at ease'. See Ray Allan, 'Jordan: Rise and Fall of a Squirearchy', in *Commentary*, Vol. 23, No. 3 (March 1957), p. 246.

23 See, for example, the interviews with Yusif al-Bandak and Yusif Bamiah, in J. B. Slade-Baker, 'Middle East Diary', Jordan, 10–21 December 1954, in which the former complained at the ' "feeling of frustration" ' felt by educated Jordanians in the 20–45-year-old age group, especially towards ' "the few old families who surround the King" '.

24 Shaul Mishal, *East Bank/West Bank: The Palestinians in Jordan, 1949–1967* (Yale University Press, New Haven, 1978), p. 56.

25 The size of the Jordanian military had risen from 6,000 in 1945 to 23,000 a decade later, with the officer corps increasing some fivefold to stand at 1,500, many of whom were young and inexperienced. Glubb worried about the consequences of this rapid expansion. See John Bagot Glubb, *A Soldier with the Arabs* (Hodder & Stoughton, London, 1957), pp. 386–387.

26 Glubb was a regular target for Egyptian propaganda, in which he was routinely referred to as 'an imperialist scorpion'. See Trevor Royle, *Glubb Pasha: The Life and Times of Sir John Bagot Glubb, Commander of the Arab Legion* (Little, Brown & Co, London, 1992), p. 439.

27 Charles Johnston refers to both Glubb's command and the treaty in just such terms. See his *The Brink of Jordan*, p. 19.

28 To quote Charles Johnston, *The Brink of Jordan*, p. 42.

29 Walter Z. Laqueur, *Communism and Nationalism in the Middle East* (Routledge & Kegan Paul, London, 1956), p. 130.

30 Yahya Fayez El Haddad, 'Social Change and the Process of Modernization. Jordan: A Case of a Developing Country', unpublished Ph.D thesis, University of Missouri, 1974, p. 141.

31 Dann, *King Hussein*, p. 43.

32 King Hussein remained an admirer throughout his long career. In an interview with the author in 1984 he would look back on the Eisenhower presidency as a golden age of American action in the Middle East, contrasting the many subsequent White House appeasers of Israel with the firm and statesmanlike stance of Eisenhower in the mid-1950s. See also King Hussein's praise for the

1982 Reagan Plan, which he described as ' "the most courageous and realistic move taken by an American Administration since 1956" ', 'Profiles Monarch', *The New Yorker*, 19 September 1983, p. 51.

33 The gusto with which King Hussein set about attacking Communism may also have had something to do with the forging of a relationship with the CIA, which for more than 20 years would see him receive funds from the agency, *The Washington Post*, cited in EIU, QER1, 1977.

34 P. J. Vatikiotis writes of the social-cum-cultural tensions between the bedouin and the *hadari* officers of the East Bank towns. He notes that: 'The bedouin was, if not inimical, at least scornfully indifferent to the *hadari* officer and NCO', *Politics and the Military in Jordan: A Study of the Arab Legion, 1921–1967* (Cass, London, 1967), p. 92. In turn, if the *hadari* officer 'did not affect an intellectual superiority or appear otherwise snooty, he was invariably well received by the bedouins', p. 93.

35 Dann, *King Hussein*, p. 56.

36 *Uneasy Lies the Head: An Autobiography of King Hussein of Jordan* (Heinemann, London, 1962), p. 127.

37 *Uneasy Lies the Head*, p. 127.

38 Despatches of J. B. Slade-Baker, sent 24 April 1957, pp. 2–3.

39 For the experiences of a typical radical, George Habash, see Walid W. Kazziha, *Revolutionary Transformation in the Arab World: Habash and his Comrades from Nationalism to Marxism* (Charles Knight, London, 1975).

40 For a contextualised discussion of Farhan's involvement in the development process in Jordan in the 1950s see Paul W. T. Kingston, 'Breaking the Patterns of Mandate: Economic Nationalism and State Formation in Jordan, 1951–57', in Eugene L. Rogan and Tariq Tell (eds.), *Village, Steppe and State: The Social Origins of Modern Jordan* (British Academic Press, London, 1994).

41 Malcolm H. Kerr, *The Arab Cold War: Gamal Abdel Nasir and his Rivals, 1958–1970* (Oxford University Press, Oxford, 1981).

42 Michael N. Barnett, *Dialogues in Arab Politics: Negotiations in Regional Order* (Columbia University Press, New York, 1998), p. 47.

43 For a discussion of earlier unsuccessful ideas for Hashemite unity see Bruce Maddy-Weitzman, 'Jordan and Iraq: Efforts at Intra-Hashimite Unity', in *Middle Eastern Studies*, Vol. 26, No. 1 (January 1990), pp. 65–75.

44 Despatches of J. B. Slade-Baker, 'Jordan Army Buildup', *The Times*, 24 August 1958.

45 Hussein of Jordan, *Uneasy Lies the Head*, p. 204.

6 THE ROAD TO DISASTER

1 For an excellent biography of Wasfi al-Tall see Asher Susser, *On Both Banks of the Jordan. A Political Biography of Wasfi al-Tall* (Cass, London, 1994).

2 Uriel Dann, *King Hussein and the Challenge of Arab Radicalism, Jordan 1955–67* (Oxford University Press, Oxford, 1989), p. 13.

3 Richard Loring Taylor, *Mustafa's Journey. Verse of Arar: Poet of Jordan* (Yarmouk University Publications, Irbid, 1988), p. 2.

4 The assessment of one British ambassador was that, while intelligent on internal affairs, Wasfi al-Tall could be 'vain, obstinate, categorical, and at times positively childish about foreign affairs'. See EJ1022/21, Parkes–FO, 3 December 1962.

5 There are many and frequent references to this in British despatches from Amman. See: FO371/164080, Annual Review, 1961, Henniker-Major; FO371/164082, Despatch #22, Henniker-Major to Secretary of State, 16 February 1962.

6 Susser, *On Both Banks of the Jordan*, p. 37.

7 FO371/164082, Despatch #22.

8 Clinton Bailey, *Jordan's Palestinian Challenge, 1948–1983: A Political History* (Westview, Boulder, 1984), pp. 16–17.

9 FO371/164082, Henniker-Major to FO, 2 February 1962.

10 For a laudatory account of the life of Sharif Abdul Hamid Sharaf see Patrick Seale (ed.), *The Shaping of an Arab Statesman: Sharif Abd al-Hamid Sharaf and the Modern Arab World* (Quartet, London, 1983).

11 Epiphan Sabella, 'External Events and Circulation of Political Elites: Cabinet Turnover in Jordan, 1946–1980', unpublished Ph.D thesis, University of Virginia, 1981, p. 186.

12 FO371/164082, Despatch #22, Henniker-Major to Secretary of State, 16 February 1962.

13 To ensure that all was fair and above board Tall set the exam questions himself and kept them in his care until the exam.

14 EJ1015/30 Henniker-Major to FO, 16 February 1962.

15 EJ1015/90(A) Parkes to FO, 27 November 1962.

16 Dann, *King Hussein and the Challenge of Arab Radicalism*, p. 120.

17 Laurie A. Brand, *Jordan's Inter-Arab Relations: The Political Economy of Alliance Making* (Columbia University Press, New York, 1994), p. 74.

18 Paul W. T. Kingston, *Britain and the Politics of Modernization in the Middle East, 1945–1958* (Cambridge University Press, Cambridge, 1996), p. 135.

19 For a commentary on the programme see Paul J. Klat, 'Jordan's Five-Year Program for Economic Development, 1962–1967', in Paul J. Klat (ed.), *Middle East Economic Papers* (Economic Research Institute, AUB, Beirut, 1963).

20 He would go on to head dar al-handissah, one of the region's largest engineering firms.

21 Less than two years after its publication it was revised due to lower levels of budget support from the US. It was then relaunched as the Seven Year Plan for 1964–70.

22 For development planning, the period between 1952 and 1962 had been characterised by 'planning for single projects'. See *Five Year Plan for Economic and Social Development, 1986–1990* (Ministry of Planning, Amman, 1986), p. 1.

23 Sir Geoffrey Furlonge, 'Jordan Today', in *Journal of the Royal Central Asian Society*, Vol. 53 (1966), pp. 277–287, 282.

24 Rami G. Khouri, *The Jordan Valley: Life and Society Below Sea Level* (Longman, London, 1981), p. 20.

25 For a discussion of the Yemeni civil war and its broader context see Paul Dresch, *A History of Modern Yemen* (Cambridge University Press, Cambridge, 2000).

26 Its air force was destroyed, it lost 80% of its armoured capability and only four of the army's 11 brigades remained operational.

27 Samir A. Mutawi, *Jordan in the 1967 War* (Cambridge University Press, Cambridge, 1987), p. 141.

28 Lawrence Tal, *Politics, the Military and National Security in Jordan, 1955–1967* (Palgrave Macmillan, Basingstoke, 2002), p. 22.

29 Richard B. Parker, *The Politics of Miscalculation in the Middle East* (Indiana University Press, Bloomington, 1993).

30 It should be pointed out that the nature of the raid was determined by the Israeli military, its ferocity shocking many Israelis, not least the prime minister of the day, Levi Eshkol. See Avi Shlaim, *The Iron Wall: Israel and the Arab World* (Norton, New York, 2000), p. 234.

31 Indeed, the first Palestinian considered to be a 'martyr' as a result of the new insurgency strategy, Ahmad Musa, was actually killed in January 1965 by Jordanian rather than Israeli security forces.

32 Bailey, *Jordan's Palestinian Challenge 1948–1983*, p. 25.

33 Dann, *King Hussein and the Challenge of Arab Radicalism*, p. 155.

34 Laura James, 'Images of the Enemy: Foreign Policy Making in Egypt and Jordan on the Eve of the Six Day War', unpublished M.Phil. thesis, University of Oxford, 2002.

35 This was neither fanciful nor paranoid, foreign embassies had been speculating about the possibility of an Israeli attack on the West Bank stretching back at least to 1963. It should also be recalled that Ben-Gurion had seriously considered a further attack on the West Bank in 1948, in the end choosing to expand Israel's territory into the Negev instead.

36 King Hussein did move Tall from the prime ministry to become Chief of the Royal Court, a close advisory position that ought in theory to have made him more influential. In reality, his well-known and trenchant views on Nasser were systematically disregarded.

37 So sudden and unexpected had been the Jordanian *volte-face* that the Egyptians were reluctant to speak to Khammash about their military preparations.

38 Quoted in Mutawi, *Jordan in the 1967 War*, p. 87.

39 This was the mobile defence concept, which had been drawn up under Glubb more than a decade before.

40 Michael Hudson, 'The Palestinian Arab Movement: Its Significance in the Middle East Crisis', in *Middle East Journal*, Vol. 23, No. 3 (Summer 1969), p. 307.

41 Kamal Salibi, *The Modern History of Jordan* (Tauris, London, 1993), p. 228.

42 See Norvell De Atkine, the US army attaché in the Jordan embassy, 'Amman 1970, A Memoir', in *Middle East Review of International Affairs (MERIA) Journal*, Vol. 6 No. 4 (December 2002), p. 4.

43 Salibi, *The Modern History of Jordan*, p. 230.
44 James Lunt, *Hussein of Jordan: A Political Biography* (Macmillan, London, 1989), p. 136.

7 ILLUSIONS OF PROGRESS

1 The third category tended to include those without clear-cut identities, such as: those from small ethnic groups, like the Circassians; those families which historically bridged the River Jordan and continued to have significant parts of their extended clans resident on both banks; those families where there had been extensive inter-marriage, affecting in particular those with strong lateral connections between such urban centres as Karak and Hebron, and Salt and Nablus; those whose ideological views partially ameliorated their ethnic origins, for example, some Transjordanian members of the Muslim Brotherhood; those of Palestinian origin who had been resident in the East Bank since before 1947 and for whom Jordan was their country, even if the notion of Transjordanian nationalism made them uneasy.
2 For example, many members of the Palestine National Council (PNC) were based in Jordan.
3 Nawaf Wasfi Tell, 'Jordanian Foreign Policy in the 1970s', unpublished Ph.D thesis, University of Exeter, 2001, pp. 88, 101.
4 Usually taken to mean the possible inclusion of the Gaza Strip, which was administered by Egypt until 1967.
5 Laurie A. Brand, 'Palestinians and Jordanians: A Crisis of Identity', *Journal of Palestine Studies*, Vol. 24, No. 4 (Summer 1995), Issue 96, p. 50.
6 Adnan Abu Odeh quoted in Tell, 'Jordanian Foreign Policy in the 1970s', p. 125.
7 Tell, 'Jordanian Foreign Policy in the 1970s', p. 152.
8 Asher Susser, 'Jordan, the PLO and the Palestine Question', in Joseph Nevo and Ilan Pappe (eds.), *Jordan in the Middle East: The Making of a Pivotal State, 1948–1988* (Cass, London, 1994), p. 214.
9 James Lunt, *Hussein of Jordan: A Political Biography* (Macmillan, London, 1989), p. 163.
10 I am grateful to my colleague at St Antony's College, Oxford, Avi Shlaim, for clarifying this point.
11 The conditionality in the Jordanian–Saudi relationship was the least prone to change. Laurie Brand neatly summarises it thus: 'Saudi Arabia paid support of various kinds to keep Jordan solvent and stable, and a consequently solvent and stable Jordan then reinforced Saudi security indirectly, and occasionally directly', *Jordan's Inter-Arab Relations: The Political Economy of Alliance Making* (Columbia University Press, New York, 1994), p. 121.
12 Brand, *Jordan's Inter-Arab Relations*, p. 105.
13 Tell, 'Jordanian Foreign Policy in the 1970s', p. 296.
14 For example, in 1977 and 1978 total commercial bank (including the Housing Bank) credit for real estate and construction came to 38% and 48.5% respectively. See EIU Jordan CR 3, 1979.
15 EIU Jordan CR 3, 1978.

16 EIU Jordan CR1, 1979.
17 EIU Jordan CR4, 1978.
18 See official Jordanian government response, 19 September 1978.
19 Ronald J. Young, *Missed Opportunities for Peace: US Middle East Policy, 1981–1986* (American Friends Service Committee, Philadelphia, 1987), p. 96.
20 Of this figure, only an estimated $500 million would be new money, the balance being the repackaging of existing pledges.
21 Tell, 'Jordanian Foreign Policy in the 1970s', p. 238.
22 Amatzia Baram, 'No New Fertile Crescent: Iraqi–Jordanian Relations, 1968–92', in Nevo and Pappe (eds.), *Jordan in the Middle East*, p. 126.
23 See Jordanian strategic expert Mustafa Hamarneh interviewed in *Middle East Insight*, May–June 1998, p. 33.
24 Amatzia Baram, 'Baathi Iraq and Hashemite Jordan: From Hostility to Alignment', *The Middle East Journal*, Vol. 45, No. 1 (Winter 1991), p. 58.
25 Exposing this connection landed the *al-Hayat* correspondent in Amman, Salameh Ne'matt, in jail temporarily in 1996.
26 This seems to have been a personal initiative by Saddam, done without the knowledge of President Ahmad Hasan al-Bakr. See Baram, 'Baathi Iraq and Hashemite Jordan', p. 54.
27 EIU Jordan CR3, 1981.
28 EIU Jordan CR4, 1981 and interview with Gennardi Gatilov, Soviet Embassy, Amman, 27 May 1984.
29 Jordan imported around 70,000 b/d of oil at the time of the Iraqi invasion of Kuwait in August 1990.
30 For example, a session of the lower house on 15 May 1984, when deputies from the Muslim Brotherhood called for: the lifting of martial law; the circumscribing of the activities of the general intelligence; and the implementation of a range of constitutional freedoms, such as equality before the law. Author present at the session.
31 For instance, he appointed a dedicated minister of state for parliamentary affairs, Sami Judeh, in order better to manage parliament as a political institution.
32 Patrick Seale, *Abu Nidal: A Gun for Hire* (Hutchinson, London, 1992), pp. 125–128.
33 William B. Quandt, *Peace Process: American Diplomacy and the Arab–Israeli Conflict since 1967* (Brookings/University of California Press, Washington DC/Berkeley, 1993), p. 351.
34 To quote former ambassador Walid Sa'di, interview, Amman, 25 September 1989.

8 HUSSEIN'S CHOICES

1 News of the default became public on 2 February, in an article in the *Financial Times*.
2 Adiba Mango, 'Jordan on the Road to Peace, 1988–1999', unpublished D. Phil. thesis, University of Oxford, 2003, p. 45.

3 There was some small-scale privatisation in Jordan, for instance of hotels and consultancy services, but on the whole the language of reform was used as a cover for inaction. An apparent decision made in 1985 to privatise the kingdom's Telecommunications Corporation was still unimplemented more than 12 years later.

4 Foreign exchange reserves fell from providing the equivalent of over six months' import cover in 1980 to only six weeks in 1986.

5 For example, Jordan is estimated to have around 37,000 qualified engineers, out of a population of four million. In Singapore, where the overall population is comparable, there are only some 5,000 engineers.

6 In 1986 the biggest and best-known in the 75-strong sub-sector, Saliba & Rizk Shukri Rizk, collapsed. The sector was closed down in February 1989 by the Rifai government, invoking martial law provisions. It returned to life, albeit in a more strictly regulated form, in 1992.

7 Affecting such institutions as the long-established Jordan–Gulf Bank and the new and aggressive Petra Bank, which had a history of sailing close to the wind. The leading figure behind the latter, Dr Ahmad Chalabi, since reincarnated as the head of the main Iraqi opposition grouping, the INC, fled the kingdom in 1989. It was subsequently revealed that Petra Bank collapsed with debts as high as $250 million.

8 The Central Bank of Jordan estimated government and government-guaranteed external debt for 1988 at JD1.7 billion ($3 billion equivalent), while the EIU estimated public external debt at $3.6 billion. The debt figure was subsequently estimated at $7.2 billion.

9 The sale, which was kept secret from both the board of governors of the bank and the rest of the cabinet, was hidden by simply revaluing the book entry of the remaining gold.

10 Interview with Hamad al-Farhan, Amman, 25 September 1989.

11 For more details on the 1989 elections see *Intikhabat 1989 haqa'iq wa raqam* (*al-urdun al-jadid* Research Center, Amman, 1992).

12 For example, the American embassy did not expect more than eight Islamists to be elected, while the British embassy predicted that the Islamists would take between eight and 16 seats in the election. The palace seemed to expect fewer than even the Americans were predicting.

13 Glenn E. Robinson, 'Can Islamists be Democrats? The Case of Jordan', *The Middle East Journal*, Vol. 51, No. 3 (Summer 1997), pp. 373–387.

14 At the end of 1991, after groups in the National Assembly had had a chance to coalesce, the breakdown was as follows: Muslim Brotherhood (23 seats); Constitution Bloc (18); Nationalist Bloc (17); Democratic Bloc (10).

15 An estimated 8,700 Jordanians had been deprived of their passports because of their political activities.

16 This included allowing the return of the boards of directors of the three Arabic dailies instead of their government appointed successors, and the return of two of the ousted editors-in-chief.

17 Akayleh was a moderate Islamist from Transjordan who had acquired a good reputation in parliament during the 1980s as a conscientious and hard-working

deputy. It is his misfortune that his career will probably be remembered more for the gym-slips policy than any of his more positive contributions.

18 For valuable information about the political parties registered in 1993 see *Jordanian Political Parties* (*al-urdun al-jadid* Research Center, Amman, 1993).

19 For a comprehensive view of the establishment and brief life of the ACC see Curtis R. Ryan, 'Jordan and the Rise and Fall of the Arab Cooperation Council', *The Middle East Journal*, Vol. 52, No. 3 (Summer 1998), pp. 386–401.

20 The king visited Iraq and Kuwait on 29 and 30 July.

21 See *al-dustour*, 31 July 1990, reprinted in the *Jordan Times*, 1 August 1990.

22 His most recent involvement in intra-Arab mediation had been between Iraq and Syria in 1989, a case that well illustrates the argument.

23 Ann Mosely Lesch, 'Contrasting Reactions to the Persian Gulf Crisis: Egypt, Syria, Jordan and the Palestinians', *The Middle East Journal*, Vol. 45, No. 1 (Winter 1991), p. 46. This was most evident at the Arab summit in Cairo at which King Hussein eulogised the Iraqi leader and hinted strongly at the existence of a conspiracy against him.

24 Uriel Dann, *King Hussein's Solidarity with Saddam Husayn: A Pattern of Behaviour?* (The Moshe Dayan Centre, Tel Aviv University, Tel Aviv, 1990), p. 1.

25 Jordan actually abstained on this vote, together with Algeria and Yemen.

26 *Jordan Times*, 17 August 1990.

27 'White Paper: Jordan and the Gulf Crisis, August 1990–March 1991' (Amman, 1991).

28 This was certainly the view of one senior diplomat based in Amman. Interview, 21 December 1996.

29 Defined as having a family income of less than JD130/month. Interview with senior official in Ministry of Social Development, Amman, 23 January 1993.

30 The Israel–Jordan Common Agenda was adopted on 14 September, and covered: security; water; refugees; borders and territory; economic and related issues. It set out the goal of 'The achievement of just, lasting and comprehensive peace between the Arab States, the Palestinians and Israel'.

31 For a detailed commentary on the negotiations between Israel and Jordan see Mango, 'Jordan on the Road to Peace, 1988–1999'.

32 For example, the Muslim Brotherhood condemned the September 1993 forging of the Israeli–Jordanian agenda for negotiations, seeing it as the thin end of a wedge that would lead to the normalisation of relations 'with the Zionist enemy'.

33 For example: in 1993 the trial took place of 10 students from Muta University, alleged to be members of the hardline Islamic Liberation Party, charged with plotting to kill the king; in January 1994 two cinemas were bombed for showing films reputed to be soft porn in content, the attacks leading to a series of arrests of Islamist and other opposition activists the following month.

34 Shbailat was arrested on 31 August 1992.

35 For full details of the outcome of the election see *Intakhabat 1993. darasa tahliliyah raqamiyah* (*al-urdun al-jadid* Research Center, Amman, 1994).

36 In Algeria, a two-stage general election had been interrupted by military intervention once it became clear that the Islamist umbrella party, the FIS, was set
to win in January 1992. After a brief period of uncertainty the country then
descended into a bloody civil war which claimed perhaps 100,000 lives between
summer 1992 and 1997.

37 Unlike 1979, when the US pledged annual subventions to Egypt of $1.9 billion
and Israel of $2 billion, there was to be no aid binge for Jordan in the aftermath
of October 1994. Even President Clinton's promise to write off $702 million
worth of debt during an address to the Jordanian parliament in October 1994
was only grudgingly honoured as a result of the Republicans capturing control
of the US Congress. However, the US did indicate that it was prepared to help
Jordan to overhaul its defence capabilities.

38 King Hussein's pragmatic willingness to do business with the Israeli right also
extended to Moledet, a radical party that advocated the 'transfer' of Palestinians
out of the Occupied Territories, the leader of which visited the kingdom as part
of a 30-strong parliamentary delegation in February 1995.

39 Under the terms of the QIZs, goods with a minimal level of Israeli and Jordanian
input can enter the US duty and quota free.

40 For example, labour rates were estimated at around 20% of the equivalent in
Israel. Interview with under-secretary of the Ministry of Trade and Industry,
Muhammad Smadi, Amman, 20 December 1996.

41 A military court found Dakamsah guilty, sentencing him to 25 years in jail for
the attack.

42 For a recent commentary on the state of the liberalisation process in Jordan see
Quintan Wiktorowicz, 'The Limits of Democracy in the Middle East: The Case
of Jordan', *The Middle East Journal*, Vol. 53, No. 4 (Autumn 1999), pp. 606–620.

43 This increased the minimum capitalisation of newspapers, made it easier
for the courts to suspend publication, quadrupled the ceiling on fines and
allowed the prohibition of papers for a range of misdemeanours, including
disparaging the royal family, the security services and friendly states.

44 A middle brother, Prince Muhammad, had long been judged mentally unstable,
and hence did not feature directly in the succession.

45 *The Constitution of the Hashemite Kingdom of Jordan*, pp. 14–19.

46 Though herself a patrician, being the younger daughter of the country's first
foreign minister, there is no doubt that in the hierarchical society of Jordan her
origins were a disadvantage to her husband.

47 King Hussein made no mention, even indirectly, of Crown Prince Hasan in his
speech on returning from cancer surgery in the US. This extraordinary omission
was taken as evidence that the king was less than completely committed to his
brother.

48 Some have speculated that had the Syrian succession, when Hafez al-Asad passed
the mantle of leadership to his shy and inexperienced son Bashar, preceded the
Jordanian succession King Hussein might indeed have been tempted to take
the gamble.

49 For the full text of the letter, see the *Jordan Times*, 26 January 1999.

9 ABDULLAH'S FIRST STEPS

1 See Lamis Andoni, 'King Abdallah: In His Father's Footsteps?', *Journal of Palestine Studies*, Vol. 24, No. 3 (Spring 2000), Issue 115, p. 79.

2 As early as September 1989, if not before, Abdullah had acquired a reputation as being 'his father's man'. Interview with senior British diplomat, Amman, 24 September 1989.

Bibliography

OFFICIAL RECORDS AND PUBLICATIONS

British archival sources of the Colonial Office (CO831) and the Foreign Office (FO371), Public Records Office, Kew Gardens, London

British Colonial Office reports to Council of the League of Nations on Palestine (including Transjordan) and subsequently Palestine and Transjordan for 1923 through 1938

British records of the Middle East Development Division, Private Papers Collection, St Antony's College, Oxford

Constitution of the Hashemite Kingdom of Jordan

Jordanian Government, *Five Year Plan for Economic and Social Development, 1981–1985* (National Planning Council, Amman, 1981)

> *Five Year Plan for Economic and Social Development, 1986–1990* (Ministry of Planning, Amman, 1986)
>
> *Majlis al-amah al-Urduni, 1921–1984* [Jordan National Council] (Ministry of Information, Amman, 1984)
>
> White Paper: Jordan and the Gulf Crisis, August 1990–March 1991 (Amman, 1991)

UNPUBLISHED WORKS

Abdul Rahman, Ismail, 'Zu Einigen Fragen der Entwicklung und Perspective der Industrie in Jordan [On Certain Aspects of the Development and Perspectives of Industry in Jordan]', unpublished Ph.D thesis, Berlin University, 1969

Allison, Norman Ernest Jr, 'A Case of Honor: Arab Christians in a Jordanian Town', unpublished Ph.D thesis, University of Georgia, 1977

Alon, Yoav, 'State, Tribe and Mandate in Transjordan, 1918–1946', unpublished D.Phil. thesis, University of Oxford, 2000

Amawi, Abla, 'State and Class in Transjordan: A Study of State Autonomy', unpublished Ph.D thesis, Georgetown University, 1992

Ameri, Anan, 'Socioeconomic Development in Jordan (1950–1980): An Application of Dependency Theory', unpublished Ph.D thesis, Wayne State University, 1981

Bissat, Nazih M., 'Jordan: From Mandate to Statehood, 1923–1956', unpublished MA thesis, American University, Washington DC, 1959

Fischbach, Michael Richard, 'State, Society and Land in Ajlun, 1850–1950', unpublished Ph.D thesis, Georgetown University, 1992

Ghosheh, Zaki Rateb, 'The Process of Administrative Change in Jordan, 1921–1967', unpublished Ph.D thesis, Southern Illinois University, 1970

Guckian, Noel, 'British Relations with TransJordan (1920–1930)', unpublished Ph.D thesis, University of Aberystwyth, 1985

Haddad, Yahya Fayez El, 'Social Change and the Process of Modernization. Jordan: A Case of a Developing Country', unpublished Ph.D thesis, University of Missouri, 1974

Hamarneh, Mustafa, 'Social and Economic Transformation of Transjordan (1921–1946)', unpublished Ph.D thesis, Georgetown University, 1986

Hammad, Khalil Nayif, 'Foreign Aid and Economic Development: The Case of Jordan', unpublished Ph.D thesis, Southern Illinois University, 1981

Hiatt, Joseph Merrill, 'Between Desert and Town: A Case Study of Encapsulation and Sedentarization Among Jordanian Bedouin', unpublished Ph.D thesis, University of Pennsylvania, 1981

James, Laura, 'Images of the Enemy: Foreign Policy Making in Egypt and Jordan on the Eve of the Six Day War', unpublished M.Phil. thesis, University of Oxford, 2002

Jreisat, Jamil E., 'Provincial Administration in Jordan: A Study of Institution-Building', unpublished Ph.D thesis, 1968

Khatib, Abdullah, 'The Jordanian Legislature in Political Development Perspective', unpublished Ph.D thesis, State University of New York, Albany, 1975

Lalor, Paul, 'Black September 1970: The Palestinian Resistance in Jordan 1967–1971', unpublished D.Phil. thesis, University of Oxford, 1992

Layne, Linda, 'The Production and Reproduction of Tribal Identity in Jordan', unpublished Ph.D thesis, Princeton University, 1986

Mango, Adiba, 'Jordan on the Road to Peace, 1988–1999', unpublished D.Phil. thesis, University of Oxford, 2003

Parris, Timothy J., 'The "Sherifian Solution": British Planning for Hashemite Rule in the Post World War I Middle East', unpublished Ph.D thesis, University of Cambridge, 1996

Robins, Philip, 'The Consolidation of Hashemite Power in Jordan, 1921–1946', unpublished Ph.D thesis, University of Exeter, 1988

Rudd, Jeffrey A., 'Abdallah Bin Al-Husayn: The Making of an Arab Political Leader, 1908–1921', unpublished Ph.D thesis, SOAS, London, 1993

Sabella, Epiphan, 'External Events and Circulation of Political Elites: Cabinet Turnover in Jordan, 1946–1980', unpublished Ph.D thesis, University of Virginia, 1981

Sarairah, Hatem A. Al-, 'A British Actor on the Bedouin Stage: Glubb's Career in Jordan, 1930–1956', unpublished Ph.D thesis, Indiana University, 1989

Sayigh, Yezid Jasper, 'Jordan's National Security in the External Environment: Threats, Constraints and Responses', unpublished Ph.D thesis, King's College, London, 1987

Tell, Nawaf Wasfi, 'Jordanian Foreign Policy in the 1970s', unpublished Ph.D. thesis, University of Exeter, 2001

Tell, Tariq, 'The Social Origins of Hashemite Rule: Bedouin, Fallah and State on the East Bank', unpublished D.Phil. thesis, University of Oxford, 2000

OTHER WORKS

Abdallah of Jordan, King, *My Memoirs Completed: 'Al-Takmilah'* [Complement] (Longman, London, 1978)

Abdul-Hadi, Mahdi F., *The Jordanian Disengagement: Causes and Effects* (PASSIA, Jerusalem, 1988)

Abidi, Aqil Hyder Hasan, *Jordan: A Political Study, 1948–1957* (Asia Publishing House, London, 1965)

Abujaber, Raouf Sa'd, *Pioneers Over the Jordan: The Frontier of Settlement in Transjordan, 1850–1914* (Tauris, London, 1989)

Abu Jaber, Kamel, *The Jordanians and the People of Jordan* (Royal Scientific Society, Amman, 1980)

Abu Nowar, Ma'an, *The History of the Hashemite Kingdom of Jordan: Volume One: The Creation and Development of Trans-Jordan, 1920–1929* (Ithaca, Oxford, 1989)

Abu Odeh, Adnan, *Jordanians, Palestinians and the Hashemite Kingdom in the Middle East Peace Process* (US Institute of Peace, Washington DC, 1999)

Allan, Ray, 'Jordan: Rise and Fall of a Squirearchy', *Commentary*, March 1957, Vol. 23, No. 3

Amman Municipality, *Amman, 'asimah al-Urdun* [Amman, Capital of Jordan] (Amman Municipality, Amman, 1985)

Andoni, Lamis, 'King Abdullah: In His Father's Footsteps?', *Journal of Palestine Studies*, Vol. 24, No. 3 (Spring 2000), Issue 115

Antoun, Richard T., *Arab Village: A Social Structural Study of a Transjordanian Peasant Community* (Indiana University Press, Bloomington, 1972)
Low-Key Politics (State University of New York Press, Albany, 1979)

Aruri, Naseer H., *Jordan: A Study in Political Development (1921–1965)* (Martinus Nijhoff, The Hague, 1972)

Asfour, Edmond, 'Problems of Development Planning in Jordan', in Klat, Paul J. (ed.), *Middle East Economic Papers* (Economic Research Institute, American University in Beirut, Beirut, 1963)

Baer, Gabriel, 'Land Tenure in the Hashemite Kingdom of Jordan', *Land Economics*, Vol. 33, No. 3 (August 1957)

Bailey, Clinton, *Jordan's Palestinian Challenge, 1948–1983: A Political History* (Westview, Boulder, 1984)

Baram, Amatzia, 'Baathi Iraq and Hashemite Jordan: From Hostility to Alignment', *The Middle East Journal*, Vol. 45, No. 1 (Winter 1991)

Barnett, Michael N., *Dialogues in Arab Politics: Negotiations in Regional Order* (Columbia University Press, New York, 1998)

Bar-Joseph, Uri, *The Best of Enemies: Israel and Transjordan in the War of 1948* (Cass, London, 1987)

Bentwich, Norman, *Palestine* (Ernest Benn Ltd, London, 1934)

Bligh, Alexander, *The Political Legacy of King Hussein* (Sussex Academic Press, Brighton, 2002)

Bocco, Riccardo, 'Espaces étatiques et espaces tribaux dans le Sud Jordanien [State Space and Tribal Space in Southern Jordan]', *Maghreb Machrek*, No. 123, 1989

 'Ingénieurs-agronomes et politiques de developpement dans les steppes du Sud Jordanien (1960–1985) [Agricultural Engineers and the Politics of Development in Southern Jordan]', in *Bâtisseurs et Bureaucrates, Ingénieurs et Société au Maghreb et au Moyen Orient* (Maison de l'Orient, Serie Etudes sur le Monde Arabe No. 4, Lyon, 1990)

Brand, Laurie A., *Jordan's Inter-Arab Relations: The Political Economy of Alliance Making* (Columbia University Press, New York, 1994)

 'Palestinians and Jordanians: A Crisis of Identity', *Journal of Palestine Studies*, Vol. 24, No. 4 (Summer 1995)

Bromage, Major T. N., 'Jordan', *Journal of the Royal Central Asian Society*, Vol. 49 (1962)

Carr, Winifred, *Hussein's Kingdom* (Leslie Frewin, London, 1966)

Chizik, I., 'The Political Parties in Transjordania', *Journal of the Royal Central Asian Society*, Vol. 22 (1935)

Cleveland, William L., *A History of the Modern Middle East* (Westview, Boulder, 1994)

Coate, Winifred A., 'The Condition of Arab Refugees in Jordan', *International Affairs*, Vol. 24 (1953)

Cohen, Amnon, *Political Parties in the West Bank Under the Jordanian Regime, 1949–1967* (Cornell University Press, Ithaca, 1982)

Conder, Claude, *Heth and Moab* (Alexander P. Watt, London, 1892)

Cordesman, Anthony H., *Jordanian Arms and the Middle East Balance* (Middle East Institute, Washington DC, 1983)

Dallas, R., *King Hussein: A Life on the Edge* (Profile Books, London, 1998)

Dann, Uriel, *Studies in the History of Transjordan* (Westview, Boulder, 1984)

 King Hussein and the Challenge of Arab Radicalism: Jordan, 1955–1967 (Oxford University Press, Oxford, 1989)

 King Hussein's Solidarity With Saddam Husayn: A Pattern of Behaviour? (The Moshe Dayan Centre, Tel Aviv University, Tel Aviv, 1990)

Day, Arthur R., *East Bank/West Bank: Jordan and the Prospects for Peace* (Council on Foreign Relations, New York, 1986)

De Atkine, Norvell, 'Amman 1970, A Memoir', *Middle East Review of International Affairs (MERIA) Journal*, Vol. 6, No. 4 (December 2002)

Dearden, Ann, *Jordan* (Robert Hale, London, 1958)

Dodge, Toby, *An Arabian Prince, English Gentlemen and the Tribes East of the River Jordan: Abdullah and the Creation and Consolidation of the Trans-Jordanian State* (SOAS, London, 1994)

Doughty, C. M., *Travels in Arabia Deserta, Vol. 1* (Jonathan Cape, London, 1924)

Dresch, Paul, *A History of Modern Yemen* (Cambridge University Press, Cambridge, 2000)

Economist Intelligence Unit quarterly and annual reports on Jordan, 1976–present

Epstein, Eliahu, 'The Bedouins of Trans-Jordan: Their Social and Economic Problems', *Journal of the Royal Central Asian Society*, Vol. 25 (1938)

Erskine, Mrs Steuart, *Trans-Jordan* (Ernest Benn, London, 1924)

Flapan, Simha, *The Birth of Israel: Myths and Realities* (Croom Helm, London, 1987)

Fromkin, David, *A Peace to End All Peace: The Fall of the Ottoman Empire and the Creation of the Modern Middle East* (Avon Books, New York, 1989)

Furlonge, Sir Geoffrey, 'Jordan Today', *Journal of the Royal Central Asian Society*, Vol. 53 (1966)

Gerges, Fawaz A., *The Superpowers and the Middle East: Regional and International Politics 1955–1967* (Westview, Boulder, 1994)

Gharaibeh, Fawzi A., *The Economies of the West Bank and Gaza Strip* (Westview, Boulder, 1985)

Ghazwi, Fahmi, 'Modernization and the Traditional System of Penal Justice in Jordan', *Journal of South Asian and Middle Eastern Studies*, Vol. 12, No. 2 (Winter 1988)

Ginat, Joseph, and Winckler, Onn (eds.), *The Jordanian–Palestinian–Israeli Triangle: Smoothing the Path to Peace* (Sussex Academic Press, Brighton, 1998)

Glubb, John Bagot, 'The Bedouins of Northern Arabia', *Journal of the Royal Central Asian Society*, Vol. 22 (1935)

'The Economic Situation of the Transjordan Tribes', *Journal of the Royal Central Asian Society*, Vol. 25 (1938)

The Story of the Arab Legion (Hodder and Stoughton, London, 1946)

A Soldier with the Arabs (Hodder and Stoughton, London, 1957)

Graves, Philip P. (ed.), *Memoirs of King Abdullah of Transjordan* (Jonathan Cape, London, 1950)

Gubser, Peter, *Politics and Change in Al-Karak, Jordan: A Study of a Small Arab Town and its District* (Oxford University Press, Oxford, 1973)

Jordan: Crossroads of Middle Eastern Events (Croom Helm, London, 1983)

Haas, Marius, *Hussein Königsreich* [Hussein's Kingdom] (Tuduv Buch, Munich, 1975)

Hudson, Michael, 'The Palestinian Arab Movement: Its Significance in the Middle East Crisis', *Middle East Journal*, Vol. 23, No. 3 (Summer 1969)

Hussein of Jordan, King, *Uneasy Lies the Head: An Autobiography of King Hussein of Jordan* (Heinemann, London, 1962)

Jarvis, C. S., *Arab Command: The Biography of Lt-Col F. G. Peake Pasha* (Hutchinson, London, 1942)

Johnston, Charles, *The Brink of Jordan* (Hamish Hamilton, London, 1972)

Jureidini, Paul A. and McLaurin, R. D., *JORDAN: The Impact of Social Change on the Role of the Tribes* (CSIS, The Washington Papers #108, Praeger, New York, 1984)

Kazziha, Walid W., *Revolutionary Transformation in the Arab World: Habash and his Comrades from Nationalism to Marxism* (Charles Knight, London, 1975)

Khouri, Rami G., *The Jordan Valley: Life and Society Below Sea Level* (Longman, London, 1981)

Kingston, Paul W. T., *Britain and the Politics of Modernization in the Middle East, 1945–1958* (Cambridge University Press, Cambridge, 1996)

Kirkbride, Alec Seath, *A Crackle of Thorns: Experiences in the Middle East* (John Murray, London, 1956)

An Awakening: The Arab Campaign, 1917–1918 (University Press of Arabia, Tavistock, 1971)

From the Wings: Amman Memoirs, 1947–1951 (Cass, London, 1976)

Klat, Paul J., 'Jordan's Five-Year Program for Economic Development, 1962–1967', in Klat, Paul J. (ed.), *Middle East Economic Papers* (Economic Research Institute, AUB, Beirut, 1963)

Laqueur, Walter Z., *Communism and Nationalism in the Middle East* (Routledge & Kegan Paul, London, 1956)

Layne, Linda, *Elections in the Middle East* (Westview, Boulder, 1987)

Home and Homeland: The Dialogics of Tribal and National Identities in Jordan (Princeton University Press, Princeton, 1994)

Lerner, Daniel, *The Passing of Traditional Society* (The Free Press, New York, 1958)

Lesch, Ann Mosely, 'Contrasting Reactions to the Persian Gulf Crisis: Egypt, Syria, Jordan and the Palestinians', *The Middle East Journal*, Vol. 45, No. 1 (Winter 1991)

Lewis, Norman, *Nomads and Settlers in Syria and Jordan, 1800–1980* (Cambridge University Press, Cambridge, 1987)

Lias, Godfrey, *Glubb's Legion* (Evans & Bros, London, 1956)

Lockhart, Capt L. K., 'The Transjordan Frontier Force', *Journal of the Royal Artillery*, Vol. 56 (1929–1930)

Longrigg, Stephen Hemsley, *Syria and Lebanon Under French Mandate* (Oxford University Press, Oxford, 1958)

Louis, William Roger, *The British Empire in the Middle East* (Clarendon Press, Oxford, 1984)

Lunt, James, *Glubb Pasha: A Biography* (Harvill Press, London, 1984)

Hussein of Jordan: A Political Biography (Macmillan, London, 1989)

Lynch, Marc, *State Interests and Public Spheres: The International Politics of Jordan's Identity* (Columbia University Press, New York, 1999)

MacCallum, Elizabeth P., *The Nationalist Crusade in Syria* (Foreign Policy Association, New York, 1928)

McCarthy, Justin, *The Ottoman Turks* (Longman, London, 1997)

Maclean, Donald, *British Foreign Policy Since Suez* (Hodder and Stoughton, London, 1970)

Maddy-Weitzman, Bruce, 'Jordan and Iraq: Efforts at Intra-Hashimite Unity', *Middle Eastern Studies*, Vol. 26, No. 1 (January 1990)

Madfai, Madiha Rashid Al, *Jordan, the United States and the Middle East Peace Process, 1974–1991* (Cambridge University Press, Cambridge, 1993)

Madi, Munib al- and Mousa, Suleiman, *Tarikh al-Urdun fi al-qarn al-'ashrin, 1900–1959* [History of Jordan in the Twentieth Century] (Maktabat Muhtasab, Amman, 1959; 2nd edition, 1988)

Migdal, Joel S. (ed.), *Palestinian Society and Politics* (Princeton University Press, Princeton, 1980)

Miller, Aaron D., 'Jordan and the Arab-Israeli Conflict: The Hashemite Predicament', *Orbis* (Winter 1986)
  The Arab States and the Palestine Question: Between Ideology and Self-Interest (CSIS, The Washington Papers, 1986)

Mishal, Shaul, *East Bank/West Bank: The Palestinians in Jordan, 1949–1967* (Yale University Press, New Haven, 1978)

Mogannam, E. Theodore, 'Developments in the Legal System in Jordan', *The Middle East Journal* (Spring 1952)

Monroe, Elizabeth, *Britain's Moment in the Middle East, 1914–1956* (Chatto & Windus, London, 1963)
  Philby of Arabia (Faber & Faber, London, 1973)

Morris, James, *The Hashemite Kings* (Faber & Faber, London, 1959)

Mousa, Suleiman, 'Jordan: Towards the End of the Ottoman Empire 1841–1918', in Hadidi, Adnan (ed.), *Studies in the History and Archaeology of Jordan* (Department of Antiquities, Amman, 1982)
  'The Impact of Oil', in Gantzel, Klaus Jurgen and Mejcher, Helmut (ed.), *Oil, the Middle East, North Africa and the Industrial States* (Ferdinand Schoningh, Paderborn, 1984)

Mutawi, Samir A., *Jordan in the 1967 War* (Cambridge University Press, Cambridge, 1987)

Nevo, Joseph, *King Abdallah and Palestine: A Territorial Ambition* (Macmillan, Basingstoke, 1996)

Nevo, Joseph and Pappe, Ilan, *Jordan in the Middle East: The Making of a Pivotal State, 1948–1988* (Cass, London, 1994)

Newhouse, John, 'Profiles, Monarch', *The New Yorker*, 19 September 1983

Nisan, Mordechai, 'The Palestinian Features of Jordan', in Elazar, Daniel (ed.), *Judea, Samaria and Gaza: Views on the Present and Future* (American Enterprise Institute, Washington DC, 1982)

Parker, Richard B., *The Politics of Miscalculation in the Middle East* (Indiana University Press, Bloomington, 1993)

Patai, Raphael, *The Kingdom of Jordan* (Yale University Press, New Haven, 1958)

Peake, F. G., 'Trans-Jordan', *Journal of the Royal Central Asian Society*, Vol. 11 (1924)
  A History of Jordan and its Tribes (University of Miami Press, Florida, 1958)

Peretz, Don, 'Development of the Jordan Valley Waters', *The Middle East Journal*, Vol. 9 (1955)
  The West Bank (Westview, Boulder, 1984)

Philby, H. St J. B., 'Trans-Jordan', *Journal of the Royal Central Asian Society*, Vol. 11 (1924)

Plascow, Avi, *The Palestinian Refugees in Jordan, 1948–1957* (Cass, London, 1981)

Pundik, Ron, *The Struggle for Sovereignty: Relations Between Great Britain and Jordan, 1946–1951* (Blackwell, Oxford, 1994)

Quandt, William B., *Peace Process. American Diplomacy and the Arab–Israeli Conflict since 1967* (Brookings/University of California Press, Washington DC/Berkeley, 1993)

Qutub, Ishaq Y., 'The Impact of Industrialization on Social Mobility in Jordan', *Development and Change*, 1969–1970, Vol. 1, No. 2

Richardson, John P., *The West Bank: A Portrait* (Middle East Institute, Washington DC, 1984)

Robins, Philip, 'Shedding Half a Kingdom', *British Society for Middle East Studies Bulletin*, Vol. 16, No. 2 (1989)

Robinson, Glenn E., 'Can Islamists be Democrats? The Case of Jordan', *The Middle East Journal*, Vol. 51, No. 3 (Summer 1997)

Rogan, Eugene L., 'Physical Islamization in Amman', *The Muslim World*, Vol. 76, No. 1 (January 1986)

   Frontiers of the State in the Late Ottoman Empire (Cambridge University Press, Cambridge, 1999)

Rogan, Eugene L. and Tell, Tariq (eds.), *Village, Steppe and State: The Social Origins of Modern Jordan* (British Academic Press, London, 1994)

Rogan, Eugene L. and Shlaim, Avi (ed.), *The War for Palestine: Rewriting the History of 1948* (Cambridge University Press, Cambridge, 2001)

Royle, Trevor, *Glubb Pasha: The Life and Times of Sir John Bagot Glubb, Commander of the Arab Legion* (Little, Brown & Co, London, 1992)

Ryan, Curtis R., 'Jordan and the Rise and Fall of the Arab Cooperation Council', *The Middle East Journal*, Vol. 52, No. 3 (Summer 1998)

Salibi, Kamal, *The Modern History of Jordan* (IB Tauris, London, 1993)

Satloff, Robert B., 'Jordan's Great Gamble: Economic Crisis and Political Reform', in Henri Barkey (ed.), *The Politics of Economic Reform in the Middle East* (St Martin's Press, New York, 1992)

   From Abdullah to Hussein: Jordan in Transition (Oxford University Press, Oxford, 1994)

Sayigh, Yezid, *Armed Struggle and the Search for State: The Palestinian National Movement, 1949–1993* (Clarendon Press, Oxford, 1997)

Seale, Patrick (ed.), *The Shaping of an Arab Statesman: Sharif Abd al-Hamid Sharaf and the Modern Arab World* (Quartet, London, 1983)

Seale, Patrick, *Abu Nidal: A Gun for Hire* (Hutchinson, London, 1992)

Shlaim, Avi, *The Politics of Partition: King Abdullah, the Zionists and Palestine, 1921–1951* (Oxford University Press, Oxford, 1990)

   The Iron Wall: Israel and the Arab World (Norton, New York, 2000)

Shryock, Andrew, *Nationalism and the Genealogical Imagination: Oral History and Textual Authority in Tribal Jordan* (University of California Press, Berkeley, 1997)

Shwadran, Benjamin, *Jordan: A State of Tension* (Council for Middle Eastern Affairs Press, New York, 1959)

Sinai, Anne and Pollack, Allen, *The Hashemite Kingdom of Jordan and the West Bank* (American Academic Association for Peace in the Middle East, New York, 1977)

Snow, Peter, *Hussein: A Biography* (Barrie & Jenkins, London, 1972)

Stevens, Georgiana G., 'Arab Refugees: 1948–1952', *The Middle East Journal* (Summer 1952)

Susser, Asher, *On Both Banks of the Jordan: A Political Biography of Wasfi al-Tall* (Cass, London, 1994)

    Jordan: Case Study of a Pivotal State (Washington Institute for Near East Policy, Policy Papers #53, Washington DC, 2000)

Tal, Lawrence, *Politics, the Military and National Security in Jordan, 1955–1967* (Palgrave Macmillan, Basingstoke, 2002)

Taylor, Richard Loring, *Mustafa's Journey: Verse of Arar, Poet of Jordan* (Yarmouk University Publications, Irbid, 1988)

Al-Urdun al-jadid Research Center, *Intikhabat 1989: haqa'iq wa raqam* (Amman, 1992)

    Intikhabat 1993: darasa, tahliliyah raqamiyah (Amman, 1994)

Vatikiotis, P. J., *Politics and the Military in Jordan: A Study of the Arab Legion, 1921–1967* (Cass, London, 1967)

Wahlin, Lars, *As-Salt: A Trans-Jordanian Town Through Time* (author publication, Stockholm, undated)

Warriner, Doreen, *Land and Poverty in the Middle East* (RIIA, London, 1948)

Wiktorowicz, Quintan, 'The Limits of Democracy in the Middle East: The Case of Jordan', *The Middle East Journal*, Vol. 53, No. 4 (Autumn 1999)

Wilmington, Martin W., *The Middle East Supply Centre* (Albany, State University of New York Press, 1971)

Wilson, Mary C., *King Abdullah, Britain and the Making of Jordan* (Cambridge University Press, Cambridge, 1987)

Wilson, Rodney (ed.), *Politics and the Economy in Jordan* (Routledge, London, 1991)

Wright, Esmond, 'Abdallah's Jordan: 1947–1951', *The Middle East Journal*, Vol. 5, No. 4 (1951)

Yorke, Valerie, *Domestic Politics and Regional Security. Jordan, Syria and Israel: The End of an Era?* (IISS/Gower, Aldershot, 1988)

Young, Ronald J., *Missed Opportunities for Peace: US Middle East Policy 1981–1986* (American Friends Service Committee, Philadelphia, 1987)

Index